Forgiveness

Sarah Brown

FORGIVENESS

A novel

With Love

Sarah

Healing Through Enlightenment Ltd
www.healingthroughenlightenment.co.uk
info@healingthroughenlightenment.co.uk

ISBN 978-0955803-802

Typeset in 12pt Bembo by Troubador Publishing Ltd, Leicester, UK
Printed in the UK by The Cromwell Press Ltd, Trowbridge, Wilts, UK

For Mum and Dad

Acknowledgements

This book took a while to write, because it took me a long time to understand forgiveness. For my current level of understanding, I am indebted to the many people who have helped me on my path: Maggie Rakusen and the other teachers at the North of England Training Centre for the Alexander Technique; the Foundation for Inner Peace, for the astonishing book that is called *A Course in Miracles;* Sarwar Osman, for pointing me in the right direction; Mark Penrose, my teacher, healer and friend; and White Eagle, my guide.

A huge thank you, too, to Ned Chaillet because you are so full of wisdom about writing and drama and life, and because you laughed at the jokes in my first (dreadful) play!

Thanks to Derrick Day, for your inside knowledge of the police; to Linda Whelan, for donning your professional counsellor hat and talking to me about grief; and to Tim Crowley, for the cover design and for all your help and advice.

To the people who read the book and made comments, thank you for the time and care you took, and for your words of encouragement and support… Clare Goddard, Erik Schelander, Barbara Henshall, Helen Grice, Anthony Mackesy, Andrew Jackson, Judith Hartley, Charlotte Penrose and Nigel Hewson.

To the team at Troubador – Jeremy, Terry and Julia. Thank you for making this a reality.

And last and most, to Mum and Dad. Thank you for everything.

Friday, 24ᵗʰ November

It happens at 6.08 pm.

I know this because I am fiddling with the timer on the oven. The display keeps stubbornly flicking back to 18:08. I want it to say 15, with a little picture of a bell, but it refuses to do as I ask.

The oven is one of those high tech things that Patrick bought to improve my cooking. It didn't work. His image comes to my mind, flying round the kitchen without appearing to move, conjuring all manner of wonderful smelling things, mere spoonfuls of which might reduce you to a blubbering heap of ecstasy. I tingle at the thought of him. His smile and his eyes − that thing they do when they see me; the pleasure thing. As if they are switched on all of a sudden and I am illuminated, and I look under his gaze like I've never looked under anyone else's and I feel a thrill because in that moment I am beautiful − because of him, and the flattering torch of his eyes. He is coming home. Nothing else matters.

Until then it is me, squinting at the recipe books, weighing ingredients and stirring and separating and whisking, creating unconquerable mounds of washing up and sprinkling the floor with things that don't come off very easily and everything I try comes out a sort of brown colour with black fringes, and tasting of mould.

18.08. My fingers are not designed to press two buttons on this thing at this angle at the same time.

"Bugger it!" I shout.

He might not come. That thought scurries through my mind as I fling the instruction book across the floor. I don't allow it to stay there – the thought, not the instruction book. Of course he's coming. So we argued. So what?

The argument won't still be there. Not now.

I was cross with him, so I didn't phone. To be fair I changed my mind, thought maybe I was in the wrong, but two days had passed and I had left it too late, so I couldn't apologise on the phone, it would have to be face to face. Besides, he was in the wrong too, and he hasn't phoned either. Now here is the fifth day and of course he's coming here this evening – where else would he go? No. It'll be fine. I can make it all better somehow. I have been charging around the flat tidying – or rather, making little piles of mess into big piles and hiding them in cupboards or behind furniture – and I am having a stab at this chicken thing that you make with the bacon and the arrowroot, and I have put the sparkling wine in the fridge, and I am rehearsing my little speech and hoping that we can skip the leathery food and go straight to bed, and now I am fighting with the bloody oven and swearing because I don't know how he is going to be. Cross or loving? Cross or loving? If the timer works this time, it will be loving. I shut my eyes and press. There is a click. I open my eyes. 18.08. I kick the oven.

There is a noise outside, on the stairs. I grab the ordinary timer and twist it round to fifteen. Then I hide it under the grill. I run to the hallway, waiting for the door to fly open, a pair of arms flung wide, perhaps clutching a bottle of something. Nothing else matters.

A knock on the door.

He doesn't knock. He never knocks. Why would he? He practically lives here.

A very nice policeman with pale skin, ginger hair and an apology in every facial expression delivers the news. He is called John, and he is a Family Liaison Officer, he says, handing me a leaflet. A female colleague hovers behind him. He wants to know what Patrick was wearing, just to be sure. I don't know.

"You're not sure it's him?" I'm searching for hope in his face.

"Pretty sure. Yes. From everything else you've told us." He looks away, seeking reassurance from his silent colleague. She avoids his gaze.

His eyes flutter around the room, seeking out information, resting on anything, as long as it isn't the girl with the hurt in her eyes.

"Would you be able to come and…" He brings his eyes to meet mine, then seems to lose what he was going to say.

"Identify him?" I say.

He nods. "Do you want to see him? Would it help?"

He is looking at me now, eager, for the first time. I get the impression he likes to be doing. I want to tell him, yes, it would help, but I can't. I picture a lifeless body on a slab. I remember my dog, when I was ten. His empty body. There was no sign of the soul in there. It left. I couldn't bear that. Hard enough with Judas, and all he ever did was pant and wag his tail. I don't want to see the bit of Patrick that has been vacated. I shake my head.

"This man," I say.

"I'm sorry?" He says that a lot. As if the tipped forward head and scrunched together eyebrows are not enough of a pardon me.

"The man in the car."

"Mr Schofield?" His colleague shoots him a look. Perhaps he isn't meant to say the name.

"The one who caused the…" I can't say it. "Why?"

"Why?"

"Is he someone who often jumps red lights? Have you come across him before? Why did he?"

"No. This is the first time. He actually has an advanced driving test."

"Oh. Oh, well that's a comfort."

"No, I mean… He says he was in a hurry to get to a meeting." He is staring at his knee, and up to his colleague, for support. If they told me his colleague's name, I can't remember it. That's bad. I'm supposed to be getting better at names and faces.

"He's an insurance salesman. He sells… Well." He blushes.

"Convenient," I say.

He laughs a little, although he doesn't find it funny. His eyes flick away again.

"Presumably he has cover, then," I say. "He'll be able to get his car repaired."

There is a muffled ringing sound from the grill. The food. I had forgotten the food. I start to get up from the sofa.

"No, stay there," says John. He leaps from the chair as if all of a sudden he thinks there might be fleas there. He glances at his colleague on the way through the archway into the kitchen area. I can't tell what her face says. She walks forward and sits down beside me.

"Is there anybody we can call for you?" she says.

"Get Patrick," I say. "He'll know what to do."

She leans across and rubs my shoulders with her hand. Sympathy. Not keen on that. Need to find something positive to say.

"He would have died anyway, one day," I say. "At least this way he'll always be himself. He won't shrink or shrivel. He won't lose his mind. I'll always know that he loved me. He won't lose that now. Nor will I."

She smiles at me and rubs my shoulders some more. Does she know I'm lying to her? I don't know that he loved me at all. For all I know, at the point of his death, he might still have felt he hated me, the way you do after a big name calling session.

I don't tell her about the row.

Ginger John comes back from the kitchen. "The food smells wonderful."

"Do you want some?"

"No. No. Thank you. It, er… It looks good though."

He is nodding.

I thank him. You might almost believe he means it. I am pretty sure the food looks a long way from good. I imagine it is doing an impression of a pair of shoes in a muddy puddle. It's nice of him to make the effort, though.

They want me to know they have arrested Mr Insurance. They will keep me informed about it all, how it is going. They want to charge him with causing death by dangerous driving, but the CPS is a law unto itself, so it might get downgraded to driving without due care and attention. They are hoping that won't happen. They are trying to reassure me.

Some things I can understand. A hurrying person, taking a risk. A bus

4

driver not quite paying attention. A swerve to avoid a head on collision. A metal post in just the wrong place, designed for safety, to give information, but instead performing a different function, bashing the bus in the middle as it hits sideways. One person in the wrong seat. One person. A miracle nobody else was hurt. Miracle. But not for the person in the wrong seat.

It could have happened at any time, to anyone, it is just bad luck. I say, "These Things Happen," and I breathe in and tell myself it can't be helped, and I breathe out and tell myself to breathe in again.

Some things I can't understand.

What the hell was he doing on a bus?

I persuaded the police to leave without calling anybody for me although, from the meaningful glances exchanged between them, I could tell they were reluctant to do that. Time alone, I said, to which Ginger John said something about a breathing technique.

I shut the door and turned off the lights. The nameless colleague was saying something to Ginger John. I could hear muffled voices and not much else. Perhaps she was admonishing him for the wittering in the door. She shouldn't. It showed he cared.

Now I am sitting on my piano stool, facing out of my bay window, staring at the darkness outside. There is no moon, there are no stars. The darkness consumes everything. I can't see the sea, although I can hear it: forwards and back, forwards and back, inexorably counting the seconds onwards, when all I want to do is turn them around and send them back where they came from.

Death is so impossible to comprehend. How can somebody be there and then not there, just like that? You don't realise, until they are not there, just how much of you is in them, how much of them is in you. Now he has gone, and I don't want to believe it, but I can feel it. I can feel it reverberating around my body. There is an empty space that wasn't there before. The emptiness spreads all around me, extending out over the sea, out to the horizon that I can't see, spreading over the darkness until that is all there is: emptiness and darkness; the same thing. Everywhere.

And now I can't breathe, because to do that is to breathe in the emptiness. Perhaps I should have listened more closely to Ginger John and his breathing technique.

Time alone was not a good idea.

Emily answers the phone in a rush. That's how she does most things. The hello comes out with heavy emphasis on the "Hell-", and practically nothing at all on the "-o".

I picture her at the other end: my 'dark friend', as my mother puts it, although why she doesn't just say black, I don't know. That's what she means. Somehow she seems to consider that racist, while 'dark friend' and a dash of disapproval are perfectly acceptable. Anyway. Emily will be standing, because there is no space in her flat to sit next to the phone. She will have one hand in her dark red hair – dyed and straightened and smothered in chemicals until it gleams. She will be playing with a strand of it now, checking the ends for any signs of imperfection.

"Hello?" she says again. Not in a rush this time; more annoyed. "Is anybody there?"

I clear my throat. No words are forming in my head, but I know I need to make a noise.

"Who is that?" she says.

Still no words will come.

"If this is a Deep Throat kind of thing, you should know Spell FM won't pay for stories. That's why we never get any good ones. Wapping's your best bet. Hello? OK. Hanging up now."

"Hi."

"Mags?"

"Yeah."

"What was all that about? Trying to scare me?"

"He's dead."

"What? Who?"

"Patrick."

There is a silence. She clears her throat too. Eventually, she says, "How?"

"He was in a crash."

"Car?"

"Bus."

She lets out a laugh. I think I may have laughed when they told me. What else can you do, with a story like this? It can't be real.

"How?" she says.

"A car jumped a red light."

"His car?"

"No, he was on the bus."

"What bus?"

"I don't know."

"Why was he on a bus?"

"I don't know."

Another silence. Emily will be twitching her nose, causing her glasses to slide gently down it. She always does, when she thinks, and I can practically hear her brain whirring and computing.

"Em," I say.

"Yes?"

"He told me he was in America."

"What?"

"He was supposed to be on a plane, coming back from America. Instead he was on a bus, ten miles away."

"Maybe he came back early."

"There aren't any airports where he's been."

"Maybe the plane got diverted and they had to bus him back."

"But there were hardly any people on the bus."

"Maybe it wasn't a very busy flight."

"Maybe. Em?"

"Yes?"

"What am I going to do?"

"Stay there. Coming over."

There was a time before I knew him, when he didn't exist to me and it didn't matter because I didn't know what I was missing. I worked, I came home, I went out to the pub. I took long walks along the beach. Occasionally I was lonely, but not really. Hardly at all, in fact. Most of the time I just lived, enjoying living, arguing with my mother, talking to my father about how infuriating she was being, making up with my mother, eating, sleeping, drinking, dancing, working, smiling, chatting, cursing, walking. So there was a time with no Patrick when I didn't feel like this. And now there is a new time without Patrick. Perhaps if I will myself back to BP, rather than AP, I shall find a way to survive this. Although I'm not sure survival is what I want. I think it might be better to curl up and stop living too. No. No. There was a time before. I will start there.

I delve through my brain, scouring it for examples of a happy me, but the images won't stay put. There is Spell FM. There is the studio. My studio, with its soundproofed, womb-like atmosphere. But I can't get the picture to stick. That is a place of safety, at least it always was. Nowhere is safe now. I place myself in my swivel chair, I see the microphone before me; with a struggle, I feel the cans on my ears. And then the thought is gone – replaced by a car jumping a red light, by a bus swerving to avoid hitting it, by a post in the ground, in the way; by crashing, bending metal. I didn't see the crash, but my imagination doesn't seem to have realised it. I need to be rid of that image, it is becoming too all consuming. I need to find something to replace it. I need to think something else, bigger, so this gets squeezed out.

The studio. I must go back to the studio. To the day we met.

It was hot. It was so hot, I remember that. It was the silly season, and we were struggling to find enough material for a programme. The green room was not really designed for the purpose of sorting out production crises, but it was the coolest room in the building, so we were taking refuge there. Jed, as was so often the case, was getting himself worked up about our latest problem. Natalie was looking nervous and biting the top of her pen in the corner of the room, in between short sharp bouts of scribbling things down onto her pad.

"It's not the end of the world," I said.

"How can you say that?" said Jed, flicking his long pony tail round to his back, away from his face, where it was in danger of being soaked in spit. I'm not sure if he's ever been conscious of this flicking habit.

I think it's such a reflex action, he has no idea he does it. The younger producers have great fun imitating this particular trait, before going into a comedy routine involving a monumental loss of temper over the stealing of a chip, or some such very minor thing.

This, however, wasn't a minor thing – he was right to be worried, but it was too hot to get worked up. That was my feeling, anyway. It wouldn't do my voice any favours.

"You don't just lose your whole show five minutes before going on and say it's not the end of the world. You don't do that. I don't know anyone who does that. You're supposed to be bouncing off the walls with rage."

"I have you to do that for me," I said. "Besides, it's not the whole show. We can always fill if we have to."

"You can't just drop the trademark interview. Ten thousand people tune in specially."

"They do?"

"Now you're being sarcastic."

"Well stop going on about bloody ratings then. If we don't have an interview, we don't have an interview. The listeners will just have to cope with a few more phone-ins."

"Um," said Natalie.

I shut my eyes and blew on my face to try to cool it down. "Weren't we supposed to be getting air conditioning?" I said.

"I don't know, Maggie. Let's see. Can we fill a whole three hours on that subject? What do you think?"

"I think I'd probably struggle," I said, thinking that I'd really rather he didn't exaggerate like this. It was a half hour segment – significant, yes, but not the whole show. Still, his anxiety wasn't going to go away, so I decided to take him more seriously. "Is there no councillor willing to talk about refuse collection, or dog wardens, or something?"

"They're all on holiday."

"All of them?"

"The ones who are good value. The rest are probably sitting by the phone, waiting for your call and their fifteen minutes of fame. Frankly, I think I'd rather put out dead air than thirty seconds more from that chap who wanted to describe accounting processes."

I laughed. His name had been Marvin Cutler. We had thought he would be unusual, perhaps even eccentric, with a name like that, and there was a lot of interest from listeners about how come their council tax was going on millions and millions of pounds in interest payments on old loans. So, much against all our instincts, we brought on a council accountant. Bless him, he managed to bore us all so far out of our minds that the hot topic of the council's borrowing somehow didn't seem to matter any more.

No. Definitely no more council employees like that.

"So we have nothing?" I said.

"Nothing. Nada. Zilch." Jed flicked his pony tail again.

"Um…" said Natalie.

"What about the story about the drying paint?" said Jed. This wasn't as stupid as it sounded. Some art students had just finished a performance thing, where they stood and watched paint drying. The art, apparently, was in their facial expressions as they put themselves through this intensely dull experience. We really were in the midst of the silly season, news wise.

"January did them yesterday," I said.

"Um…" said Natalie.

"What's January doing with that material?"

"Same as us," I said. "Scratching around for something to say. What is it Nat?"

"Well, it was just…" she said, then stopped, looking doubtful.

"Just what?"

"We don't have time, Natalie," said Jed. "We've got to get on."

"I had a call yesterday, on the telephone." The words dashed out of her mouth, which she clamped shut again as soon as she was able. Nervous girl, Natalie. What she was doing in broadcasting, I didn't know. It didn't seem the obvious career choice.

"From whom?" The irritation in Jed's voice was growing. He tended to come over a bit Royal Shakespeare Company when that happened, the frustrated thespian in him desperate to burst out. The voice deepened and swelled, with rolling Rs and super sibilant Ss. For Natalie, it was an intensely uncomfortable experience, and one she liked to avoid as much as possible, often by locking herself in the Ladies.

"Let her speak, Jed," I said. "Come on, Nat, what you got for us?"

"It was this old lady. She was really sweet."

"Marvellous. A sweet old lady. It just gets better. Wants to tell us stories about the war, perhaps, or how adorable her grandchildren are?"

"She said she had Alzheimers."

"Aha!" said Jed, his interest at last beginning to warm up. Not that we're mercenary types, of course, but a good bad luck story is generally of interest to the listeners.

Jed plonked himself on the chair next to Natalie, excitedly running through the possibilities. "So she's just been diagnosed, and the doctors got it wrong for ages? And she hasn't had the help she's needed? Yes? Something like that?"

"No. No. She sounds quite well off."

"Oh."

"Don't be too disappointed, Jed," I said.

"Well, it's not as good, is it? Better to get the underdog. People aren't all that bothered about these pampered types, no matter what their problems."

Natalie was staring at her pile of press releases and nervously biting on her pen.

"What did she want, Nat?" I said.

She looked at Jed, then looked back at me quickly, a blotchy rash rising from her neck to her forehead. Poor girl didn't just blush. She kind of lit up like a purple beacon with blotches on it.

"She says she had it."

"Yes."

"And she doesn't have it any more."

"But you can't cure Alzheimers."

"That's what I thought."

Jed sighed.

"Fruitloop," he said. "We've got no time to check it."

"You've got the first half of the show," I said. "Off you go."

"This is ridiculous."

"It's something," I told him. "And something is better than nothing. Let's get her in."

Natalie looked relieved. She had gone out on a limb, and it hadn't misfired. I never understood that. She always expected it to, and it never misfired. She was a bright girl. But the self doubt corroded her every thought process and her every impulse to take action so that, more often than not, she ended up sitting in the corner, biting her pens and saying nothing. Our station manager Harry wanted me to do something about it. "Take her under your wing," he would say. But I didn't get it. And how could I help her if I didn't get it?

The old lady's name was Lottie. She was sitting very upright on the chair next to mine, without leaning against the back. She had a poise that was quite beautiful. I wondered if she had been to finishing school. She was of an era and a class that might do that sort of thing, before coming back to Blighty for "The Season". She had a dry voice, with a few creaks in it. Every so often she would clear her throat and I would glance across to Jed on the other side of the desk. He doesn't need to be in there with me, but he likes to be. I think it makes him feel more part of the show, somehow. I don't mind, just so long as he keeps the rustling to a minimum, and doesn't pull too many faces while I'm trying to make out what the interviewees are saying. He was making a face now. Either Lottie's eyesight wasn't too good, or she was ignoring him. There was no sign that she knew what he was doing. I glared at him and turned back to my interviewee.

"So Lottie," I said. You were diagnosed with Alzheimer's... when?"

"Oh, do you know," she said. "I find time very difficult."

I felt that crunch I sometimes get in my stomach when I feel I will be embarrassed on somebody else's behalf in the very near future. I dared not look at Nat, who must have been thinking we should never have done this one at such short notice. If she turned out to have Alzheimer's after all, we would simply be making a fool out of a sweet old lady. No programme was worth that.

"I'm not bonkers," said Lottie, laughing a little at my concerned face. "I just don't bother with time any more. You go through an experience like that, when you really don't have a clue what's going on for vast chunks of the day or week or month, and you come out and you think, well, what does time matter? Isn't it the moment that counts?"

"So you have no idea when your diagnosis was made?"

"It'll be three years, perhaps three and a half. I think it was the winter. After Christmas, because we'd tried goose for the first time and we were thinking why bother? You know? Turkey isn't all that special, and goose certainly isn't. Although they do have a point about the roast potatoes. So I think we'd decided to just do beef next year. And chocolate, of course. Not on the same plate! But none of us is terribly fond of Christmas pudding, you see, so there really isn't any point when you can get a perfectly good ready made chocolate spongey thing from Sainsburys with that gooey sauce oozing out of it."

I wasn't following her line of thought all that well, so I looked for a detail that I *could* get hold of. "When you say we…?"

"Oh, my son. And his girlfriend of the time. Although she isn't there any more. I think he decided – oh, no. Sorry. You won't get me to tell you about my son's private life!"

"So January, then?"

"What? Oh, yes. Very probably. February at the latest. My son had been worried about me for quite some time. I was forgetting things, you know. Not just silly things like appointments and so on. Names, of course. I always forgot those. But now I do it and everybody looks at me as if I'm losing my mind again. I'm sure you've been known to forget the odd name in your time."

"Only important people," I said. "The sort that really get offended by it."

She chuckled. Her face spread into a warm smile.

"I thought this was going to be difficult," she said. "But you're very kind."

I felt my face heat up. Jed grinned on the other side of the desk and licked the end of his finger, then put it to his cheek and made a hissing sound.

"Careful," I said to Lottie. "People will start to think you're senile."

She leaned forward and put her hand on mine. "Why do you do that?" she said. "It was a perfectly innocuous little compliment. I've noticed this before, on your show. You just don't take praise well, do you?"

Her eyes were a very intense blue. It was a gaze I was finding difficult to meet, so I turned away and looked at the notes Natalie had put together for me, freeing my hand from hers as gently as I could in the process.

"So you were getting forgetful. Is that all?"

"Not just forgetful. I kept falling out with people. Not the people one normally falls out with, you know, friends and family and so on. But the people to whom one normally manages to be polite. The window cleaner. The drain chap. That sort of person. I was yelling at them about things and refusing to pay and that sort of thing. And I was paying for other things twice, of course. I hardly had any money, even though my husband left me really rather well provided for. I was spending all of it and then panicking that somebody was stealing from me. And I always assumed that the thief was the person who was around when I opened up my bank statement and discovered the state of my account. I fear I may have chased after the postman one day, although I don't really remember. Some I do, but for the rest I must rely on the people around me to fill me in. Then I pushed the window cleaner off his ladder one day. Poor chap had to go to hospital."

"You assaulted somebody?"

"That is precisely the term the police used. My son was horrified, having to pick me up from the police station. He felt very ashamed. Well, you would, wouldn't you? Nobody thinks it's an illness, they just think you are a bad, bad woman. You know, rotten to the core. Nobody thinks, well, maybe she's not very well. And I paid for him to have a private room and everything."

"Your son?"

"The window cleaner. We're best of friends now, of course. Water under the bridge. It helps, I think, that I have a very large number of windows."

"Let's talk about your cure," I said. "How did you find it?"

"There isn't a cure, as such."

"Sorry?"

"Talk to any medicine man. Or woman. Look in all the journals.

14

They have some tablets now, which are supposed to slow it down, but not stop it. No. If you look at it purely in scientific terms, there is no cure. For some reason unknown to the doctors and so on, large lumps of protein form in the brain and attack the rest of it. It's no wonder there are so many old dears sitting around looking vacant. They've hardly got any brain left!"

"I'm sorry, Lottie, you've lost me. If there's no cure, and you haven't got Alzheimer's, but you were diagnosed with it 3 years ago, how come you don't appear to have it now?"

"Ah. Well, there's the question, isn't it? I was healed. Not cured."

"What's the difference?"

"All the difference in the world. A healer looks at the whole person. Mind, body, soul, spirit. The scientific part, that's just about the body, really. But why should a body turn on itself? What led to the situation in the first place?"

I looked at Jed. He was rolling his eyes.

"Um. So what are you saying here? If you're ill, you've done something to cause it? It's your fault?" I could feel my hackles rising.

She smiled. "No," she said, "No. But it is very easy to get out of balance."

"How do you mean?"

"If you think of a healthy human being as a compass which points North, then an unhealthy one has a magnet next to it, pulling it off to the East or the West. That magnet can be made up of a number of different things. It can be unhealthy attitudes, such as an overindulgence in anger or so on. It can be unhealthy lifestyle, such as drinking too much, eating unhealthy foods, never getting any fresh air, that sort of thing. Or it can be unhealthy beliefs."

"Beliefs?"

"Yes."

"Like what?"

"People believe all sorts of things about themselves. Some believe that they are failures. Others believe that they are not lovable. Others believe that somehow they need to change other people, or improve them. There are all sorts of beliefs that take us away from our true North."

"So you're saying that people believe things that make them ill."

"I did."

"Forgive me, but, if you were senile, how do you know?"

"My senility was a shield. It protected me from things I didn't want to see or know. It took me away."

I stared at her. It was difficult to argue with her, because I wasn't quite sure what she was saying, but I wanted to argue. I wanted to fight back on behalf of all those people out there who didn't find life as easy as she seemed to be painting it.

She dropped the smile and looked deep into my eyes, no expression at all on her face but one of – what? Openness. That was all I could think. An open expression. "I was a very bitter woman," she said, shaking her head. "I lived my life in bitterness. I loathed everybody. My belief was particularly destructive. I thought that I was substandard. Because I saw that in myself, I looked for it in other people. I spent my life looking for faults in everyone around me. Of course, it didn't make me terribly popular. So that confirmed my belief in my own shortcomings, and on it went. Do you know, there was an afternoon while I was recovering when I suddenly smiled! And it occurred to me that it was a very alien thing. I'm not sure I smiled for years before that. Years and years."

"But you're smiling now."

"Wouldn't you be?"

"So you're a different person now? Doesn't that mean that you've just been brainwashed, not cured?"

"Healed."

"Healed."

"It would have been a job to make anything stick, if you were trying to brainwash me, bearing in mind how far gone I was."

"How far gone was that?"

"A lot of it I don't remember, because I wasn't there. It takes the spirit to keep the brain working, you know. And my spirit was off somewhere else."

I leaned back in my chair and pulled the microphone towards me. I felt tired, suddenly. It would be lovely to think that you could just throw off Alzheimer's by changing your views on a few things, but I couldn't see it. We were being conned, I was sure of it. And conmen always dress up in a costume you can trust – why not as a sweet old lady?

"You were off somewhere else," I said, showing the listeners not to trust what was being said by the tone of my voice.

"I hid. You see I thought everybody hated me. So I would hate them, just to get ahead of their decision about me. I didn't know I was doing that at the time, of course, I just did it. That was normal for me. And you always behave in a way that is normal to you, don't you? That's why changing your habits is so jolly hard. Well, if you believe that everybody hates you, there comes a point when, if you could choose to be away with the fairies, why wouldn't you?"

"So you're saying that people who have Alzheimer's hate everybody."

"No. I'm not saying that at all. I'm saying that I did. That was my route into it. Other people will have their own beliefs, their own reasons. This was mine."

"OK. OK. So if you were away with the fairies, how come you're sitting here now? Looking normal as you like? If a bit balmy."

She chuckled again.

"Balmy is good," she said. "It keeps people on their toes."

"So?"

"So. So a very kind man came to see me. And he brought me back."

"Just like that?"

"Well, it took a while. I met him quite by chance. He had the strangest job for a healer, you know. He was a shop detective. And I'm afraid he caught me walking out with some goods! I was terribly rude to him."

"But he helped you?"

"He was jolly helpful. He talked to me in a way that made me want to stay in the room. It was most extraordinary. I saw him every week for almost a year."

"And he brought you back."

"Yes."

"How did he do that?"

"Well, you'd have to ask him that, really. But he helped me to understand some things. He removed some physical and spiritual blocks to my being well. He would put his hands on my head, or my back, and I would feel strange whooshings, as if something was being pulled out of me. Which of course it was."

"What was?"

"Darkness."

"Darkness?"

"Yes. We all vibrate, did you know that? Our bodies are made up of thousands of electrical connections, and lots of different fields of energy. They vibrate at different frequencies, each of which has a colour associated with it. So he would look into my system, with his mind's eye, not his physical eyes, and see colours. And because darkness is so overwhelming, when it is out of balance – when the compass is off North – well, you need to take it out. He took mine out. And replaced it with more healthy energies, like yellow, blue, green and so on."

"He changed your colours?" I was trying not to sound incredulous, but I wasn't managing very well.

"Yes. And he talked to me a lot. Not the usual rubbish you hear people saying to the senile. He was very direct. He didn't treat me like a child."

"What sort of things did he say to you?"

"Well!" She laughed again. She was more nervous now. This was harder territory for her. I felt myself warming to her once more. "One of the first things he said to me was, he wanted to know what was my opinion of death?"

"What did you say to that?"

"I have no idea. It seems such a long time ago. I probably said I was frightened. Because I was."

"You were?"

"Yes. Very frightened."

"But you're not now?"

"Good lord, no dear. Are you?"

"Isn't everybody?"

"Death is simply change. Our souls carry on. They just go to a different place. Perhaps a more interesting one."

"What are you talking about?" I said. "This is death! It's not change, it's the end! That's how it works. You're born. You live for a bit, then you die. And it's over."

"Then I feel sorry for you my dear."

"Well, there really is no need."

"No. You're right, of course. There is no need. You'll get there in the end."

That response was almost too much to tolerate. But I have never shouted at an interviewee, no matter how provocative they were trying to be. I decided to try another tack.

"What about the doctors?"

"Sorry?"

"What do the doctors say?"

"Oh, you know doctors. They say I can't have had it in the first place."

"So what do they say you had?"

"They seem to think I had a virus. That is so much easier for them to live with than the idea that I might actually have been healed. There are some broad minded doctors, but the vast majority are happier to believe in the power of the virus to cover all eventualities."

"So they're saying they got the diagnosis wrong?"

"Yes."

"Are you going to sue them?"

"What would be the point in that? They didn't get the diagnosis wrong. They're getting their assessment wrong now."

"Look, this all seems a bit far fetched. If this healer that you went to – what was his name, by the way?"

"He has asked me not to give it out on air. He says he will see anybody who approaches the radio station with a need for healing, but he is not doing this for fame."

"Very convenient. All right. If this healer is so good, why aren't we hearing more about this sort of thing? Why are you the first one we hear about?"

"You hear what you want to hear my dear. You hear what you want to hear. And most people don't want to hear this."

"Why not?"

"Because it challenges their beliefs. Makes them feel vulnerable. Makes them feel tired, drained of energy, because they will need to look at everything a different way, and they don't feel that they can do that. People are terrified of having been "wrong". They would rather turn away from something wonderful than admit that they may ever have been wrong about anything. Of course, it's not until you admit that you've been wrong that you understand it couldn't matter less."

At that moment, the door opened. I held my hand up in its direction, assuming it was Miles with the weather, signalling for him to stay where he was. Lottie looked up, surprised. She smiled in recognition, then looked concerned. I turned to see what the matter was. It wasn't Miles in the doorway. It was a tall man with black curls cut very short. He had to duck slightly to fit in the door frame. What with that and the breadth of his shoulders, and the look of rage on his face, he seemed somewhat larger than the studio could accommodate.

"What the bloody hell are you doing?" he said.

"Shhh. No swearing, dear," said Lottie, pointing at the microphone.

I signalled to Jed to get him out, but Jed seemed to be shrinking on the other side of the desk, as if perhaps, if he tried hard enough, he could make himself invisible.

"Do you enjoy making fools out of little old ladies?" said the giant. Large and furious as he was, there was a grace about him. He had on a charcoal suit with a blue shirt and a plain, slightly paler blue tie. He didn't hunch his shoulders like most men of that height. There was a groove down the side of his face, which was flicking in and out of existence with the way he was clenching and unclenching his jaw. His eyes were the same piercing blue as Lottie's. I realised I knew who it was.

"We're nearly finished," I said. "Would you like to wait outside?"

"You're finished now. Come on Mum. You're coming home."

"I am doing no such thing. Wait outside, Patrick. I do apologise to your listeners, Maggie. These outbursts are so unnecessary."

"Mum..."

"Patrick. It is very kind of you to give me a lift. It will mean I don't have to get this nice young chap to drive me. Where is he? Oh, there you are Jed. No. It will give us a chance to have a chat, and perhaps a cup of tea. I haven't seen you for a little while."

The rage swirled around a little bit and settled into hot embarrassment. A blush appeared on his cheeks. "I've been busy."

"Yes, dear, and I understand. Now would you be so kind as to understand that I am busy now, and to wait for a few moments?"

The man's face froze. He looked as if he might have been carved out of rock anyway, without the frozen face. He had deep craggy lines down his cheeks, and, as I think I may have mentioned, he was very tall and broad. And rather well put together, I thought. Then I blushed and turned back to my microphone to wrap it up. The interview had lasted longer than any of us had intended, and we were fast coming to the news. I heard the door swing to a close behind me. I handed over and Jed transferred the transmission to the newsroom.

"Oh, I did enjoy that. Thank you so much," said Lottie.

"Well, um. Thank you," I said. "Most, um, illuminating."

She laughed. "You don't believe a word of it, Maggie. I know that. But not to worry. Perhaps it will help some people. And if it does, then I'm very happy to have done it. You didn't mind my saying that about people contacting the station, did you?"

I thought of poor Miles. General dogsbody, traffic and weather man. I didn't imagine he would be too thrilled with the influx of calls from nutcases that we were sure to receive.

"I'm sure it'll be fine," I said.

"Now, you really must come and meet my son. He's a big fan, you know."

I laughed.

"What's amusing you?" she asked.

"Big, yes. Absolutely. But a fan? Come on. I think if he was ever a fan those days are well and truly past."

"Oh, you don't want to worry about Patrick. He gets angry, lets off a little bit of steam, and then it's all in the past. He'll be gentle as a lamb now, you mark my words."

We left the studio and Lottie led the way along the corridor to the green room. She had an easy way of walking, very upright, and with no jerkiness. It was almost as if she was gliding. I found myself looking down at her feet, just to make sure they were on the ground. They were. It crossed my mind that there weren't many 72 year olds who could walk with such easy grace. But then, there was a lot about Lottie that defied the average.

The green room was empty. We tried the open plan production office. Just Miles, busy answering the phones in the corner. No dark haired giant.

"He's gone without me," said Lottie, a hint of sadness dimming her features. "I may have to prevail upon you for a lift after all," she said to Jed, who nodded and went to fetch his keys.

"I do apologise, Maggie dear. How rude. It's all in the upbringing, you know! I fear I may have done a horrible job!"

"He was a bit cross," I said. "I'm sorry if we've made things difficult for you."

She gave me a quiet smile and looked directly into my eyes, as if she was looking through me to the other side. "You mustn't work too hard," she said. "And you must stop skipping meals and making up for it with chocolate. You really must."

"What?"

Jed arrived behind Lottie and tapped her on her shoulder. She patted her pockets and looked around her, as if she thought she might have forgotten something, then smiled at me and left.

I went straight to the bathroom and stared into the mirror, looking for signs of excessive chocolate consumption. I wasn't skinny, that was for sure, but neither was I fat. My skin was okay. A bit grey, but then I never spent much time in the sun. What was I expecting to see? Chocolate wrappers lining my face?

She could have got that information from anyone. Or made a guess. Perhaps I mentioned it on the show. Except I didn't. I never talk about stuff like that. I make it a rule. Very boring, going on about diets and make-up and shopping and all that other girlie stuff that I can't stand. I leave that stuff to January. Her listeners are into that sort of thing.

The door opened, and Emily walked in. I pulled myself away from my reflection and smiled at her.

"Mirror, Mirror on the wall," she said. "Who gets the nuttiest interviews of them all?"

"That would be me."

"What was that all about?"

"Oh, God. I don't know. Nat found her."

"Well Nat ought to be fired."

"We were short of stuff. It was all we could come up with. Not Nat's fault."

"You should send her down to man the phones with Miles. Have you seen all the calls that are coming in?"

"It'll calm down."

"It better."

She grabbed the bag that was hanging over her shoulder, pulled out mascara and lipstick and expertly touched up her already pristine make-up. She nodded at her reflection with approval, glanced at mine with disapproval, and took my arm. "Time for a drink," she said.

"It's not even lunch yet."

"Yeah, but I did the night shift. I'm ready for a gin and tonic. You coming?"

Which is why, when a considerably more gentle version of the curly haired giant returned to apologise, carrying a box of chocolates and looking sweetly shy, I was sitting in the production office, giggling manically, and helping myself to a third gin. Emily was sitting under her desk hunting for a contact lens.

"Excuse me," he said, as if we were two professionals sitting perfectly normally in an office. "I'm sorry to bother you."

"My what good manners you have," I said, staring at his suit and wondering how he was managing to look as if he wasn't melting – which he surely must have been, in that get up.

"And my, how drunk you are," he said, before turning to Emily and saying, "Mr Wolf, I presume?"

"What?" said Emily, hitting her head on her desk as she clambered out from underneath it.

He blushed. "Never mind," he said.

My stomach felt as though it were being pulled towards my feet. He's flirting with Emily, I thought. And why that should have troubled me, I couldn't fathom, because men always flirted with Emily in front of me. I should have been used to it by now.

He turned to me. "I'm sorry. I hope I didn't spoil your show too much. I don't normally... I just... She's very old, you see. People take advantage."

His blue eyes were spookily similar to Lottie's in the intensity of their gaze. But somehow when I looked at Lottie, I didn't get this strange lurching thing going on in my heart. I blushed again. I wanted to tell him it wasn't a problem, that it actually enhanced the show because listeners love it when there's a real life drama going on, but I couldn't form the words. I just stood and looked at him, looking at me. I wanted to look away. So badly. But I couldn't. And I think it's because, much as I wanted to, I didn't want to at the same time.

Emily coughed.

"G & T anybody?" she said.

Patrick said nothing. I said nothing. We just stood there, locked. Well, I was. I couldn't tell if he was locked as well, or just toying with my lockedness.

"I'll, er..." said Emily, then waited for a response. "I'll just go, shall I?"

I felt her waft past me, and I heard the door close. We were alone, me and this unknown being, this strangely powerful presence that I knew nothing about but couldn't tear myself away from. I tried to smile. It was harder than I could have imagined. Then I saw the corners of his mouth lift up a little and it became easier. His stern face broke into this glorious, sunny smile and I wondered how on Earth I could stand, I was trembling so much. I hadn't noticed it. I had no idea when it started. I wished I hadn't had that gin.

I don't know how long we stood there like that. I was waiting for him to do something; to break this spell that he was casting on me. Perhaps he was waiting for some signal from me, but I didn't know what that might be. The door opened behind him. Emily reappeared and gently nudged his back until he walked forwards a step. She waited there. He didn't move. She nudged him again. She got sick of the game and grabbed his arm, then grabbed mine and pulled us towards each other. As soon as we were close enough she put her hands on each of our backs and sort of launched us at each other.

Patrick recoiled.

"Emily!" I said. "What are you doing?"

"Well somebody had to do something," she said.

Patrick was standing off to the side, blushing once more and looking deeply uncomfortable about the whole thing.

"I'm sorry," I said to him. "I don't know what happened."

"No, it's my fault," he said.

"Oh, my God, you're so bloody polite, you'll never get anywhere," said Emily. "Here's what's going on. Maggie, you daft cow, you are in the process of being desired by a male of the species. Of the opposite sex. Get me?"

"Emily!" I said. I didn't know where to put myself. I sat down at the desk next to me and hid my darkening face in my hands.

"Oh, for God's sake! Now you. What's your name?" she said.

"Patrick," he muttered. I didn't dare to look at him. I was sure he was dying to get out of there, away from this desperate woman. I pictured him arriving in a smart city flat, dropping his keys in a bowl on a sideboard by the door, and slipping his jacket off. That image was a mistake. I blushed more beetroot than I had ever gone before.

"OK, Patrick. I can see you suffer from the same insanity as my friend here. You too are in the process of being desired. That's why she's sitting in a heap over there and wishing the ground would swallow her up, because she never believes that anyone finds her attractive."

"Why not?" he said.

"Well you'd have to ask her that, and I don't think you'd get much sense out of her at the moment. So here's what you do. Walk over to her. Come on. We haven't got all day."

He didn't move. She sighed heavily and took his wrist, then she dragged him over to me.

"OK. Now, Maggie, you are going to have to stand."

"I can't."

"Patrick, help me out here."

Emily took one hand and Patrick took the other. Gracelessly I was heaved out of the chair by two graceful people. I was standing, but wobbly.

"OK. Now, Patrick," said Emily. "Repeat after me. Would you like to go out with me tonight?"

There was silence. I couldn't see anything, because I was looking at my feet and wondering why I had worn these old trainers today.

Emily tapped Patrick on the arm. "Go on," she said.

"Would you like to go out with me tonight?" said Patrick.

Once again, silence. Emily sighed again. "Oh, for God's sake. Maggie. Will you answer him please?"

I couldn't say anything. I tried to clear my throat, but I couldn't.

"Oh, look," said Emily. "We're going to be here all day. The answer's yes. Meet her in the Cricketer's Arms at 7, OK?"

"Um. OK."

"OK. Bye then."

"What? Oh, yes. Bye."

Hesitantly, he made his way towards the door.

"Um," he said.

"Yes?" said Emily. If she was trying to hide her exasperation, she wasn't succeeding very well.

"Will you be there?" he said.

"Good God no."

"Oh good. I mean... Sorry, that didn't quite come out how I meant."

"I understand. Bye then. Bye."

The door shut behind him. I flopped back down into the chair.

"What the Hell are we going to do with you?" she said.

I remember this. I lost someone before. I remember how it goes. You don't lose them all at once. It takes a while to persuade your mind they're not coming back. Ridiculous as it sounds, it takes a while to persuade your body. There's a certainty about them being there. And you don't lose certainty straight away. If you did, we would be an entirely neurotic species. Certainty can only be chipped away, bit at a time, piece by little piece, fragment by fragment, until you end up with a *new* certainty. He's not coming back. Of course, with that certainty there is a loss of solidity too. Memories are harder to recreate. The comfortable feeling, or the excited feeling, or whatever feeling that person used to produce in you – it becomes less there.

Less there, and less there, and less there, until it's no longer a familiar part of daily life, and one day you get a bolt of it, produced by an entirely different stimulus, and you're plunged headlong into a memory of a feeling and all the guilt of having forgotten it for a while.

That's how it goes.

Last time I lost my big brother. He used to sit on me on the sofa so that he could control the telly channel without me interfering. He liked programmes about cars. I used to worm my arms free and tickle his feet – then he would sit on my arms, which left the rest of me free to wriggle out and rub my smelly feet in his face. We giggled a lot. Sometimes, when I push my shoes off after a long day, or when I giggle, I think of him.

And today I'm not giggling, but I'm still thinking of him. So perhaps there is now a new feeling associated with him, not to do with giggling at all, but to do with crying. I know he wouldn't have wanted that.

Is this what Patrick will eventually become? A memory that gets stirred up only when I'm upset about something?

I don't want it. I don't want it. I don't want it.

I want him back.

That picture again in my head. A car, a red light, a bus. I want the bus to squash the car. I want the one dead person from this situation to be the person who caused it. Can wishing make it so? But I shouldn't think like that. The daughters of country vicars don't think like that. I shall have to make do with a prison sentence. Yes. Then he can think about what he has done. Mr Insurance.

19.24. An hour and... Whatever. Feet, clattering on the stairs outside. High heels. Not Patrick. The door wallops open, bashing the bay tree and causing it to wobble. Emily is there, breathing hard, running towards me, then standing in front of me, her hands clutching mine, her face a pop eyed caricature of itself, her scarlet hair soft and sleek, cascading down her back like a burnt waterfall. She always has time to do her hair. No matter what.

"It's all right," she says.

"No, it isn't," I say.

She raises one hand to my face and brushes my hair away, then her eyes dart from my left eye to my right and back again, very quickly, like you see heroines doing in films as they stand, clutching the dimple cheeked hero by his broad shoulders.

"You're right," she says. "It isn't. What can I do?"

I pull away. People always want to know that. And what can you do? Actually very little. Buy flowers, write letters, bring fruit. That's what they did when Ben died. Lots and lots of fruit, as if they thought the sensations inspired by his departure could be relieved with the consumption of fibre.

"Is it me?" I say.

"What?"

"The men I love seem to die in car crashes."

"Honey, no," she says. But she can't think of a sentence to follow it up. The fear is left there, waiting to be crushed. I *could* be the reason.

"I am a character from an Australian soap opera," I say.

Her arms find my shoulders, hugging, crushing, as if they could squeeze the self pity out, like tomato ketchup or HP sauce. The thought of food makes me feel sick. I hope she won't try and make me eat.

"Do me a favour," I say.

"Anything," she is pulling back so that she can look at me, small, rapid nods of the head emphasising her readiness to help.

"Don't say, 'Life goes on,' 'Time's a great healer,' any of that shit, yes?"

"What?"

Somewhere in history, someone was first. Had they been through it themselves? If they were the first, then they wouldn't have known exactly how you feel when someone sees fit to say it to you. They'd have been saying it from the perspective of time, which, as we all know, is a great bloody healer.

"Nobody is going to say it to me. Not this time."

"Sweetheart, I think they might."

"Not yet," I say. "I want them to treat me normally. Till I'm used to it. If we leave it long enough it'll be too late for them to say anything at all."

She doesn't know what to say to this. She wants to make it better, and she doesn't know how. I look away from her dancing eyes, out of the window. "People say it all the time, as soon as they hear. They think it makes it better."

"And it doesn't?"

"It's what you say to it. If you take it at face value and think, well, they're just being kind, and you nod, or say yes, then you're agreeing with them, which is all right, maybe, but you feel odd about it." I can see the lights, further along the shore line. "If you don't say anything, they think you're rude, and they go away and tell your mother."

"Is that what happened?"

"His life doesn't go on, does it?"

"No."

"It stops."

"Yes."

"Yours goes on."

"Yes."

"And maybe you don't want…" I can't finish the sentence. I watch a man throw a stone across the water. I can't see if he manages to skim it, in the darkness. "It doesn't matter."

"You mustn't think like that."

"No."

She shakes her head.

"You've still got me," she says. "Your parents. Memories."

I smile at her. "Memories?"

"Lots of them."

I try to say something else, but tears are gathering in my eyes, and I know if I open my mouth they will fall down my face. Instead, I clamp my teeth together. She notices the tears and pulls me towards her, her arms around my shoulders once more, the side of her head touching the side of mine, as if we can squash the pain between us, which sets the tears rolling anyway, accompanied by great gasping sobs.

"Did I mention you had me?" she says.

21.02. Nearly three hours, AP. Emily has given up coaxing me to eat and is clearing away my romantic dinner for two, in the kitchen. She disappears to make clattering noises, never longer than three minutes at a time, and then emerges, casually, around the doorframe. Checking, but trying to make it look as if she isn't.

"What did you do to this poor chicken?" she says.

"Mmm?"

"It looks as if it's been in an accident."

I laugh.

"Oh shit, I'm sorry. Oh God. Me and my big mouth. Oh God." She comes towards me, checking both eyes again.

I pat her arm. Emily has very big feet.

The door squeaks behind us. We jump apart, as if we were doing something wrong.

"Sorry," says a voice. I wipe my eyes. It is Barney. He is shaking. There are tears in his eyes, too. I should have called him.

He takes my hand. "Erica called me. They asked her to go and identify his body. She said would I come too, but I couldn't go in. I couldn't go in." Barney is a big man. Not tall, particularly, but big. He used to be a prop forward, which means that he was in the front of the scrum.

"She went in on her own," he says, in that North Eastern lilt that seems so odd in a rugby player. Some part of me expects them all to talk like they went to Eton, or Rugby of course, or else why aren't they playing football? There are great, racking sobs coming out of him, as if they are being excavated from a place deep within him and from there they take over his whole body.

He is holding me now. Hugging, squeezing, wailing.

"I can't believe he's gone," he says.

Neither can I.

"So Erica's... seen him, then?" I say.

He nods. I can't see it, but I can feel his head next to mine. I am struggling to breathe.

"And it's definitely...?"

He nods again. Another anguished cry. It releases another wave in me, and our wailing joins arms against our shared pain. Together we find ourselves kneeling on the floor, clinging to each other. I am embarrassed. There is something not quite right about wailing and crying. I should pull myself together. Patrick wouldn't want this.

"Where was he, Barney?" This is Emily's voice. She is over by the bay window. Sensible Emily. Journalist Emily. There's a mystery. Who better to ask than Patrick's best friend?

"What?"

"Patrick. Where was he? Where had he been?"

Barney freezes. The sobbing has abated for now, but he is still clinging on. I can feel his big chest heaving as he tries to regain control of his breath. He pulls back and looks at me. Not at Emily. He never can look at Emily.

"I thought he was still in America," he says.

"Still?"

"Well, I knew when he went, like, but you never do remember other people's travel plans, do you? I just knew he'd be back in time for the match against the Jesters next weekend."

"I think he came back early," I say.

He nods. That sounds about right to him.

"Did he fall out with Danny again? They're too alike, man."

"I don't know."

"Didn't he tell you?"

"No." I'm not going to tell him Patrick wasn't speaking to me. Not yet.

"Why would he be in Strayfield on a bus?" says Emily.

"Strayfield?"

"Yes."

Barney has the same look that I imagine I wore for the police when they told me. The same look Emily was wearing after I told her. Utter bewilderment. Strayfield isn't on the way to anywhere, particularly. It's on that sticking out bit of coast. If you go to Strayfield, you go to Strayfield. You aren't going through it. He shakes his head. "What's in Strayfield?" he says.

Saturday, 25ᵗʰ November

Time is passing, and I don't seem to be here. Whole conversations are happening, and I know I'm a part of them, but I can't remember what is said. I don't seem to have volition, let alone memory, over anything that is going on or has been going on since yesterday at 6.08 pm.

Perhaps I can take refuge from the present in the past. But memory is so little. It's all in the mind, after all – there is no physical presence to it. How is remembering a comfort when it is so thin?

Useless, and I can't stop.

I'm thinking of the Cricketer's Arms. I'm thinking of that first date, of how clumsy I felt, walking towards the pub I always walked to, but somehow this walk was different. This evening the pub was different. It was darker. It was as if someone had twisted a giant dimmer switch, and the night had drawn in quicker than usual, despite the cloudlessness of the sky. Emily had arranged this. How awful. He probably didn't want to meet me at all, he probably felt sorry for me because of what she said, he probably was dreading this evening, longing for it to be over so that he could go back to his life with his batty mother and no obligations forced onto him by sexy newscasters who always managed somehow to cast a spell on men. It was her. It was her power over men. That was the cause of this date. It had nothing to do with him or me or attraction, or any of those things. It had to do with Emily, and the power of her will.

Except those blue eyes had been looking at me.

No. It was down to her. And she wouldn't be there. And how

awful was this meeting going to be? My legs had never been heavier, or so difficult to move.

I would start with whisky. I would get through the door and go straight to the bar, and I would start with whisky. A good drink for courage, because you had to have a certain amount of courage to drink it in the first place.

I pushed open the door, trying to avoid touching the various notices. Pilates classes in the town hall on Tuesday nights. Choral Society on Thursdays. Dog training Sunday afternoons, "Please bring something to clean up after your dog." Spell FM, of course. "What's it all about?" News and views at breakfast time with Maggie Olds. Mornings with January Newsome. Drive with Philip MacAffrey. Times. Events. Places. Distracted by these notices I read almost every day, I mistimed the push on the door, and it flew open, landing against the wall the other side with a loud and attention grabbing bang, before flying back towards my face and hitting my toe instead. I pushed it forwards once more, gently this time, so that it must have seemed as if I was creeping in nervously, which, of course, I was, but I didn't want anyone to know it. Especially the quiet man with the blue eyes drinking whisky at the bar.

He stepped down from his bar stool and came towards me, taking my hand. "Are you all right?" he said. "Did you trip?" His hand was warm. It sort of tingled. He drew me forwards, putting his other hand in the small of my back, which made me jump. He took it away again quickly.

"Sorry," he said. "Force of habit."

"Oh?"

"Just – my mother. I worry that she'll fall."

"Oh. Oh. No. It was... Nice."

We stopped walking. I don't know which of us decided to do that, but we stopped together. We looked at each other. That smile again. That wonderful smile. I smiled back.

"God, this is awkward," he said. "I can't... speak. Um. Look, why don't you go and sit over there?" He pointed at the little booth over in the corner by the dart board. We would have to move if they wanted to play darts, but there were only a couple of old men in so far, and they were absorbed in their separate worlds, one tutting and shaking his head while he read the Daily Mail, the other alternating a contemplative silence with flirting with Lynne at the bar. "I'll get the drinks in. What will you have?" said Patrick.

"Same as you're having."

"Johnnie Walker?"

"Perfect."

I remember watching his back as he chatted to Lynne. I remember tracing the line of his shoulders with my eyes. I remember thinking that he must have played rugby or something. He had that sort of tapering thing going on, where the shoulders are really broad, and the rest kind of tapers down towards a narrower waist. He was wearing the posh boy uniform, a striped shirt and jeans, no socks, loafers.

I remember I was holding my breath, waiting for him to turn round and walk towards me.

I remember his smile as he did just that. What was it about that smile? It was a little like the sun coming out. Without it, he seemed very intense, very thoughtful. When it broke out, it saved him from that darker state, and in doing so, it seemed to have the power to save the world.

I remember thinking that, and then thinking how ridiculous to be thinking that, he was only human, after all. And only a man.

He sat down next to me.

"Your whisky, madam," he said.

"Thanking you kindly, sir," I said.

He looked at me oddly. It was an odd thing to say. I looked at my whisky. Took a sip. Placed the glass down very carefully on the table. Picked it up again. Held it. Took another sip. Thought about taking another, but I was getting through mine, and he hardly seemed to have touched his. I put it down. He was still looking at me. I cleared my throat.

"You don't say as much as I thought you would," he said.

"Sorry?"

"You never seem lost for words on air. I thought you'd be, you know, difficult to shut up."

"Oh, sorry."

"No, don't be. I wasn't… It's just different to how I expected, that's all. Not in a bad way."

"Oh."

There was another silence.

"So, what do you do, then," I said, "when you're not barging into live broadcasts?"

He blushed. "Sorry," I said. "I was only joking."

"No, it's fine. Just… Look, this is really awkward."

I held my breath. This was it. This was the point at which he realised that he was in a completely different league to me and walked out. It was inevitable, had always been inevitable. It was only a matter of time. I had just hoped that it would last a little bit longer, that's all. I looked down at my whisky, waiting for the excuse, for the chair to be pushed back, for the slight waft of air as the door swung open, for the pain to arrive in my heart as soon as the feeling returned to it. I waited.

He kissed me.

It was very gentle, very tentative. Then I kissed him back and he took my head in his hands and it all got a bit more, well, involved. A bell rang. It was Lynne at the bar. "Bit early for that, isn't it? We don't do rooms. Have you told him, Mags?"

We broke apart. Laughed. Looked at Lynne. She gave me a thumbs up sign. This one she approved of.

"Sorry," he whispered in my ear.

"Me too."

"Mind you, broke the ice, didn't it?"

"I don't understand," I said. "I don't know anything about you. You just turned up today. And here we are. And it just doesn't happen this way. How has it happened this way?"

"What do you need to know?"

"I don't know. Something."

He drew back, sipped his whisky, and took in an exaggerated breath, like a diver before a leap from a high board.

"I'm a physiotherapist. I'm 32. I live alone in a small house in a village, five miles out of town. It's next door to my mother, who lives in a vast house which she can't cope with but refuses to leave. I cycle to work every day at the Royal Infirmary, and at weekends I patch up rugby players and send them back out onto the field of play. I used to play, but not any more. I am not and have never been married. I have no children. I have a dog. I like taking her on long walks. She runs away a lot. The local police know me quite well, because I have to go and pick her up from the pound every couple of months. I wanted to climb Everest before I was 30, but somehow that never happened. I have decided I'm too old and set my sights on Ben Nevis before I'm 40. Um. Favourite film, *The Fisher King*, which is odd because I don't really like Robin Williams in many things. I'm a Capricorn, although I don't see what that's got to do with anything. I like roast beef and Yorkshire puddings, with a really strong horseradish sauce. I'm anyone's for an apple crumble. Cream, not custard. Ice cream at a push. I have a brother who I haven't seen for five years. He moved to America when he was 17 because he fell out with our father, who is now dead.

"Um. Have I missed anything out?"

"How would I know?"

"Is it enough to be going on with?"

"I suppose so. How did you feel about your father?"

"What?"

"You said your brother fell out with your father, and he's now dead. Do you miss him?"

"Not really."

"Don't want to tell me?"

"Not much to tell. He was my mother's greatest mistake. Ask her, she'll tell you."

"I'm sure she would."

"So what about you?"

He was giving me the full force of those blue eyes again. He had one hand on my elbow, the other on my hand. It was as if my arm was a barrier between us, to stop us getting any closer. But it wasn't working. I kept finding myself leaning in towards him as he talked, and then I'd notice and pull myself back again. But it was tiring, doing that. There were these big broad shoulders, right there, and I just wanted to rest my head on one.

So I pulled my arm and hand away and I did. I leaned my head on one of his shoulders. He laughed. Then he waited for a moment or two. Then his arm appeared around my back, his hand on my hip.

"Just wanted to see what it was like," I said.

He laughed again. "Now you have."

"Mmm."

"You can stay there if you want."

"I intend to."

He gently kissed my forehead.

The pub was starting to get busier. I didn't care. Normally, I would have been embarrassed. I would have pulled away and acted normally, whatever that was. I certainly wouldn't have been nestling up against a stranger. But he wasn't a stranger. He suddenly seemed really familiar. And I didn't want to have to break away, not now, not ever.

I need to find that shirt. It's his favourite. It has to be here somewhere. Unless he was wearing it when he went to America.

It isn't in the cupboard. I try the linen basket. It is half full, but only with a tracksuit and some teeshirts. It might be at his place, but huge as his house is, he doesn't keep many clothes there. It should be here. I pull out a sweaty teeshirt and hold it to my face. Oh, Patrick, are you laughing at me now? Do you see what you have reduced me to? Sniffing your sweaty sports gear. Wherever you are, is this what you wanted, you bastard? Is it?

Sorry.

I didn't mean that.

But I don't understand. I don't see why you had to... I don't know why you were on... I don't know where you'd been and where you were going. I don't get it. You were supposed to be coming home. Why didn't you?

Sunday, 26th November

My flat is too full of his absence. And Emily, who means well but has stayed too long. I waited for her to go to the loo, and I left. Now I am in Patrick's house, watching the minutes tick by until the sun comes up. It is empty of course. But there are his shoes, just inside the door, same as always. Indoor shoes. A habit left over from Lottie. To keep the muck out.

This is more his house than hers, and she was here for fifty years. He had it for just three months. How he managed to stamp himself so indelibly onto it in such a short time, I just don't know. I wonder if Lottie minds, looking down on us from her little place in heaven, where she must surely be.

It's nice to think about Lottie. It's comforting. Perhaps he's with her. I used to tease him about being a Mummy's boy. Perhaps he missed her too much, and had to go. Which begs the question, doesn't he miss me now?

And this line of thinking is not doing me any good at all. Need to stop with the self pity, for goodness' sake. How would I handle a caller who was wallowing like this? I'd tell them to pull themselves together, most likely. That's what I must do. I will pull myself together and have a look around his house, because life goes on.

Here is his office. I don't usually go in here, it seems an intrusion somehow. He has the designs in here for his silent lawnmower which one day he says will make him fabulously rich. He's doing OK. The physio job doesn't pay particularly well, but he has his inheritance, and it isn't as if he lives in an extravagant way. I don't know why he needs more. But there you go. The air is damp. He was supposed to fix the leaky radiator. Perhaps he didn't have time before he left. I pat the carpet, but it doesn't seem to be wet. Maybe he did fix the radiator. Maybe the smell is left over from when it leaked before. I'm trying not to think of him with his toolbelt on. He loved that toolbelt. He felt like a gunslinger from one of those Spaghetti Westerns. I have lost count of the times I have been held up by an adjustable spanner set, before it has been twirled and returned to its place in the holster.

I am smiling. I shouldn't be smiling.

There is his chair. I will sit down in his chair and take some deep breaths.

There is his rugby ball, signed by the Kestrels, high up on the bookshelf where only he can reach it. There is his desk, with its ordered untidiness. A pile of post waiting to be filed. A post it note on the computer screen. "Dentist Tuesday. Must not miss." He won't go. Wouldn't have gone. My big burly rugby player. Never liked the dentist. I had to drag him there and hold his hand when he had an abscess. Promised him apple crumble if he behaved. But he couldn't eat it of course. Then he accused me of not keeping my promises for ever afterwards.

There is another post it note under the one about the dentist. "Friday 24th, CT. 4 pm."

Friday 24th. That was the day he died. But 4 pm? He should have been on a plane at 4 pm. Unless the time in Atlanta is sufficiently different to make a 4 o'clock meeting possible. CT. What is CT? Somebody in Atlanta? His diary isn't here. None of his stuff is here. It should have been with him, but the police haven't said anything about suitcases, or briefcases, or anything. I must ask them. Ginger John's mobile phone number is on the board at home. I pinned it up as he left. I'll call him when I get back . I might as well find out. Maybe it'll help, if I know more about where he was and what he was doing.

The rest of his desk yields nothing of interest. Envelopes stacked in order of size, a hole punch, a stapler, a box of staples. Sellotape. Some pens. I glance around at the rest of his office. I can't work out if it's better to be among his things or worse. On the one hand, a bit of him is here, but on the other it isn't, and the lack of it is so much clearer here than I think I can stand. I go through to the living room. His telly, his armchair, his sofa, his coffee table, his lamp, his bookshelf, his books, his DVD collection. I can't breathe.

Here is the kitchen. The oven gloves folded on an opened cookery book. The surfaces all clean and shining. There is his porridge pan, waiting, ready for tomorrow's breakfast. Only man I can think of who would do that. Wash it up and put it right there ready to use. Most would just leave it unwashed, wouldn't they? And if they were washer uppers, they'd put it away.

A lot of people call, listen to the outgoing message, and hang up. So there are clicks. Lots of them. I tried it too. One of those clicks is mine.

It doesn't even say anything interesting. Just a few words. And his voice is mangled by the digital recorder. I knew we should have bought a better machine.

I sit. That's my new occupation. Sitting, in his house. Letting time pass, without any sort of contribution from me. Letting noises outside just happen. Not thinking. Not doing. Not. Not living. I can't even see his smile. When I see him he's accusing. It isn't his smile, or his eyes. It's… ugly. He wasn't ever ugly. So not thinking seems the best option. Everything else seems complicated.

It might not be true. Erica didn't know him as well as me, she's just his boss. And she's short sighted. He might just be delayed with Danny in America and have very similar looks to another tall person with curly black hair, who happened to steal his wallet. Perhaps he's just cross with me still. He's decided to make me wait. They could be out at a bar, he and Danny, getting drunk and falling out about their mother. Perhaps they've hit the magic number of hours when it all goes sour. Perhaps Patrick has only now stormed out to get the taxi to the airport. Perhaps he is flying home, and will turn up at my flat any time now with a smile and a hug and a chuckle about how stupid we were, fighting. He'll say he didn't mean it. I'll say the same. He'll say have I changed my mind yet? I'll say yes. I'll hold onto him and never let go. Never again. I'll move in here. Whatever he wants. What was I thinking staying in that stupid flat? What was I doing? How long has he been asking? That's what this has been about. He's not dead. He's not dead. He's just late.

I am clutching at straws, aren't I? Stupid.

Danny. Somebody should tell him.

The phone goes again. The answerphone message comes on. There is a click and a beep as the caller hangs up. I pick it up before it can ring again. I dial. Long number. All those American codes. I go wrong a couple of times and have to start again. Then at last there is ringing on the other end.

"Yah?"

I don't recognise the voice. It sounds clogged and strained.

"Hello?" I say. "Is that Danny?"

"Yeah right." The voice belongs to a woman and now she is cross. I hear the phone drop, and there is banging and buzzing while another person picks it up.

"Danny here."

"Oh, hi. Sorry. Did I wake you?" My voice doesn't sound like my own. It sounds too far away.

"Two in the morning. What do you think?"

"Sorry."

"Is it Maggie?"

"Yes."

"Maggie, baby, whaddya *want*?"

Even loaded with sleep, Danny can make you forget not to laugh. It's that odd combination of Deep South American and posh Brit. It never sounds quite right, but somehow it fits with his sense of humour. I have never met Danny. But I have had long, easy conversations with him on the phone, on the rare occasions he phones his brother, and his brother is not there. Phoned.

"Danny, I think you'd better sit down." Seems the right thing to say, somehow. Perhaps sitting makes things easier to take.

"Haven't got up, baby. Come on. Can't be that bad."

What do you say to that? How can I say this so as not to hurt him? Is there a way? A gentle way to deliver this news that doesn't cut to his heart and leave him curled up and crying like I have been doing? Is there a way to stop this from spreading?

"Danny, Patrick's dead."

He laughs again. Then he stops laughing.

"It's a mistake," he says. The relief floods through me like a warm drink. A mistake. Of course. Of course.

"Oh, thank God. Is he with you?"

"What? No. Did you just say he was dead?" The relief was premature.

"Yes."

"Is it a joke?"

"That would be good, wouldn't it?" I am cross with him for some reason I can't fathom. Why did I have to tell him? Why doesn't he already know?

"What are you… What happened?"

"He was in an accident."

"Are you sure it was him?"

"No. Yes. They are, anyway."

"What if they got it wrong?"

"Is he there with you?"

"No. I said that. I think. Maggie…"

"He isn't here either."

"Oh."

"Yes."

Silence for a minute. Danny doesn't like to think.

"Are you still there?" I say.

"I guess."

"Why didn't you call?" I ask.

"I don't call every five minutes, you know that. Neither does Patrick."

"It wasn't every five minutes. I thought you might call to check he got back OK, for God's sake."

"Maggie, what are you talking about?"

"Why did he leave early?"

"Leave where?"

"You. Were some of the meetings cancelled?"

"He wasn't here."

"He told me... He said...He was meeting some lawn mower people in Atlanta. Staying with you."

"First I heard."

Another silence, as the same thought hits us both.

"You've not got to leap to stuff, you know?" he says. "It's probably innocent. He's not like me, you know that. He's not... There'll be another reason. Yeah?"

I am finding it hard to breathe.

"He lied," I say.

"You got to stop thinking what you're thinking, OK?"

I am not thinking anything, not now. Except that he lied.

"Hello?" says Danny.

"I'm still here."

"Is there going to be a funeral or something?"

"I don't know. I suppose..." I haven't thought. Did Ginger John mention anything about that? I can't remember. I don't remember much of what he said. I probably have to arrange something.

"You take care, babe." The words sound uncomfortable, coming out of his mouth. He doesn't know what to say. He wants to get off the phone.

"Yes."

"It's not what you're thinking."

"No."

The phone slips from my hand, missing the cradle. I think about picking it up and replacing it. It is sitting on the floor now, the end you put to your ear resting against the floorboard, the other end suspended by the cord. If it stays here then there won't be any more calls for a while. I could just leave it.

I pick up the receiver and put it back where it belongs. The phone rings. I let it.

"Leave a message," says Patrick. "I might even ring you back."

A click and a beep as the caller hangs up.

I grab the receiver again and bash the answerphone with it. I hit and hit until the receiver is covered in little black marks and the answerphone flies off the table, detaching itself from its cord.

"Leave a message. I might even ring you back," says Patrick. I have hit my hand. There is swelling on the knuckle. I stare at it, trying to remember.

I want to hit myself again, but I can't find the energy. I could have broken it. The machine. I could have taken away the last thing I have. I mustn't do that.

CT. Oh, God. It suddenly seems very possible that CT is a person. A female person. A blonde, maybe, good looking. She sways when she walks. She hypnotises men with her beauty and they will do anything for her. She has hypnotised my Patrick. My Patrick. As if he was ever mine. How could he have been mine? We weren't even in the same league. How could I have been so stupid? It was only a matter of time. He had to wake up some time. He had to see. There was no way he was just going to love me for ever, if he ever did. Perhaps it was all just an illusion. I wonder how long he stayed with me, wishing he could finish it, wishing he could just move on. He wouldn't want to hurt me. That was the sort of man he was. And at the same time, he would hate deceiving me. No wonder it was so difficult these past few weeks. No wonder we had been fighting. Poor man had been looking for the chance to piss off.

I look at the answerphone with its slowly blinking light. Is the answer in there? Do I want to hear it, if it is?

I decide I can't not, which is as good a reason as any to press the button.

"Hi Patrick. Steve. Listen, did you forget about the squash game? I'm at the court, and if you can get here in the next 10 minutes we've still got time to get a sweat on. Anyway. I'll try your mobile. OK. Bye then. Bye."

He didn't tell Steve he was going to America then. But he must have gone somewhere. Tuesday night was squash night, and he went wherever he went on Monday.

Beep.

"Hey Patrick. It's Ginny. Listen, Erica suggested you might swap shifts with me this weekend. Any chance you could? Got the chance to go to Twickenham and catch the match. And you wouldn't want a girl to miss that, would you? All those sweaty thighs!" A giggle. Beep.

Ginny. No. No way. Anyway, she always talked like that. Patrick didn't mind Ginny, but he found her posh girl behaviour irritating. I always thought it was ironic, bearing in mind just what an upper class so and so he could be at times, but I could see what he meant. There was a sort of unquestioning acceptance of privilege that so many of his contemporaries had, and he questioned everything. It made him quite intense, sometimes, and he would have long discussions with Emily about things that I didn't really see the importance of, like some letter a politician had written and what it all meant for the wider world. He was too intelligent for people like Ginny. I had no worries there.

"Patrick, hello. It's Martin Holloway from B&Q. I've had a look at your lawnmower design, and I do think it's very clever, but I'm not convinced there's a market for it. You don't seem to have researched that side of things. Do me a favour, mate. Do a bit of test marketing and see what's what, for me, will you? Great. Bye."

Beep.

Beep.

Click. Beep.

Beep.

"Patrick. Steve again. Where did you get to? And why aren't you answering your mobile? Give me a call. Want to know if you're still up for watching the match in the King's Arms on Saturday."

Perhaps I should ring Steve. Perhaps he doesn't know.

Beep.

"Patrick. Don't come today. I'll tell you about it later. Don't come."

The last voice was female, with a local lift to it. Low. Confident. Urgent, but not hurried. It was left on Friday.

My heart appears to have stopped.

I am not sure where the time has gone. First I played and replayed the messages for hours. Then I sat and played and replayed them in my head. Why didn't she say who she was? How well did she know him?

I'm not getting anywhere with any of this. I'm just going round and round and round again. He lied. Who's CT? Is it the woman who told him not to come? And why didn't she say her name? I have no answers, just questions. The same questions. Over and over and over again.

Shit. What time is it? I'm late. I must be. It's daylight out there. Shit. I've missed my show. Jed will be furious.

I go to the wardrobe, open the door, then sit down on the bed for a bit. Baby steps, as Emily would say. I feel my head shaking. Don't remember the decision to shake it. Feel strangely in my body but not. I look at the wardrobe. The next step involves choosing the clothes. There aren't many in here. They're mostly at my place. So it's not a difficult choice. I opt for black. Most of my things are black. I usually wear a belt or a scarf or something that has colour in it. Red, usually. I'm not going to today. My black knitted dress that ends just above the knee. The kind of dress you feel hugged in. One of his favourites. He likes the long knitted jacket that goes with it, as well. I look at them, hanging there, waiting. I'll get them in a minute. Got to take off this teeshirt first. It's stupid, because it's already lost its smell of him. It now smells of me. What was I thinking, wearing it? Even so, can't take it off. It's the chill. Every time I go to lift it over my head, I feel a chill wind blow, like the grave's got something to say about it. Got to stop this. Got to pull myself together. Got to do something other than sit here, sitting. I try again. I can't do it. The smell of rain is making its presence felt in my consciousness. Where has that come from? It isn't raining outside. I shut my eyes. I see a street. I remember that street. It was early on in our relationship, maybe a month in, maybe two.

It was raining. Warm drops of heavy rain, the way you remember it from childhood. Fun rain. I jumped forward and splashed in a puddle. A hand gripped my wrist and pulled me backwards, so I couldn't jump forwards straight away to minimise the wet to my feet. It didn't matter. Wet feet were part of the fun.

I grinned at Patrick, who was looking worried. I started to jump forward again, but he gripped my hand tighter and hissed at me to stop it.

"What's the matter?" I said.

"It's raining."

"I know."

"I hate the rain. Anyway I'm late."

"Well you would buy a British car. British cars always break down in the rain. It's the law."

It was the wrong time to make a joke. Something was bothering him. He looked around him, searching for something.

"What you looking for?" I said.

"Taxi."

"It's half a mile."

"It's raining."

"I know." I kicked the puddle I was walking through over his shoes. He clenched his teeth together.

"Maggie." He looked cross. I swung round and took his other hand, the one that wasn't clasping my wrist. I pulled my body towards his. I frowned at him. He tried to pull away. I stepped on his foot to hold it there.

"What are you doing?"

"You're already wet," I said.

I stood on the other foot. If he was going to move, he would have to dance with me. It was a game we'd played before.

"Aaaaaagh," he said, in mock exasperation. Then he let go of my arm and brought his hands to my face and held it there. The slow smile started to build across his face.

A bus pulled past us slowly, easing in towards the stop across the road. I broke away from him and ran towards it, pulling him along behind me.

"What are you doing?" he said.

"You're late. Come on. This one stops outside the hospital."

He stopped. I couldn't move forwards.

"No," he said.

"What?"

"No. No buses."

"What?"

"I'll be late."

"What?"

"It doesn't matter."

"What?"

"Are you going to say anything other than what?"

"You'll be late. Late. Late."

"So, I'll be late."

He was trying to sound calm, but his jaw was doing that flicking thing.

"Come on, get on the bus."

"No."

It was too late, anyway, because the bus was pulling away. I looked up at him.

"Come on," he said. "We better run."

"Why?"

"I'm late."

"Why wouldn't you take the bus?"

He stopped running and faced me, brushing a stray hair out of my eye and tucking it behind my ear. "I don't do buses. Come on."

"Why?"

"Bad things happen to me on buses."

A sound in the hall makes me jump. I get up to see what it is. Someone has pushed a newspaper through the letterbox, but it is too big to fit through. Sunday. I'm not late. I don't have to be in work. Why did I not know it was Sunday?

When I get home, Emily is frantic. She's been ringing Patrick's house. Of course. I don't say anything. Just sit on the piano stool, looking out the bay window. Watching the sea.

She calms down. Sits on the sofa watching me, watching the sea.

"What shall I do about work?" I say.

"I called them. Miles is doing your show for now."

"Poor Miles, he hates going on air."

"Well he shouldn't, he's a natural. He'll be fine."

Ginger John is on his own this time. He seems a little disconcerted to see Emily. Perhaps it's the scarlet hair. Perhaps when you're born ginger – and you're shy anyway and you've been through the whole school experience – it makes no sense to you when people pick red for their own head. Or perhaps it's that short skirt. Yes, I should think that's probably it. My mother would describe it as a pelmet, with a disapproving tut. But there isn't anything to be disapproving about – Emily has a very beautiful pair of legs; it makes no sense to hide them away.

Apparently I'm making him repeat himself. The doctors at the hospital registered the death. I don't need to worry about it. He told me this the other day, it seems. And he talked about some funeral people, but he also said I should check in case there were arrangements made by the deceased. He uses that word. Deceased. As if it's a normal word to use when talking about somebody.

I don't know about the funeral. I don't know what he would have wanted. We never discussed this. Never even thought about it. I know he doesn't like cremation, because he didn't like seeing Lottie disappearing behind those curtains. But I don't know what he feels about holes in the ground either. We didn't find these things out. We should have done.

There wasn't a suitcase. He had a briefcase on him, but they need to talk to his brother about that, and see if he wants it sending there.

"Why?"

"You weren't living together. It's just tricky. We've talked about it, because obviously he has you down in his wallet as the emergency contact, but we have these things we have to follow. We just need to check. I'm sure he'll be fine about it."

"What about the mobile phone?"

"That too. I just need to get his permission."

"Can you do it today?"

"I'll do my best."

"Thank you."

He stands to go, then waits again. It is just as if he doesn't know how to leave, how to stop a conversation. He always seems to have more to say. "OK then," he says, after a pause for thought. "OK."

It wasn't worth waiting for.

"Goodbye," I say.

"Oh, yes. Oh right. Goodbye. Yes. Goodbye."

Poor Ginger John. He reminds me of Patrick, a little bit. Only sometimes, when Patrick was feeling unsure of himself, he turned into a very large little boy. I would feel like I wanted to ruffle his hair and give him a bag of sweets. It didn't happen often, but when it did he would tilt his head down, and his eyes would flick away from you and then back, just the way that Ginger John's do when he is trying and failing to take his leave.

It makes me think of our trip to the Dales.

It was one of those glorious sunny days, where nothing catches up with you and everything seems wonderful. We had a week off. It was Friday, so I was free as soon as the show finished, and we had set off, Meg in the back of Barney's estate car, which was much more practical (and reliable) than Patrick's, our clothes for a week of walking stuffed into bags on the back seat; maps, water bottles, sandwich boxes, dog food and bowls, boots, waterproofs and rucksacks piled so high that there was no looking out of the rear view mirror.

I had never seen the Dales before. Patrick was over the moon to be showing me.

We stayed at Lottie's cottage in Camberdale. She was thrilled that he wanted to take me there. He never took girls there, she said. He usually went there alone to brood over his inventions and invariably came back in a worse mood than when he left. "Whatever you do," she said, "don't let him think about that wretched lawn mower – not even for a second."

It was tiny. You walked in through the front door to a kitchen which doubled as living space by virtue of a solitary sofa cramped in between the front door and the door to the stairs. There was a small table in the centre of the room, with two chairs tucked into it. There was a range cooker set into an alcove, and there were a few white cupboards with wooden handles either side of it. The sink was under the only window. It was a dark kitchen, even today, but it was cosy and welcoming all the same.

Patrick took Meg out to the garden to "get her settled," and I went on up the stairs. One bedroom, one bathroom, both decidedly snug. It was a holiday let most of the time, but someone had cancelled at the last minute, which gave us the chance to get away.

Back in the kitchen, there was a note from the lady who looked after the cottage in Lottie's absence, telling us to make ourselves at home, and that there was a bottle of milk in the fridge, and to look for the teabags in the cupboard in the corner.

Patrick and Meg returned. "What do you think?" he said.

"It's gorgeous," I said. "Does Lottie know there's only one bedroom?"

He squeezed round the kitchen table and came to perch on it behind me, as I faced out of the kitchen window. The table made us roughly the same height. He put his arms around my middle, pulled me back towards him, and leant his head against mine. "It's an awful thing to be the daughter of a country vicar," he said. "What does he think you get up to? Prayers before bed, and nothing between the neck and the knees?"

I laughed. We'd heard someone on the radio saying that thing about the neck and the knees, ages ago. He sets the radio alarm to go off at really odd times of the day, all over the house. I have never worked out why or for what purpose. I certainly couldn't find the logic to it. Anyway, we were in bed at the time, and it made us laugh so much we couldn't concentrate on what we were doing.

And now I don't even know why it's funny.

I leaned to the side and turned my face so I could kiss him. "Want to investigate between the neck and the knees right now?" I said. Or something similarly awful. The sorts of things you say to each other when you're in the mood, and you'd hate anybody else to hear them.

He pushed me away and stood up. "No," he said, all business-like. "Come on. The day is shot!"

That was the signal to get on. It was something one of his uncles used to say to him, and it meant that time was passing and the day would soon be over. He said it as a joke, more than anything. He wasn't exactly a morning person. Mind you, he'd never used it to turn down sex before. I watched him in amazement, as he grabbed both sets of boots from the porch. "Here," he said, proffering mine.

"You've just turned me down," I said.

"Later, woman. We have a hill to climb."

"Are you feeling all right?"

He stopped mid tie of the shoe lace and looked up at me. He checked his watch. "All right," he said, kicking his boots off. "But if you're not screaming in ecstasy in 15 minutes I'm going for it anyway, and you can bloody well wait till tonight for your jollies. Got it?"

"No pressure there then."

He makes me laugh. Even now, he makes me laugh.

Anyway. Yes. Stonesett. It was a long way up, I remember that. We parked near a ruined abbey and walked through the woods there and along the river. Then we started going up. And up. And up. On and on we went. Patrick used to run to keep fit; I viewed the walk to my car as exercise enough – but he was very sweet to me: solicitous, as my mother would say. He was longing to get to the top, and yet he waited while I caught my breath and suggested that we stop and look at the view as soon as I seemed to be struggling. It was amazing, looking down over the grouse moor at the hills beyond. The view disappeared behind the brow of the hill we were standing on, which suddenly seemed to spring large clumps of rock. It was very lunar. Of course, I doubt the moon has heather in between its rock formations, but there was definitely something of the one small step for man about it. It didn't look as if it was designed for human beings, more for people with pointed ears and laser guns. I thought about saying that to him, but it would only invite endless impressions of Yoda and I thought I could live without that. And then, finally, we were near the top and the view of the surrounding valleys reappeared. There were the softly sloping contours of Camberdale laid out in front of us, with all its green fields and tiny villages. I stopped, not really out of breath, but breathless all the same. It was the most beautiful view I'd ever seen.

"I knew you'd like it," he said. "Blue sky. Slight breeze. And that." He swung his arm round to indicate the view. "Doesn't get much better than this, does it?"

I shook my head, and breathed in the beauty of the place.

"Come on," he said.

He took my hand and helped me to climb onto the top of the rocks. There the view was even more extraordinary than before. A wisp of white cloud which didn't seem to be much higher than where we stood seemed to be racing towards us across the valley. I couldn't take my eyes away from the view. There was a tiny lake over on the right, and a miniature stately home in between it and us. Everything looked soft, gentle, quiet. I thought I could stay there for ever.

"Sort of place you could forgive anyone anything," he said.

I turned to face him. I wasn't sure what he meant. He had on his little boy lost look. Had I done something?

"What is it?" I said. "What's the matter?"

He just stood, with his head tilted over, looking at me. I searched through my brain, looking for whatever it was I could have said or done.

"Have I upset you? What have I done? Whatever it is, I didn't... God, what is it? I didn't mean it." I said.

He shook his head. "No. No. Not you. Maggie, can I ask you a question?"

I felt as though his eyes were piercing my face. It all seemed very serious, all of a sudden. "What?" I managed.

"Could you forgive me if I did something...?"

"What sort of something?"

"Not good."

Again, the big little boy with the nervous look on his face. He wouldn't have looked wrong in short trousers with buckled shoes. I laughed. This was too ridiculous. What could he have done?

"Well, if you've been shagging another woman, I think you should just come out and tell me."

"Not that," he said. But he didn't smile. Why was he being so serious?

"And I think I'd struggle a bit if you turned out to be an axe murderer. Where is it? Where's the axe?"

I started to pull off his rucksack, getting it a little way down his arms so that he couldn't move, then I pretended to look through it. I turned him round to face me. "Can't find the axe," I said. "So it must be OK." I reached up and stroked his hair back away from his face. "What is it?" I said. "Can't be that bad."

There was a moment, a long one, where it felt as though we were standing on the edge of a cliff. Which of course we were, but I mean metaphorically. It was as though he was about to tell me something momentous. I held my breath.

"I forgot the chocolate brownies," he said, shaking the rucksack down and loosening his arms.

I laughed. "You bastard."

"Sorry. I remembered everything else. Look, we have sandwiches, and iced buns, and everything. Just no chocolate brownies."

I couldn't seem to stop giggling.

"You had me going there. I thought you were going to tell me something awful."

"So you forgive me, then?"

"For the chocolate brownies? We'll see. Iced buns, you say?"

I often thought about that day afterwards. Was he going to tell me something? Of course, I always told myself no, it was just a joke. But was he? Was there some big secret? And does it have anything to do with not going to America, or going to America, or whatever? What am I supposed to think?

When Ben died I used to make believe he was there, in the room. People said it might happen, that you imagine it, to get over someone. You hear the person's ghost and talk to them as if they're still there. Part of the denial phase. Shock, denial, anger, acceptance – the calibrations of bereavement. A scientific way of explaining why you behave like a rhino with colic who is allergic to all the other animals in the zoo.

My imaginings of Ben produced nothing. An emptier room than the one I inhabited alone before I tried to find something of him. At fifteen I ended my experiments with the occult in the knowledge that no spirits existed after death, because Ben would not have left the sister he had squashed on the sofa, twirled round the living room, and held upside down in a swimming pool suffering such a loss as this, without some words of comfort. Ben would have made contact, if he could. He didn't. He wasn't there. Of course he wasn't. And all that stuff my father preached over the years, the Father, Son and Holy Ghost business, well that was a falsehood. A lie. We are what we are. That was my decision. One that had kept me sane through the years of longing for my absent brother. He didn't come back because he couldn't. He wasn't there.

All the same, maybe it is worth a try.

Maybe Ben was cross with me because I missed his funeral and that was why he stayed silent. Maybe Patrick will be different. I light a candle. That's what they told you to do in the magazine I read when I was fourteen. It was not aimed at teenagers. Its market was rather older, which is why we liked to read it, or to be seen to read it. When you got past all the unspeakable sexual positions involving bodily fluids I really didn't want to know about, they had snippets of information about other parts of life, and once they talked about contacting the dead. It was my friend Sarah's magazine. That's what I told my parents when they found it. It wasn't mine. I was banned from seeing Sarah for three weeks.

I take the candle to the bathroom and place it on the floor in front of the long mirror on the back of the door. I sit on the edge of the bath, looking into the mirror beyond the candle, attempting to empty my mind. These are the instructions. I don't need to see the magazine to remember it; I tried so many times it is fixed in my brain.

Empty the mind. This was the bit I always struggled to do. My mind refuses to be empty. As soon as I think the words, "Empty your mind," it starts chugging away, repeating the instructions over and over and filling itself up with useless rubbish like the idea that unconsciousness is surely the only way to truly empty the mind so perhaps I should hit myself over the head. I move onto the next phase, which is to imagine a white light. My brain jiggles around some more, questioning how an empty mind imagines things, or follows instructions for that matter. I remember the white light always takes a little time, and the candle helps. Perhaps that is its purpose, to provide a white light for the souls which lack the imagination to produce one of their own.

White light. It is a sort of greyish light, but it is the best I can manage. I stare into it and let my eyes go soft, out of focus, waiting for a figure to emerge. The magazine had warned this part might take some time. When I was fourteen it took all my time, because it didn't work. I carry on staring, trying to ignore the numbness in my left ankle, which is crossed under my right. The grey light swooshes a little and reasserts itself. Is that a message? Are the spirits trying to tell me something?

"Patrick?"

The grey light shifts once more, and disappears. My eyes are crossed, that is all. I softened the focus a little too much.

I blow out the candle and leave the bathroom. Stupid. Stupid playing with candles. Thank goodness Emily is asleep.

There's the piano. It is too late to play. Emily will wake up. I sit on the stool and touch the keys. There is a tingling feeling, like electricity, but ever so faint. It's hard to describe, but it kind of draws my fingers along the keys, mapping out a tune. I watch my fingers. They seem to belong to someone else. As my fingers that aren't my fingers gently brush each key without playing it, I hear its note in my head. Words form to join them. "I like New York in June, how about you?" My fingers are playing a song that isn't mine. It belongs to him. The tingling sensation is buzzing through my hands and up my arms. It is too much. I pull my hands away.

"Patrick?"

There is no response. Of course.

It's gone cold and I only just noticed. If this moonlight piano thing is going to be a regular feature, maybe I should reset the central heating to come on in the middle of the night. Alternatively, maybe I should wear a few more layers over his pyjamas. I think of anything, other than the piano being played, or rather me being played, by the dead. I touch the keys again. No signals this time. No electricity. It was just my imagination.

"Patrick?" I say. The room is empty, and yet there is me in it, and Emily asleep on the sofa.

Monday, 27th November

A red sky. Shepherds' warning. Or is it shepherd's? Several or one? How amazing, the things the brain will do to make you think of other things. This isn't my first quibble of the day. I have already spent several minutes in the bathroom, staring at the ceiling, wondering about the origins of that word. Not a very English word, I have been thinking, as a spider eased down from it, apart from the 'ing' part, of course, before I realised that it really doesn't matter anyway. I am wrong. Not about it not mattering, about it not being English. Middle English, apparently, from the verb to ceil which has a lot to do with plaster. (It may not have mattered, but I looked it up all the same.)

Now I am standing at the bay window in the living room, watching the waves and wondering about that warning. What could the red sky warn of today? It wasn't red on Friday. Maybe it only denotes awful things happening to sheep. Maybe it would be an equally appropriate, if less poetic, saying, if it went, "Red sky in the morning, radio personality's recap of recent unpleasant events." A post modern proverb.

Dad arrives flushed. He hates motorway driving and avoids it if at all possible, preferring to trundle gently through country lanes for days on end, making a holiday of the journey, rather than choosing a holiday destination. However, Emily's tone on the phone has meant that needs must. She called him while I was in the bathroom. She is worried because I didn't sleep, and I won't take

57

the pills she wants me to have. She hasn't told him, she says. She wants him to get here safely and she's not sure that this news is the best for that. She just said could he come and she'd explain when he got here. And now she's not here. She had to go home and get some clean clothes and her hair straighteners. She's coming back as soon as she can.

He is standing in the doorway looking confused and worried.

"Where's Mum?" I say.

He looks behind him down the steps, as if trying to remember, then turns back to me and says, "I haven't told her about Emily's call. I thought it best. I thought she should perhaps stay. I thought that you and I could have a little talk."

I hug him. The presence of my mother has a tendency to make things worse. She never intends to, but she reacts to all bad news as if it belongs to her. She isn't one for making room for other people's grief. Hers is so overwhelmingly powerful. It often amazes me that their marriage survived the death of my brother, but it seemed to become even stronger, somehow − as if by being forced to grieve quietly my father was able to come to a richer understanding and acceptance. He never did like wailing. Perhaps my mother did his wailing for him.

"Shall I come in for a bit?" he says.

"Sorry. Yes. Cup of tea?"

I clank around with the kettle and the cups and he stands, watching me. He doesn't pay any attention to the mess in the flat, which Mum would have done. He simply stands, his head on one side, and watches quietly; the essence of the country vicar meeting one of his parishioners.

I hand him a mug and we go through to the living area. I sit on the sofa. My father walks to the bay window and gazes out at the sea.

"It's Patrick, isn't it?" he says.

I feel the awful over the edge feeling again, as if I'm on some sort of roller coaster ride and my insides can't quite keep up with the gravity. I stare at my mug. It is my favourite mug. There is a chip on it I have never noticed before.

"Has he done something?" says Dad. He is trying not to give

anything away. He is trying not to judge this man, Patrick, who has so clearly hurt his little girl. He is trying to pull himself up into a form that can understand all behaviour and forgive it. He has to, it isn't just his job, it is his whole being. My father turns the other cheek.

Even so, I don't want him to think that Patrick has done anything bad. I'm not sure I believe it myself. I stand and go over to him, joining him in looking out to sea.

"Patrick died on Friday," I say, my voice flat and unwavering, slicing through the rhythm of the tide.

Dad is very still. He says nothing. He carries on staring out to sea, although I have a feeling he isn't seeing a great deal of it any more. I tip the rest of the details into the silence.

"He was in a bus and it was in a crash – a car jumped a red light. There was a post and the bus hit it side on. They think it was an accident, but they want to get the car driver for dangerous driving. Only one person died. The rest just had cuts and bruises. Not even that, some of them."

Dad waits for me to say more. He puts his hand on my shoulder to show he is still listening. He has found, over the years, that parishioners tell you much more if you don't speak. It is a technique he has perfected, one that I have never managed to master. I fear my mother's genes take over in the talking stakes.

Of course, I tell him everything. The row. The fact we didn't speak for five days. The first time we missed a day since we met. The awful things I said. The bus. The phone call to Danny. CT. The woman on the phone.

"Let's sit," he says. We walk to the sofa, and he sits down, pulling me down onto his lap the way he did when I was five years old.

"I'm too heavy," I say.

"There's nothing of you," he says. "And anyway, you need a cuddle."

He holds me there, not moving, for I don't know how long, and eventually the tears come again. I sob, and he rocks me and holds me. This wouldn't have been possible with Mum here. Mum would have been railing against the injustice of it all, demanding to hang the driver of the car, and screaming with hysterics at that God of my father's. He is always Dad's God when things go badly. He becomes the God of everyone when things are going well.

"Danny's right," he says.

"What about?"

"There will be an explanation. Patrick doted on you. Your mother and I were so happy when you found him." His voice is breaking up. He stops speaking, breathing deeply to get back his composure. "Sorry," he says. "This isn't helpful. But he wouldn't be messing around. How could he be?"

"I don't know, Dad. But he lied."

"Then it must have been important."

The phone rings. I want to pick it up, but Dad holds me still. "You've got an answerphone," he says. "Use it."

We listen.

The caller hangs up.

"I don't want to leave," I say.

Dad made eggs which neither of us ate. Now he is washing up, I am drying. It is a solemn little ceremony.

"Just for a few days," he says.

"No, Dad. I can't. Patrick's here."

He looks around him, playing for time, trying to come up with the argument that will win me over. He puts the last of the dishes on the draining board and dries his hands.

"Don't you want to come home? You haven't been back for such a long time."

He is cross with himself for this comment, I can tell. He pushes his tongue over his top teeth and into the back of his top lip, and he shakes his head. I knew he was hurt. I have known for some time. The remaining child doesn't even want to come home any more. It must feel as if they lost both of us. But I can't do it. I can't go from this place with its memories of Patrick to that place with its memories of Ben. I can't substitute this aching feeling for that one, not at the moment. And I can't say that to Dad.

He knows anyway. "You've still got Ben's watch, I see," he says.

"Yes. Always."

"You don't want one that tells the time, then?"

"I'm sorry, Dad."

He picks up the cloth and begins to wipe the taps, searching for the words that will drive me home.

"I need to be around his things," I say.

"Of course you do," he carries on wiping. "You want some company?"

"What would the people of the parishes of St Mark's and St John's have to say about that?"

"They are a little more charitable than you give them credit for."

I am sorry. His work means everything to him. Even though I can't believe in the same things, I can at least see that he does some good. I find it hard to forgive some of his parishioners, though, when they wouldn't forgive me. In the aftermath of Ben's death, which I discovered so much later than everyone else, owing to a small coma, I went a little 'off the rails', as I heard it described. Some of my father's parishioners decided I needed to learn a lesson. It is their idea of godliness that I can't come to terms with. And it is this that floods through my head whenever I think of Dad's church. Highly unfair on him, but there it is.

"You… I don't think you should stay, Dad. I don't want to pull you away from your work. I'm feeling a lot better, really."

"Is there someone who can look after you?"

"Emily."

"Ah. Of course." The look of slight distaste crosses his face before he can wipe it clean. Forgiving he may be, charitable, certainly. Racist, well, I am very much afraid he shares that with my mother. Not intentionally, of course. He just lives in a small village in the South East surrounded by people who look a lot like him. He frowns on black skin as a reflex, not a decision. Much as I love my father, it is one of the things that separates us. It is one of the things that means we can never be as close again as once we were, when I was small and my world was all white.

I don't want him here. The thought horrifies me. Have I grown so far apart from my family? Would it have happened if Ben was still in place, moderating and mediating and driving them demented with pride in his accomplishments? No, probably not. But then, I wouldn't have moved away. I would have carried on in my narrow little world with my narrow little focus. I would be a completely different person.

So maybe, in some ways, Ben dying was a good thing. No. That thought should never have happened. I want it out. I shake my head.

"What is it love?" says Dad.

"Nothing. Nothing. Just... Nothing."

"All right," he says, and he rubs my back and whispers "Shhh." When I have stopped shaking, he says, "I'll stay until after dinner, then I'll leave you in peace."

"I love you, Dad." It isn't something I have said to him before. To either of them. It isn't the right thing to say.

He looks at the carpet and doesn't answer.

Emily loves the term "flip-flop." If she can find a way to slot it into an interview with a politician, she will do. They can't get away with simply changing their minds in Emily's presence – they must have committed the terrible sin of flip-flopping. I have often wondered about this. I mean, if you never allow a politician to change his mind about things, how can he act on things he has learnt through experience? Or she. I think that's why I can't be a news journalist. I can't get my head around attack for the sake of attack. I don't understand the thrill of the chase, and the excitement of making someone look bad just because you can.

I think I probably understand flip-flopping more than I understand the reasons why it's a bad thing to do.

So I probably couldn't be a politician either.

I have been flip-flopping since Friday. Either I can't move, or I can't stay still. I can't be here and I can't be at his house. I can't be at work and I can't be at home. I can't see why he wouldn't cheat on me and I can't see how he could. I love him. I resent him. I want him to hold me. I want to shake him until he hurts as badly as I do.

Flip-flop, flip-flop.

Dad says I must find out where he was, and why he was on the bus. He mentioned Patrick's car. I hadn't even thought about it. There's no sign of it at home – his or mine. I sent Emily to the hospital car park to see if it was there. It wasn't. I called Ginger John, and he said he would put out a something-or-other, some three letter acronym, and see if they could find it. He said not to worry. He said Danny had given permission for me to have Patrick's briefcase and phone. I said did he want me to come and collect them and he said no, there was something he wanted to talk to me about in person.

So now I'm waiting for him to arrive. I'm playing an old piece of Chopin that I haven't played for years. My fingers are struggling with it, and I keep going wrong, but somehow the dischords work today, rather than the chords. Chopin à la Schoenberg. Poor old Chopin. I hope he's not listening, wherever he is.

And there's the doorbell. A reprieve for the neighbours.

He looks as if he might have spent the night in his car. His shirt is crumpled, he has a sort of sleepy look about the eyes, and there is a white mark on the side of his mouth, which might be milk or it might be toothpaste. I am trying not to stare at it, so I can't really tell what it is.

He is panting slightly, although the stairs aren't that steep and he is a policeman. I always thought they were supposed to be fit.

"Sorry," he says. I wonder if that's always the first thing he says. I wonder if he is aware of it, if it is.

"Are you all right?" I say.

"Sorry," he says. "That should be my question. How are you?"

He is blushing again.

"You first," I say.

He seems taken aback. It is not supposed to go like this, it seems. He wants to tell me he is fine, but he is struggling to answer at all.

"You look like you could do with a coffee," I say.

"I just er… had… Yes. Thank you. Coffee would be good." He follows me through to the kitchen, placing Patrick's briefcase down on the sofa as he comes through. "I, er… that's… there's the briefcase, there, for you."

"Thank you." I have been avoiding looking at it. I don't want to seem too eager. I don't want him to know there is something wrong between us. Patrick and me, not him and me. I don't know why. I shouldn't care what he thinks. But I'd rather not let on that there are unanswered questions about Patrick. For now.

"No sugar, thanks. Can I use your loo?"

"What? Oh. Yes. Sure."

And now it's just me and Patrick's briefcase. I sit next to it on the sofa. I touch its soft leather. I open it. It belonged to his grandfather – Lottie's father. There are pictures of him in Patrick's house. He looks a sweet, kind man. He's always patting a dog, or clipping roses, or doffing a cap, or something. I would like to have met him. I click open the catch and look inside. His mobile phone is here. His lawn mower sketch that he takes everywhere. His wallet. A few opened envelopes. A pen. A screw driver. Some screws. And a tape measure. This makes me laugh. He would have a screw driver. For eventualities. He did love eventualities.

"What have you found?" says John. He makes me jump. I didn't hear him come out.

I show him the screw driver and the tape measure.

"We wondered about those," he says. The toothpaste, or whatever it was, has gone from the side of his mouth. His hair looks smoothed down and perhaps a little wet. It is the look of someone who has done their best in the absence of a brush. He looks tired.

"Do you have many people like me?" I say.

"Sorry? What? Radio personalities?"

"No. Grieving people."

"Oh. Oh, I see." He looks at his feet. He is blushing again. "A few. It's been a quiet week, really."

"That's good."

"Yes. Yes, I suppose it is."

"Are you going to tell me what's the matter?" I say. It is perhaps a little forward, bearing in mind I hardly know the poor man, and he is only here because he has a job to do, but if you don't ask, they don't tell you, and frankly, anybody's angst is a diversion from my own at the moment.

He looks shocked.

"I don't know what you're… I, er… There isn't… Anything. You know, the er, the matter."

I don't say anything. I just look at him. Perhaps my father's genes are bashing some of my mother's out of the way.

"Can we sit down?" he says.

The kettle is reaching boiling point. It is perhaps the loudest kettle in the history of kettles. I wish I had tested it in the shop. Finally it clicks off and I pour out the coffees and take them through to the living area, where Ginger John fidgets on the sofa.

"Sorry. Thank you," he says, as I hand him his drink and kneel on the floor on the other side of the coffee table.

"I prefer the floor," I say to the worried look on his face.

"Right. Sorry. Um... I have something to tell you. I'm not sure how... er... Well... It's probably best just to come straight out with it."

I think my heart may have stopped. Patrick? Was he doing something dodgy in Strayfield? Was he some kind of criminal overlord, running his affairs from the middle of a bus? Why, when my body won't work, is my mind working overtime to come up with this drivel?

"It's about Mr Sc... the, er, the driver of the car," he says.

"The bastard who jumped the red light?"

"Well, sort of."

"What do you mean?"

Silence. Ginger John pulls his hand through his hair and looks into his coffee. He stands up and goes to the window. He remembers himself and turns around to face me. He tries to say something. He stops. He comes back to sit on the sofa once more.

"There isn't any evidence."

"What?"

"Nobody saw. Anything. People looked when they heard brakes, and they looked when they heard the er, the impact itself, but nobody was actually looking at the time he ran... may have run the red light. And the camera wasn't working that day. Which, rest assured, we will look into."

"I'm not sure what you're telling me."

"It's not ideal, I know."

"What isn't?"

"The CPS say we can't prosecute."

"The CPS do?"

"Yes."

"And the CPS is a law unto itself."

"Yes."

I have been hit in the stomach. I can't even look at my visitor.

"How?" I manage.

"We thought it was clear, but we can't prove it. The bus driver got a bang on the head and can't remember any of the journey at all. And the car driver stopped saying anything as soon as he was cautioned."

"So he admitted it before?"

"It doesn't… It really doesn't serve any purpose to worry about that."

"But did he?"

He is embarrassed. He looks into his coffee. He doesn't deny it.

"I'm sorry," he says.

And now I have an image of fat Mr Schofield the insurance man, on his sofa eating his crisps. And laughing. Laughing and laughing and laughing. Why not? What has he lost? Nothing. His car will be insured. His life will go on as it did before. And what is he to think about some stranger on a bus, some bloke he'll never meet, would never have met?

They can't prove it.

And so he walks. He takes someone's life. He ruins mine. And he is just going to work today? Just like any other day?

This is not right.

This is not bloody right.

Tuesday, 28th November

Barney has taken over the funeral, which probably wouldn't ever happen if left to me. I didn't know what he wanted. We never had that discussion. Barney did. They talked about it all the time, apparently. He left five minutes ago, brochures in hand. Didn't want to step on my toes, he said. He loved him too. Of course he did. I didn't mean to imply that he didn't. I don't think I did imply that. But I didn't react the way he wanted me to and so I have upset him.

He is cross about CT, too. "How could you think that?" he said. "Didn't you trust him? After all he went through for you? You think he was fooling around?"

What did he go through for me? What did Barney mean? I should have asked him.

I can't get this wretched mobile phone to work. I keep pressing it, but nothing happens. I've tried charging it, but nothing lights up. It has a little dent. It may have been the impact.

Emily arrives from doing the breakfast news.

"I don't want to be cremated," I say.

"OK. Can I come in, though?"

"Yes."

She throws her coat over the back of the sofa, pulls her miniskirt down a little bit to preserve her modesty and tips herself backwards over the arm of the sofa, long legs left draping there, back sinking into the cushions. I lean my elbows on the back of the sofa. I press the button on the top of the mobile phone again, just in case it has changed its mind.

"No cremation," she says, taking the phone from me and trying the button. "Buried at sea?"

"Compost."

"What?"

"I heard about it on the radio. It's the most environmentally friendly way of dying, apparently. Compost."

"Right."

"Patrick's being cremated. He told Barney."

"Oh."

"I didn't think he would, after Lottie. But he told Barney at the pub. Cremation."

"Well, it's quite normal, isn't it, to be cremated?"

"He didn't tell me."

"No, love. He wanted to live with you not die from you. Anyway, did you tell him about the compost?"

"No."

"No. Because you're not morbid and gloomy, and you weren't before either, and there really isn't anything to feel guilty about."

"There isn't?"

"No."

"Simple as that." I am aware I spat those words out. That wasn't necessary. I reach for her hand. She gives it, dropping the mobile phone beside her with the other.

"Compost. God, you're weird."

"He wants to be scattered in the Dales."

"He always liked it there."

"Yes."

"When are we going?"

"Sorry?"

"We *are* all going? You, me, Barney?"

I haven't thought.

"Think about it," she says. "Plenty of time. He can sit in an urn for a bit, till you're ready."

I shudder at the mention of the urn.

"I'll never be ready."

"Think about it."

I haven't told her about fat Mr Insurance. But he hasn't been far from my thoughts. I want to sit him in a bus and find a way to fling it at a metal post. See how he likes it. I want to crush him to death, crumple his face like Patrick's was crumpled. That's the face I see now. A crumpled face. I don't have access to the creases in his face any more, just this one that's folded in on itself. And yet Mr Insurance, whom I have never met, I see in all his fat, tortilla chip dipping glory.

"Penny for your thoughts," says Emily.

"Nothing."

"Have you heard any more from Danny?"

"He's coming over on Thursday."

"Oh. Well that's good."

"Yes."

"He'll get to say goodbye."

"Yes."

"You'll get to meet him."

"Yes."

"OK."

She has run out of things to say. She shuts her eyes. I sit down on the floor, my back against the sofa. She puts her hand on my shoulder. There isn't any need for the talking. The talking can stop, that's my feeling. For good. We can just sit here with our thoughts. In mine, Mr Insurance is crashing horribly and bumpily over a cliff. I may or may not have pushed him. Emily's eyes have fallen on Patrick's briefcase. I pick it up. I click open the catches and empty it out on the floor in front of me. Emily leans forward and picks up the screwdriver, a sad smile crossing her face. His diary is here. I didn't spot it before.

CT. There it is. Friday. 4 pm. I flick back through the weeks. Thursday, the week before, 6.30 pm. CT. And the week before that. And the week before that. Going back over several weeks. Going forwards over the next one, two, three, four, five weeks. Thursday evening. His night for helping out with OT. No. His night for visiting CT. Shit. But not this week. This week it was Friday. It couldn't wait a week while he was in America, or wherever. And I nearly let Barney convince me there was nothing going on.

"What is it?" says Emily.

I show her. "Bloody Hell," she says. Too right. "Who the hell is CT?" she says. It's a question we keep asking. Barney doesn't know either. Nobody knows. This must be evidence of something, surely, because lies are involved. He hasn't been at Occupational Therapy, because if he had it would say OT, or Martha, whom he helps there. Or maybe he doesn't. Didn't. I have met Martha. She certainly told me he helped there. I call the hospital.

"Martha please," I say.

"Martha who?" says a grumpy voice on the end of the line.

"I don't know. How many Marthas are there?"

The woman sighs. Which department?

"Occupational Therapy."

I hear the ring tone. "OT," says Martha. I recognise the voice. It is quite high and breathless, as if she had to run to the phone, but she always sounds like that.

"Martha? It's Maggie."

"Oh, Maggie. Oh, I'm so so sorry. I heard what happened. We just can't believe it. None of us can believe it."

I shut my eyes. I say, "Martha, you know Patrick used to help out with OT?"

"Yes." She is crying.

"Thursday evenings?"

"Oh, no. No. He used to give up his lunch hour, when he worked days. He was so generous. You'd think he'd want to go off and get a sandwich or something, but he did seem to enjoy coming down and helping get people started with things. He said it was like watching them get their life back."

"Lunchtimes."

"Yes."

"So no Thursday evenings, then?"

"No. We don't work evenings."

"Oh. Right."

I hang up before she can tell me she's sorry again. Emily is looking over the top of her glasses at me, biting her bottom lip.

"He wasn't at OT," I say.

"Have they found Patrick's car yet?" she says. I think of Ginger John. The apology and the shake of the head. Then another apology as I left the police station. No sign of his car. Not in a pound. Not spotted out and about. No car.

"No."

"Mystery."

"Yes."

I can't think where it might be. I think of that old black and white film with the freaky old silent movie star keeping some poor young writer prisoner. Sunset Boulevard. At the start of the film, while he's running from the Mob, he parks his car in an abandoned garage. But silent movies weren't really Patrick's thing. Besides, he wouldn't just park his car in some stranger's garage. He loves that car. Stupid thing. Always breaking down. He is always thumbing lifts to garages, or calling me up from the roadside.

That car must have let him down hundreds of times since we've been together.

I never knew him to catch a bus. Never.

I'm back on this again. I don't know why I bother. None of it makes sense. None of it is going to make sense. I should just stop thinking about it. As Ben would have said, it's doing my head in.

That thought is a mistake.

Patrick's crumpled head returns to my vision.

"You OK?" says Emily.

"Yep."

"It's just you sort of yelped."

"I did?"

"Yeah."

"Oh."

I didn't know.

The smiling man at the Mobile Place doesn't hold out much hope for the phone.

"Did you save your numbers?"

"Sorry?"

"On the SIM card?"

"What's a SIM card?"

He sighs heavily, preparing to adjust his approach. He realises he is talking to a technophobe, it must dawn on him that more than half the spiel he has tried on me so far is utterly wasted. I don't have a mobile phone. I never had one. I don't see the point. If I want to talk to somebody I can always find a phone, and if I don't, why should I carry something around that makes it easy for people to talk to me? Then there's all this business with a SIM card, which I have no interest in understanding. Except that I must try, because it may hold the information I need. If I can understand this and somehow get to the information held there, then perhaps I can find CT.

"Then you probably didn't. If you don't know what it is."

"Didn't what?"

"Save your numbers so you could transfer them to another phone."

"I'd better have another phone," I say.

The light that switched itself off only moments ago, flickers back into his dark eyes. "What sort?" he says, reaching for a brochure and thumbing through to display a selection of remarkably similar looking pieces of metal.

"The cheapest," I say.

"Well what do you want to do with it? Do you want to be able to take photos, because this one has a 3 mega pixel camera? Or do you want a Blackberry? Yeah? Then you can synchronise your diary and everything on it. And this one's got extra memory. Is that what you're looking for?"

"The cheapest," I say again.

"But that's not a very good phone," he says. "It hardly does anything. The one you've got is top of the range."

"Will it accept this — SIM — was it? Card?"

"What? Yes. I suppose."

"Then it's fine."

He seems less sure of himself. He is not used to this. There must be very few people who don't leap at the chance of 60 billion pixels of RAM, or mega Bluetooth, or whatever it is he's been trying to sell me. "Right," he says. "What colour do you want?"

"I want a phone."

The metal stairs to the flat seem noisier than before. Perhaps a screw has come loose and the metal is reverberating with more force. Or perhaps I just hear things now in a way that I didn't before. There was always a peace about these stairs, even though they clattered. I know that sounds ridiculous. These stairs signal the end of a working day, they signal home, space, privacy. You round the building away from the rush of the sea and the screeching of gulls, and you reach the back yard with its wheelie bins and the little scrub of grass I can never be bothered to do anything with, and there you are at the steps to my home. Nobody here. No demands. In more recent times, the need for there to be nobody here was replaced by the need for there to be somebody here. But it was always home. It was always a safe place. Once I'd reached those steps.

Now I wonder if a safe place exists at all. And the steps clank and clatter, and the door is too big for its frame and the plant in the entrance needs attention and the curtains are falling off the rail and the sofa is pushed sideways and the piano is covered in dust and the bathroom light is still on from this morning and the plate of uneaten toast is still on the coffee table and the flowers I have been sent are thirsty and going brown and the rug has a ruffle in it and there are clothes all over my bedroom floor and my flat is empty.

It's empty.

I mustn't think.

I must somehow get this phone to work. The man with the dark eyes put the old SIM card in here for me. He showed me where to find the on button, but I can't see it now. I tip the box out onto the sofa and sort through various plastic wrapped wires until I reach the instruction book. An instruction book to find an on button. Something tells me I will not get on very well with my new purchase.

It's there. It doubles as a "no" button. I suppose that makes sense. They are made up of the same letters, after all.

It makes a noise and a bright logo flashes up and shrinks back again. It is working, at least.

Somehow I find the address book. No contacts. He said something about saving things onto the SIM card. The instruction book is too frustrating for words. Rather than flicking through pages, I might as well just look through the options on the phone. At least then it feels like I'm doing something.

Nothing in File Manager, nothing in Settings, nothing nothing nothing. I try every possible option. Nothing. I come back to the "Contacts" menu. The one I tried first. There is an "Options" button. I try that. SIM contacts. Fourth one down.

No CT. No C anything. Or T anything. It's just directories and 1471. Nothing.

After all that. But then, I don't think I expected to find anything. Not knowing is becoming more familiar than knowing. Perhaps I will have to be content with that.

There must be something at his house. Something I missed.

I leave the phone on the sofa, with the box it came in and their various contents. More mess, to add to the existing mess. I will sort it out later. It will give me something to come back to.

I slam the door shut behind me and clatter and clank my way down the steps. There must be a screw loose, they are starting to feel unsteady. Why couldn't he have just saved his contacts onto the card? Why wouldn't he? He was always one for saving effort. Well, surely that would have saved effort when he came to change the phone. There is someone on the bottom step. It is Emily. I haven't noticed, because I have been preoccupied with rubbish. What does it matter about why he did or didn't do whatever he did or didn't do with his bloody mobile phone?

"Hey, you," she says. "You OK? Where you going?"

"Patrick's house."

"Wait a minute."

She is barring my way.

"I need to go."

"Hold on a minute."

"There must be something there. CT. There must be. I need to know who it is."

"Mags, calm down. Mags. Look at me. Look at me. Please, love. Please. Wait. Talk to me."

"Why?"

"Because if you get in your car in this state, I'm going to end up with two funerals to go to."

"Would that be such a bad thing?"

She looks as if I have slapped her in the face.

"Sorry," I say.

"I know who CT is."

"Why didn't you say?"

"Are you going to calm down now?"

"Who is it?"

She does the dancing eyes thing, looking from one eye to the other. She looks worried. She reaches into her bag and takes out a folded piece of paper, which she gives to me.

"A press release?"

"Look at it."

I read.

"Amanda is flying high with garage that pampers your car," says the headline.

"Read on," says Emily.

"Amanda Milton has always been a tomboy," it says, under a photo of a car flying through the air. "But when the blonde mechanic from South Shields got the chance to fly her car over a bus, she jumped at it." There is a contact email for photographs and a list of names and numbers.

I look at Emily. "Why send a photo story to a radio station?"

"PR darling. You don't have to be intelligent, you just have to be pretty," she says. "Look at the notes."

I flick over the page.

"Notes for Editors: Amanda Milton is founder and owner of Car Treats, a pioneering new service for people who love their cars. She and her team will lovingly service, fix and pamper your car, because you need to know it's being cared for as you would care for it yourself. With love."

I am starting to feel sick.

"Car Treats," says Emily.

"Yes, I get that."

"Well, he did love his car."

"Every week?"

"You don't know where it is, though, do you? At least it might be there. Isn't it worth a try?"

Everything is pink. Even the socket things have pink handles to them. We have come in through the garage bit and are standing on pink concrete. Looking through the glass doors to the reception area, there are pink fluffy cushions on the chairs in the office, although they do at least seem to have the good grace to have oil stains. Amanda herself couldn't be less of a pink female if she tried. She is older than I imagined her to be. She has a broad set of shoulders and a sort of masculine swagger. Her hair is tied back in a tight ponytail, and there is oil on her forehead, right next to a livid looking bruise.

"Hello ladies," she says. She has a cylinder of metal in her hand. She points at a hole in it and says, with a shake of the head: "Look at that. Been driving round like that for weeks. No wonder it's been keeping the neighbours awake. Still, always do your own last, don't you?" She chuckles. I have no idea what she is talking about, but I like her smile. Did Patrick like it too?

"What can I do for you?" she says.

Emily gives me a little nudge. I can't speak. She decides to take over.

"You don't happen to have a red TVR in here, do you?" she says.

"No. TVR, though. Gorgeous. What model?"

Emily looks helplessly at me. I am just rather impressed that she knew it was a TVR. She looks back at Amanda, who says: "Griffith, Cerbera, Chimera?"

"It was sort of low to the ground and curvy," says Emily.

Amanda laughs. "Not your car, then," she says. "Why do you want to know?"

"Do you know Patrick? Patrick Miles?"

She hesitates. "No. No, I don't think so. I know a Derek Miles."

"Tall, curly black hair. Quite posh."

She laughs. "No, sorry. Never met anyone like that. I'd like to though, is he available?"

There is a stabbing feeling in my heart. Emily takes my arm and turns me towards the exit. "No," she says. "No. Sorry to have bothered you."

"Is she OK?" says Amanda. "Here." She pushes open the door to the reception area. "Sit her down in here. I'll get her some tea." She looks at me. Another person who is going to cure my grief with tea, or try to.

Emily wants to get me home. Amanda persuades her to wait a while. "Come on," she says. "Just a cup of tea. Save me from my exhaust."

"I think it's a clean cup," she says, handing me my tea. "I wiped it with the cleanest cloth I could find. Sorry. Just the way of it, I'm afraid, when you work in a garage. What happened to you, then?"

I don't know where to start. Words form in my head and then jump out again. I look at Emily.

"Patrick was Maggie's… boyfriend. He died in a crash last week. In a bus."

"Oh, God. That bus crash? Terrible. Do you know, I saw the ambulance. It was just round the corner."

"Was it?" Emily's grasp of geography is similar to mine. We know it was vaguely in this area, we just couldn't tell you how the streets fit together. "Well, you see, that's even more weird, because we can't work out why he was out here, and why he was on a bus, and we can't find his car, and he's got this CT in his diary for that day, and… are you sure you've got no TVR?"

"Positive. Been a bit quiet. I'd remember, because I'd love to get my hands on one of those. So are you Maggie Olds, then? Spell FM?"

"Yes. How do you know?"

"Been in the papers. Haven't you seen it?"

Emily takes a firm grip of my hand.

The silence is broken by beeping. "Shit," says Amanda. "Stay there. Be right back." She goes through to the garage and disappears under a silver car.

"I thought it was better not to tell you," says Emily. "I didn't want to upset you."

"What did they say?"

"Not much. Usual stuff. Radio personality. Boyfriend. Death. That sort of thing."

"Shit!" shouts Amanda from the garage. When she comes back, there is another mark on her forehead. "You'd think I'd learn, wouldn't you? Always banging my head on the buggers."

She sits down next to me again, on the other side to Emily. "You've had a rough time of it, pet. But he's gone. Do you see? And you might never know what he was doing there. You might never find out. You're better off putting your energy into remembering him how he was. Remembering how much you loved him. How much he loved you. Do you see? There isn't any point clouding it with some mystery you'll never solve. He lived his life, and there were things he didn't tell you, but that doesn't mean they were bad things, just that he didn't think to tell you. That's all, love. That's all."

I know she is being kind. But I can't look at her. I hand her back her mug, half drunk.

"Thank you," I say. I stand up. Emily takes hold of my arm, as if I might fall. I don't think I will. "I'm feeling better now."

"Oh. OK."

We get to the door. She calls after us. "If a red TVR comes in, I'll let you know."

It was a big game, or I wouldn't have been there. It was a bit cold, and although I was beginning to get into rugby, I preferred, on days like this, to watch it on the telly, with the benefit of a commentator explaining why penalties were being given and who was offside and when. Today was different. It was exciting. We hadn't been expected to get to the finals. We were the underdogs. So we had driven all the way to Cardiff on a freezing cold day, in amongst the dozens of coaches all with scarves hanging out of the sides, full of people shouting and singing and generally having a good time. Patrick was nervous. He kept losing the team coach in the rear view mirror, because his accelerator foot had a tad too much adrenalin in it. He always got nervous before a big match. It was as if he was part of the team himself, which, I suppose, he was. He sprayed stuff on their legs and massaged them and sent them back out to get beaten up again, so his role was pretty vital.

Barney couldn't speak. He hadn't eaten, which the trainer had a go at him about, but he said he wouldn't be able to keep it down. He was on the team bus now, probably listening to a CD Emily had given him to try and calm him. It was a hypnosis thing she had been asked to cover on the news and never got round to listening to. She said she had no idea if it would work, but it might distract him a bit.

She was working, back up North. She never let on to Patrick, but she hated rugby. She avoided it whenever possible. So there was usually a big story that she had to go after, whenever there was a match coming up. I don't know why she didn't tell him. I'm sure he wouldn't have minded. He and Emily had a sort of battle going on. They were always arguing about something or other – it didn't usually bother her, so why she didn't own up to the rugby thing, I have no idea. But there you go. Perhaps I should ask her. But now she is engrossed in whatever she is reading, and I am in Cardiff in my head, willing myself back into the days of rugby watching and the physio on the pitch with the tender eyes and the grabbable backside. I may have a touch of a masochistic tendency because I have chosen to remember this rugby match, rather than any of the countless others that didn't end in the unhappy way that this one did.

It happened in the scrum. Someone knocked the ball forwards, which isn't allowed, and so all these big beefy men huddle together and try and shove each other. The crowd yelled, "Heave!" But something was wrong. It collapsed. There were men on the floor. Slowly, they got up, one by one. But one man was still on the floor. Others gathered round him. People gesturing. Where was Patrick? There he was, on the sidelines. He looked frozen. Somebody shoved him from behind. He started forward slowly, then quickly.

"Who is it?" I said. I was sitting next to Mia, the girlfriend of the scrum half. She shook her head, and looked through her programme.

"Can you see the number?" she said.

I couldn't. He was down. I looked at the others. I was starting to have a horrible twisting feeling in my gut. Barney wasn't among them.

"Where's Barney?" I said.

"Oh my God," she said. "It's him. It's Barney."

He still hadn't moved. If you didn't move when a scrum collapsed, then there was a very good chance you had a neck injury. I didn't want to think about it. Wouldn't think about it. Maybe it would be all right, if we just willed it to be so. The crowd around us had gone quiet. Were they all willing it too?

The stretcher came on. They were putting a neck brace around him. I couldn't see Patrick amongst all the shirts. Then I could see him. The stretcher was on a little golf cart type thing. Barney was being moved. And Patrick had his hand. The crowd started to clap. There was no movement from the stretcher.

There was an argument at the touchline. The referee had started up play again, but Patrick was arguing with someone on the touchline, and Barney was disappearing through the tunnel.

Patrick would want to go with him. Of course. And he couldn't. Of course. He had a job to do.

I squeezed past Mia and out into the aisle. The yelling was starting up again. From the fever of it, somebody must be running with the ball. I didn't look. I had to get out. I ran out of the ground, barely able to see for the tears in my eyes from the cold. These places are so huge. At the gates I asked where they would have taken him. Someone shrugged and said, "The hospital." Perhaps there was only one.

I ran out into the street, searching for a taxi. There was hardly any traffic at all. I kept running. There was a taxi rank up ahead, with three taxis in it. The drivers were all grouped round one car, listening to the radio.

"Excuse me," I said.

"We're on a break, love," said one. "Try again at the end of the match."

"No," I said. "I need to go to the hospital. Please."

A short bespectacled man detached himself from the group and said, "All right, love. Which one?"

"I don't know. Is there more than one?"

"About four."

"Where would they take an injured player?"

"Rugby player?"

"Yes."

"James Rubbel?"

"Yes."

"Come on, love. You his girlfriend? Come on. Get in."

They were best friends all their lives. Born on the same ward on the same week. Lottie tried to keep them apart because she didn't approve of Barney's Mum who was a dinner lady in Patrick's school. It is hard to believe that Lottie could have been such a snob back then. She certainly wasn't when I knew her. Patrick loved Barney. We all did. Do.

When we first got together, Patrick was very nervous about my meeting him. I had to pass the Barney interrogation. It was intense, but I passed. Barney says I scraped it, but he usually winks when he says that.

Standing there in the hospital corridor, waiting for news, I wondered if there was anything worse than this, waiting and not knowing. It must have been like this for Mum and Dad, waiting for news of Ben and me. And then of course I realised, there is something worse than the waiting: it's when the waiting is over.

It wouldn't be like that. I would make sure of it. Somehow. I thought about praying, but how ridiculous was that? If there was a God, he certainly wasn't going to listen to me. I sat. I stood up. I paced. I sat down again. I waited.

Patrick arrived. He rushed past me. "Where is he?" he said.

"They're working on him," I said. "They say they'll tell me when they know something."

He tried to push through the doors to the mysteries beyond but a large and immovable male nurse was barring his way.

"I have to see him," he said.

"You need to wait, sir. I'm sorry. I will do my best to find out what's going on, but you have to wait. You'll only be in the way."

I thought he was going to punch the nurse for a second. They were staring each other out, in the same way you see animals on those wildlife programmes before they set about killing each other. There was a sense that whoever looked away first would probably die a horrible and bloody death. I stood up and took his hand. "Patrick," I said. "Patrick. Sit with me."

He blinked. He blushed. "Sorry," he said to the man. "Sorry. I don't know what came over me. I don't know..."

"I know," said the nurse. "I know. Can I get you a coffee or something?"

Just like that. The two lions on the Serengeti moved away from the fight, and one was offering the other a bit of the gazelle he had left over from the morning's hunt.

He sat down. He was sweating.

"How did you get away from the match?" I said.

"Ginny was there. She volunteered."

"Oh. Good for Ginny."

"She has her uses."

He was sitting next to me, but he wasn't there. That big, beautiful face looked so haunted. I reached up with my hand and touched his cheek. His hand came up to mine. He held it there. Tears started down his face. I kissed the cheek I wasn't holding. I kept my face there, nestled against the side of his, breathing in his smell.

"This is all my fault," he said. His voice was cracking.

"What do you mean?"

"It should have been me."

I took my hand from his face and reached round until I had him in a tight hug.

"Don't be silly," I said. "It's an accident. A horrible accident."

"It's my fault. You don't understand. It's my fault."

"What are you talking about? You weren't even on the pitch. It was a huddle, for heaven's sake."

I could feel him smile. He couldn't help himself. I called a scrum a huddle, to wind him up. It usually wound Barney up far more.

"Scrum," he said.

"How is it your fault?"

"It's punishment."

"Don't be ridiculous. It's just the shock of seeing Barney like that."

He didn't say any more. Great, rasping sobs had hold of his body. I held on as tightly as I could as he jolted and convulsed in my arms. My big, beautiful bear of a man. The softy.

"Penny for them?" says Emily.

I am looking out over the sea. The sky has turned a charcoal grey colour. The water is rushing and dancing. This is the warm up – the overture before the first movement of the storm. It is saving its energy for later, when it will really start to swirl and dive. I like days like today. I like the feeling of being inside and watching what nature can do on the outside. It won't be long now. The rain will start to fall in the very near future. The wind, which is whining softly at the moment, will start to howl and roar. The steps outside will rattle. The windows will whistle. And we shall be here. Cocooned in the warmth of an untidy flat.

"I've been thinking about Barney," I say.

"What about him?"

"Neck."

"Oh."

She returns to her book. I return to my contemplation of the sea. There it is. The first big wave hitting the rocks over to the right. Somebody was standing on there once a couple of years ago when the wind started up like this. He wasn't standing for long. I think they found him. The lifeboats were out pretty quickly. And there he was, bobbing in the waves. Miracles do happen.

"I'm not being funny," she says.

I sigh. "What?"

"You seem to be dwelling on the bad stuff. There's lots of good stuff you could be thinking about. What about that time he took you ballooning? Or when he hired that ridiculous limo to take you to the Sonys? Or, you know, all those times in Studio 3?"

"How did you know about Studio 3?"

"We all knew about it."

"It's sound proof."

"Yes. But the blinds don't quite fit in the corners."

I picture Jed, peering through the gap in the blinds and calling others over to have a gawp. Patrick liked to take the opportunities when they presented themselves. Studio 3 hadn't been used for years, except when people wanted to edit something in peace and the other studios were in use. It was our little naughty assignation. We thought it was our secret. My temper is hovering in the background, awaiting an invitation to erupt, but somehow I can't seem to make it go off. Not at this. This is a memory I'm happy to have. Sharing it with other people, well, it's not ideal, but at least it won't die, even if it fades in my mind. I turn away from the sea and face Emily.

"How do you know I'm not thinking about Barney's recovery?"

"Are you?"

"No."

"So stop it."

Why are people so afraid of pain? All I have is pain at the moment. I might as well indulge it. Don't cry. Don't think like that. Don't be upset. Don't what? Don't grieve? Don't care?

I lost count of all the people who told me to pull myself together after we lost Ben. It didn't help that everyone else was so much further on with their grief than I was. Dad was the only one who seemed to understand the value of a good cry. He sat there with me, with his hand on my shoulder, or my head on his, and he didn't say anything. Not even shhh.

I have this big pain where my heart used to be. And people want me to think happy thoughts. I didn't think Emily would be like that. But if you haven't lost, can you understand loss?

And then the pain gets too much, and the mind kicks in to steer you away from it. So you think about things like Barney with his broken neck, and the horrible smell at the hospital, and Ginger John's face as he broke the news, and that fat little man sitting eating his potato crisps and laughing off the accident, as if it's just something that happens every day and it's all jolly unfortunate and why should he care? I have been trying not to think about him, but he creeps back into my thoughts again and again, in all his self satisfied smugness. Oh yes. This is how you get away with causing an accident, you just deny everything and keep your fingers crossed. If nobody else has seen anything then that's just marvellous, isn't it?

I wonder if he is in the phone book.

"What you doing?" says Em.

"Just, er... Just looking for something."

"Oh, God. You're not going through the Ts are you? Do you have any idea how long that would take?"

"No. I'm not." That hadn't occurred to me. A project for later, perhaps.

Schofield. I don't know his first name. There are 2 columns of Schofields. And of course it doesn't tell you which ones work in insurance.

"Bugger," I say.

"What?"

"Nothing."

"Tell me."

I sigh. I might as well tell her. She might even be able to help.

"You know the person who killed Patrick? The one who jumped the red light?"

"What about him?"

"His name is Schofield. I don't know if Ginger John was supposed to tell me that. They're not prosecuting, because there is not enough evidence."

"Oh, honey. I'm sorry. That bastard. So he's sitting at home feeling all smug? After he jumped a red light? Irresponsible git."

"The CPS is a law unto itself. That's what Ginger John said."

"The CPS is useless. You see it all the time."

"The thing is, it's driving me nuts."

"I bet it is."

"I want him to pay for what he's done. I want him to see what happens when you do something like that. I want him to know..."

"Know what?"

I can't find the words for it. I gesture at the space around me. "This."

She nods. "Yeah."

"How do you find a Mr Schofield who works in insurance?"

"Why, love? What are you going to do? Don't you think you should leave it to the police?"

"They aren't going to do anything."

"I don't know what to say to you."

"That you'll help me."

"It wouldn't be helping you."

"How can you say that? How do you know what would help me and what wouldn't? You have no idea what's going on in my head. None at all. How can you possibly? You didn't even like him."

There is a silence. I know she is looking at me. I know I shouldn't have said it. And I know that if I look at her I will have to back down and apologise. But I don't want to. She doesn't deserve it. There is a little germ in the base of my gut that wants to punish her.

"How can you say that?" she says.

I don't say anything. I am looking at the rain outside. There is so much of it you can hardly see the sea. I hear her put her magazine down and shuffle her papers together. I hear her stuffing them into her bag. I hear her pick up her coat and put it on. I hear her walk over to the door. She pauses.

"You might want to have a little tidy up," she says. "If people are brave enough to come to see you, they need to be able to get in the door."

I hear the door open and close, and high heels clanking down the stairs. She will get wet. There will be no option.

I am sorry. Now. But it's a bit late for that. I turn to the piano. There is fat Mr Schofield, sitting there in my mind's eye, troughing his way through his big bag of crisps. Still these crisps. I have no idea what that's all about. There is a piece by Kabalevsky. It starts with three staccato cords, then goes very Russian. I like to race myself, see how fast I can play it. Perhaps in the playing of it I will erase what has just happened from my mind. I didn't mean to hurt Emily. But that's what I do now. I pity myself and I hurt my friends, because I can't hurt the person who hurt me. That's who I am now. So Mr Schofield has done way more than just jump a red light. He has destroyed every part of my life. I can't imagine ever working again. I have lost the will to go into that studio and chat to people. I can't be trusted anyway, even if I feel like going back. I keep taking swipes at everybody. My havens of safety are my flat and my studio. Neither remains. There is no safe place. There is just me, alone, with this horrible pain and this over the edge feeling as if any moment I might fly off the Earth's surface and end up God knows where.

I reach the end of the piece. The final run of notes leading up to the big end chord comes faster and faster. My fingers have become something that is not part of me. I bring down that final chord as if the piano is Mr Schofield. The notes are left there. Reverberating round the building. I wonder if Edith in the flat below was bothered by it. I decide not to care.

"That was dramatic."

Emily is dripping in the doorway. I shut my eyes and put my hands on the lid of the piano, as if to shut it but not. I never shut it. It is just something to hold.

"I'm sorry," she says.

I can't say anything. That should be me, saying that. And I can't.

I hear her coat dropping onto the chair behind me. I feel a hip touching mine, as she perches on the piano stool next to me. I leave my eyes shut.

She plays the opening bars of chopsticks. I can't stand it. I stand up and move away, into the bay window. My eyes are open now and taking in the dark grey of the scene outside. She stops playing.

"What do you want me to do?" she says. "How can I... How can I make it better?"

There is a tear. I can feel it. It is falling down my cheek. There is another one falling out of the other eye. I don't want this. I don't want her feeling guilty. What has she to feel guilty for? But I can't speak.

She brings down her hand onto middle C and the B below it, hard. The discordant sound reverberates around the room. That is what I am feeling. Exactly.

"I don't want this," I say.

"What?"

"These things happen. That's right, isn't it? These things happen.

You have to accept them and move on. People die. And you have to just carry on. Put it behind you. Progress. These things happen. They happen, they happen, they happen. And I can't. Move on. I can't. I'm supposed to let this creep get away with it, am I? Just, what is it? Turn the other cheek? Let him do this to Patrick? Let him do it to me and not care? Is that it? Oh, well. Can't be helped. How do you do that? How? Because I'm trying. I've been trying ever since it happened, and I can't. Do you understand? I can't. I want him to pay for what he did. I need him to pay. I need for him to be in jail right now, eating porridge or whatever it is they do in there. I need that."

She doesn't say anything. What is there to say? She hits those two notes once more, then lets go of the B and moves it to a B flat. Slightly less discordant. A tone apart. Then an A. Minor third. A melancholy sound. She doesn't take it further. The major third is a happy chord. We don't want that one. She doesn't know anything about music, but she knows enough not to play a major third.

"I'm sorry," I say. "I know you loved Patrick."

"He did piss me off sometimes."

"I know."

"I'll regret this," she says. "But I'll find your Mr Schofield. OK? Just promise me you're not going to commit murder or anything."

"I promise. I just need..."

I don't know what I need. The sentence hangs in the air.

"I know," she says.

There is a glimmer of sunlight outside. It has a lot of work to do to push through the grey, but it wasn't there a moment ago. The storm may be coming to an end soon. I can see the waves. I couldn't see them before. The wind must have died down a little, because they are not so high as they were. I can make out the rock over to the South. It is definitely clearing up. Emily went out in it five minutes ago. She should have waited.

I love the smell of the air after a storm. I get my coat. I will walk to Patrick's. I will use up another half an hour and breathe in the unsettled air, while I'm at it.

I am looking at the sea, but not really noticing it. As I walk along, the wind blowing at my side, I am back again in that hospital, watching another storm. It's amazing how so many of the key players in your life can be gone, just like that. I am looking at Barney, lying on the bed with all sorts of machines keeping him alive, and I can see Lottie, who hasn't been with us for maybe six months. But there she is, in my mind's eye, as if she never went away. It surprises me that I still have access to her – to the things that she did. What is missing, I suppose, is all the things she may yet have done. Same with Patrick, but he is not in the picture. Not yet. This picture has Lottie and Barney and me. This picture has Lottie looking as cross as I ever saw her.

She wasn't having it. No way was Barney going to be paralysed. "5% chance, my bottom," she said. It made Barney smile. It was the first thing that had made him smile since it happened.

"You tell 'em, Mrs M."

"I shall," she said.

She put her hand on his head. It was as if she was taking his temperature, except that people usually do that with the palm of the hand on the forehead. Hers was on the very top of his head.

"Close your eyes. Relax," she said, putting her other hand on his chest.

"Not this again," I said. "What are you going to do, Lottie? Magic this away? It's a broken neck, for God's sake."

"Mmmm. Maybe."

"This is cruel, Lottie. You're giving him false hope."

"Hope is never false, dear."

Barney whispered something. I crept forward. "What, Barns? What do you want?"

"I want you to go away," he said.

Patrick was talking to the doctor. I went to find him. No point staying and upsetting Barney, however much damage Lottie might be doing. It was his choice. Although it wasn't, because he was hardly in a position to make up his mind about anything sensibly. But there was nothing I could do about it without upsetting him further.

"Thank you, anyway," Patrick was saying.

The doctor put her hand on his arm. "I'm sorry," she said. "You're the best person to help him now. You're the rehab man, after all."

Patrick didn't answer. The doctor's beeper went off.

"Excuse me," she said.

He turned around. He looked such a little boy. I suddenly had a clear picture of him and Barney in short trousers, sticking plasters on their knees, racing around in circles, with a young Lottie laughing at their antics.

I held him. It was all I could do. He clung on. I could feel hot tears falling down my neck. I didn't tell him what Lottie was up to. No point. It would only upset him.

The tears dried up and he started to breathe more evenly. "Better go and see him," he said, stepping back from me.

"I think he's busy at the moment."

"Doing what?"

"Talking to Lottie about something. Private."

He looked confused. He took my hand. "We'll wait," he said.

We sat outside for half an hour. He told me some of what the doctor had said. It wasn't what either of us wanted to hear. Her five per cent estimate had been a kindness, it seemed. People did recover function with this type of injury, but it was incredibly rare. Now it was just a matter of wait and see.

When Lottie emerged from the room, we were both in tears again.

"Well, he doesn't need to see you two blubbing, that's for sure. Poor chap. Positive thinking, that's the key."

"Mum…"

"Patrick, dry your eyes and let's go home. Barney is jolly tired and having a little sleep. There is nothing to be done. Come on."

He rarely disobeyed his mother. Even today, when she seemed so cheerful in the face of such tragedy.

The next day there was no difference in Barney, of course. I don't know what I'd been expecting. There was no difference that day, or that week. They turned him over in his high-tech bed. They bathed him in there. They fed him through tubes. Ginny came in and brushed his hair for him. He smiled. All these indignities he suffered, he smiled at all of them. Smiled at the nurses, the doctors, Patrick, me. Perhaps it hadn't gone in that he was in such a state. Perhaps that was a blessing. We would be there for him when the news eventually hit home.

Then one day his hand twitched.

I am looking at that picture on Patrick's desk. The one with Barney sandwiched between Lottie and Patrick. It was the day he took his first steps. They are all grinning. Lottie and Patrick are looking at each other across Barney's back. Barney is hunched forwards over a walking frame. I remember taking it. Patrick had made some quip about Mr Zimmer. Barney was laughing. It was a good day.

The answer phone light is flashing. I press the button. There are some clicks and beeps. Then:

"Mr Miles? Mr Miles, it's Sandy Emerson. I've been trying your mobile. Haven't you got the messages? I don't know what to do. You'll recall you were supposed to pick Meg up on Saturday? Well, it's now Monday, and I have no idea what to do with the poor thing. She looks very sorry for herself. I ran out of her food, so she's been on the stuff we give ours, but really you need to pick her up. Do you think you could ring me back? It's odd, because she's usually so easy going and she's been decidedly off it. I'd like to take her to the vet, but I'd rather you did it, and anyway I'd like to talk to you first. Please, could you ring me back?"

Shit. I hadn't even thought about Meg. She wasn't there, so I didn't think where she might be. How could I forget about her? I scoop up my car keys and run to the door. The answerphone is still playing, but I'll have to pick those up when I come back. I know where the kennels are. They're only a mile or two down the road. Poor Meg. He never leaves her there for long. If he's going away for any length of time, he pays someone to come in and look after her. He dotes on that dog. Funny he didn't ask me to look after her. But then he wasn't really speaking to me.

It's a straight road, and even so you can't really see the kennels until you're right upon them. I have a car on my backside. I am going quite slowly because I'm not sure exactly where the turning is. I don't know why he doesn't overtake. There it is. I indicate right and brake. Now he chooses to overtake. I'm assuming it's a he. The windows are blacked out so I can't see. Idiot. My car rattles and squeaks as if it is about to fall apart. I'm not worried. It's always done that, right from when I first bought it when it was only two years old. It's done a good few years since then.

The drive has a deep rut in it. Too late, I remember that from last time, because Patrick swerved to avoid it in the TVR. There is a loud bang, and my little car lurches and jolts, then rights itself. It amazes me how this car keeps going. I've been expecting it to give up on me for years now, and still it keeps on, keeping on.

I can see Sandy, over by the stables. She is a skinny girl with short blonde hair that she scrapes back into a tiny ponytail that hardly looks worth the effort. Some stray curls escape, giving her a cherubic look. She has a horse by its headcollar and she is talking to the backside of a man who is bent over, examining its right hind leg. She has a look of studied concentration on her face. Last time I met her she was all smiles.

I get out of the car. The yard is muddy after the last few days of weather. I am wearing my trainers. I can hear yapping and barking from the long low kennel building behind the stables.

"Sorry about the mud," she says. "You know how it is. Are you here for the kennels? Oh, hi. Maggie, isn't it? Oh, thank goodness."

She hands the horse to the man and comes running over in her wellies.

"I just haven't known what to do with her. It's just not like Patrick. He's normally so conscientious. Are you all right?"

That worried look again. It happens whenever anybody looks at me these days. I am getting used to it.

I break the news to her. She hadn't heard about the bus accident. She had no idea. She is very upset. I hand her a tissue. I have plenty on me.

"I don't understand," she says.

"No."

"I'm sorry. I'm sorry. You don't need me, do you? Like this? You need people to be strong and calm round you, don't you? I'm sorry."

"I don't mind. Really."

She takes a deep breath, stuffing her hands deep into her pockets and pulling her tears back under control. "Meg," she says, as if she has found a new decision in the pocket of her Barbour jacket. She turns and leads the way through the mud to the kennels.

There is a golden retriever barking his head off in the first cage on the left as we go in. He looks quite distressed. I wonder, not for the first time, how an animal lover can run a dog kennel. They just always seem upset to me. Patrick hated leaving Meg here, although he liked Sandy and he knew that Meg would take it all in good part. Meg takes everything in good part.

The next two cages house yappers. There is a King Charles Cavalier and a Jack Russell. High class of kennel, this. No mongrels here.

She is in the fifth cage. It is dark in there, and she is a black dog. I nearly walk past her, she is so quiet. Then I notice a shadow moving and I realise it is Meg. There is a slight wag of the tail, but her head is down. Sandy opens the door, and she crawls out, the way she used to when Patrick was cross with her, as if she is trying to slither across the floor.

"I've been worried about her," says Sandy. "She's not been right since Friday."

She licks my hand, softly, her sad eyes looking up at me. This isn't the usual Meg. I crouch down and put my arms around her. She licks my face.

"It's you and me now, kid," I say. I think she knows. Isn't that madness? She's a dog. But I think she knows.

"What do I owe you?" I say to Sandy. We are letting ourselves out, away from the howling retriever and his yappy companions.

She shakes her head, embarrassed. "Oh, no. No. Nothing. Patrick paid up in full before he went to Scotland. And I'm not going to charge you for the last few days, not after… You know."

I think my heart has stopped.

"Scotland?"

"Well, no, sorry. It wasn't quite that far, was it? He said it was just this side of the border. Somewhere in the middle of nowhere, that's why I assumed it was Scotland. Sounds gorgeous. We had a conversation about it, because I go up to the west coast quite a lot, it's so beautiful up there. It's just so lovely. You can walk through these woods and if it's the right time of year there are bluebells everywhere, and the sea is just glorious. Obviously that's a bit further on. But I love it up there."

Scotland? What's in Scotland? I am not sure what's going on. She is looking at me, waiting for a response.

"Oh. Yes. Yes, that's right."

"I was kicking myself because I didn't get the name of the hotel, you see. And when he didn't come back on Saturday I tried ringing round, and eventually I found his hotel and they told me he'd checked out on Friday, which is when he said he was coming back to pick up Meggie here. And I thought it doesn't add up. Because he wouldn't ever leave her here and not call me. He loves her so much."

"Yes.

"Shit," she says. "I just can't get my head around it."

"Which hotel was it?" I say.

"What?"

"He didn't tell me, you see. He wanted a few days peace and quiet to, er… to work on his invention. You know he invents stuff? He knew I would be calling him every five minutes."

"Oh, yes. He said that. Peace and quiet. Exactly those words."

"Really?"

"Yes. Anyway, yes. It was the Glen Chase Hotel. Sounds gorgeous. Very out of the way."

She looks away from me, at the horse that is still standing in the yard, but now has nobody examining its leg. I realise I am staring at her.

"Thank you," I say. "For, er… Looking after Meg. Thank you."

"Oh. No problem," she says. She seems to want to say something else, but she doesn't. I get in the car and start the engine.

She taps on the window. I wind it down. She opens her mouth to speak and pauses.

"I'm so sorry," she says.

And now my little car is stuttering and sputtering towards Scotland. I haven't told anybody where I'm going. I'm not even sure myself. I have just pointed north and put my foot down. Meg is very quiet on the back seat. The radio ceased to work after about an hour, so the car is very quiet too. I am doing my best to fill it with noise. For some reason, the only songs that will come into my head are hymns, so I am singing those, raising my eyebrows ironically whenever there is any mention of God or praise or anything like that.

I feel the need to turn left soon. I see a turning up ahead, and in the absence of a map I take it. Now we are on a narrow lane, the sort you have to pull off when there is something coming in the other direction. Having left the very straight road, this one is a surprise with all its little twists and bends. I should go slower. Someone might come round one of these bends in a minute and there will be nowhere for either of us to go. I put my foot down instead. We will get there quickly or we will die trying. The state Meg's in, I don't think she would mind that either.

I can't sing any more. My voice keeps breaking up. I can't inflict this noise on the dog. I have no idea where I am going. I didn't check a map. I didn't phone the hotel. I didn't do anything. I just pointed the car and now we're here on this stupid little road in the middle of who knows where and I don't care I just want to keep going forward. If I stopped and did my research I would never go. We have to keep moving. I am trying not to think about what we are going to find. Every time it crosses my mind, I see some sleazy honeymoon suite with the sheets all crumpled and defiled. I see some sleepy naked woman lazing in bed and calling Patrick Mr Miles, then I stop myself before I see him grab a big bucket of strawberries and feed her one and call her Mrs Miles.

My imagination needs censoring. It is way way too out of control. I try that deep breathing exercise that Ginger John mentioned. Breathing out first, he said. Then letting the air back in. Well, I'm sorry, but isn't that the same as breathing in? He didn't seem to think so. The car seems to be slowing down. The breathing seems to affect my accelerator foot. Most bizarre. Still, it's quite a comforting feeling, so I keep on with it. And somehow a naked Patrick with his naked floozy are not quite so present in the front of my mind.

I mean, let's get this into perspective, shall we? He lied about America, yes. He lied about Scotland. Or not quite Scotland. So he lied. But that doesn't mean that he went and got married to somebody else without telling me, now does it? Mind you, it doesn't look good for the other possibility, which is some sleazy affair. And does it matter how much you love somebody, are you ever in a position to trust them unconditionally not to do that? I mean, I thought I was, before this. But then this happened, and I can't think of an explanation. Why else would he lie? Why else would he?

The road is petering out into a mess of mud and ruts. I wonder if I should turn round. The breathing has kept me at a slower pace, so the car is not suffering as much as it would have been if we had got here ten minutes ago, although the rattles are getting louder and they've been joined by a new one which is coming from outside the car. I suppose this is when a mobile phone might come in handy.

Meg grunts on the back seat. I shoot a look over my shoulder and she is looking at me, her big sad eyes imploring me to do something, but I don't know what. I usually wish she could speak when she does this, but not today. I would rather not hear what she wants me to do today, because I'm pretty sure I'm not humanly capable of doing it. And now I really am going mad. Anthropomorphising, that's what Emily would call it. She would probably be right.

There is another bend up ahead. It is quite overgrown with bushes and so on. If the road doesn't look any better beyond it, then I'll just turn round and head back while there's still some daylight to help me.

It's no better, but I don't want to turn round. Something is propelling me forward. Then I see it. Another road, a couple of hundred yards ahead. A proper road. We're about to hit a real road.

"Well, we survived that bit, Meg my love," I say. "What do you reckon, left or right?"

She has gone back to sleep. She has no interest in any of this. She is caught up in her own private misery.

I have switched on the right indicator. There is nobody there to see it, so quite why I have done it, I don't know. Still, now it's flashing, I might as well turn right.

We haven't seen any towns or villages for ages. After it went dark, I thought it might be a good time to ask somebody if they knew where this place was, but there hasn't been anyone to ask. I'm not at all sure I haven't been driving round in circles. I have no clue where I am. It occurs to me that a petrol station wouldn't be entirely unwelcome at this point, but for those you need civilisation, and for that you need a little more luck than we've been having.

The road has started to undulate. We go up and up and up and up, and there is a moment of doubt as we reach the peak because we can't see over the top, then we're past that and plunging down and down and down. I think I saw a light though, as we went over the top. Perhaps there will be people over the next crest. The trees are very tall here. The moon has been with us until now, but it can't compete with these trees. We have reached the dip and are now on the ascent once more. It is particularly steep. I have to change down a gear for fear of going backwards. It starts to level off a bit towards the top and the poor engine is now making a high pitched noise. This is a particularly blind summit. Oh my God. The car bounces off the road, airborne for a brief moment. The road plunges away from us, down and down and down. I take my foot off the accelerator and the car seems to breathe a sigh of relief as gravity takes over. I was right. There are lights here. There is a village at the bottom of this hill.

My petrol light comes on.

I will have to stop and ask where I am. "This is too ridiculous, this driving around without knowing where we're going." I've been talking to myself for some time. I have been justifying it by telling myself that it is for Meg's benefit, but it's not. It's for mine.

There is no place name as we drive into the village. There haven't been many signposts at all, to be honest. The first house is painted white. It is so close to the road that for a moment I think I'm driving straight towards it. Next there is a little stone terrace, set back, this time, behind a low wall and some bits of garden. Then there's a gap and another couple of houses further up. They all have lights on. I can't see any pubs or anything, so I had better try one of these houses. I pull off the road and walk back towards the row of terraces. I pick the first one. The gate doesn't quite fit, so I struggle to close it behind me. Dad was always very hot on that. I think it's because he grew up on a farm. You always shut a gate or tie it back, you never leave it swinging. The front garden here is full of neat rows of vegetables. There are some leeks that I can see, and then some other leafy things, but I don't know what they are. It doesn't seem the right time of year for growing vegetables. I don't think I would want to be out tending soil, or whatever it is you do, in the wind and the rain. Each to his own.

As I ring the doorbell and hear something chime inside the house, I start to wonder what the accents are like here. You don't think about border country having an accent, do you? We're still in England, so will they sound English? Or Scottish? Is there a cut off point? Does the accent suddenly change as you pass the sign that says Scotland on it?

A light comes on in the hall. A man appears, looking as if I might have just woken him up. I check my watch, to make sure I haven't lost a few hours and arrived in the middle of the night. No. It's only 7.

"Yeah?" he says.

"I'm really sorry to disturb you," I say. "I have no idea where I am."

"Where you looking for?" It is a London accent. How disappointing.

"Glen Chase Hotel?"

"Glen Chase?"

"Yes."

He looks confused. Then he points down the road. "That way. About a mile. Then you go off the road and down this track through the woods. What you driving? It's not the best of roads."

About a mile?

I must be looking surprised, because he says, "What?"

"Nothing. Thank you."

I didn't know where it was, and yet I've driven straight to it. That seems more than a little strange to me.

I go back to the car and tell Meg we're nearly there. She couldn't care less. It occurs to me I didn't pick up any food for her. I'll have to see if this hotel can supply it.

It is pretty much exactly a mile, because I set the mile thing on the dashboard to zero. 0.9, it says now. And here is the turn. There is a sign, but it is much smaller than I was anticipating. I imagined a giant green board with logos and such like on it, and some kind of welcoming message. This is a white sign with hand painted writing on it. "Glen Chase".

He was right about the road. I'm not sure how much more abuse my little car can take. We are bouncing and sliding along, on a track that is in the process of being reclaimed by a dense wood. It doesn't seem very hotel like. A cattle grid signals the end of the wood, and the road becomes a little more stable. There is a building up ahead, through some stone gate posts. The gate posts are not attached to anything. There is no fence. It seems very odd. As if there is a dislocation in reality. The building itself is unremarkable. Quite pretty, but not the rambling country house hotel I had been expecting. It looks like a farm house with a series of farm sheds behind it.

There are a couple of cars parked in front of the house, so I follow suit. I climb out onto gravel. "Meg," I say. She should probably have a toilet break. It's been a good couple of hours. She doesn't budge.

"OK," I say. "Have it your own way."

I shut the door and look at the building. It doesn't seem the sort of place you would come for a romantic assignation. It smells of bread. It's not very… well, *impressive*. It's quite pretty, you can say that for it, but it doesn't strike me as a particularly popular destination for philanderers and all round bastards.

His crumpled face comes into my vision again. Perhaps I would trust him if I could see his face whole, but I can't. I can only see this. This damaged image. That's what I'm left with. The partnership we had, that feeling of knowing him, like I've never known anybody before, and being known, like I've never been known before, those things are too hard for me to remember. Whatever he was doing just before he died, he didn't tell me. And there can only be two reasons for that. Either he was doing something wrong, which meant that I couldn't trust him, or whatever it was he felt he couldn't tell me. Which meant he didn't trust me.

There was never an issue of trust. Not before now. We always trusted. I would have thought that trust would survive anything, even his death, but I would have been wrong.

The door opens. A woman in a blue dress and a very clean white apron comes out. She must be at least seventy.

"Are you all right?" she says. I think the accent is Scottish. She has a round face, and you might, if you were being unkind, describe her as being well cushioned. I think she looks comforting. She smiles at me. "You've been staring at the house. Do you want to come in?"

I am confused. Is this a house or a hotel?

"I'm baking for the morning," she says, pointing at her pristine apron. It doesn't look like she's been doing anything of the sort. It looks like she's been doing something that involves no mess at all.

The front door opens directly into the kitchen. It is enormous, with a great big wooden table in the middle of it. The table has benches, rather than chairs. There are several wire cooling trays upon it, and she is in the process of tipping out bread onto the trays.

"Sit down," she says.

She hasn't asked me who I am.

"Cup of tea?"

Actually, that sounds good. It's been a long day of uncertainty and strangeness and something as normal as a cup of tea would be good. I leap up off the bench and offer to make it.

"You'll do no such thing," she says. "Guests are guests." She has finished taking the bread out of its containers and is turning towards the sink with them. She leans across and grabs the kettle.

"Now, you're not booked in, and we're pretty full this week. I don't know what it is about the nights drawing in. People seem to decide it's time for them to have a little peace and quiet. But you can have the guest bedroom. It's all made up and ready, just in case."

"Just in case of what?"

She smiles at me. It is a big, beaming, sunny smile, in an open and trusting face. It is odd. I've turned up out of the blue, why isn't she suspicious of me, at least?

"In case somebody turns up needing a place to stay," she says.

"Is that a frequent occurrence?" I say, hearing the sarcasm drip out of my mouth like poisoned spittle.

She chuckles. "Fairly, yes," she says.

I start to wonder if I've ventured onto the set of some horror film or other. But there is no wind howling, and I don't think I've seen any bats. Besides, if this were a horror film wouldn't there be a feeling of nerves, or disquiet, even? It feels... Warm. That's the only word I can think of that comes close to describing it.

"Don't look so worried," she says. "People come and they don't know why. They just need to come here. It's a very special place."

"Sorry?"

"Listen," she says.

I listen. I can't hear anything. Nothing at all. Not even a traffic hum.

"What?" I say.

"The silence," she says. "We're shielded from the road by the woods, and we're in this valley here. People need silence in their lives. They just don't know it. So they are guided to come here, to experience it."

"What?"

"Drink your tea," she says, "and tell me why you've come here." Finally, she does want to know why I am intruding upon her. I check her face for hostility, but there is none. Just that open, questioning look.

"Do you know Patrick? Patrick Miles?"

"Patrick? Lovely boy. Lovely." She looks sad, for an instant, but brightens quickly. "Did he recommend us?" she says.

"Not exactly," I say.

"How do you mean?"

My eyes feel full to overflowing again. I bite my lip. I have to say it. Again. This is my punishment. My life is now a constant flow of telling people about Patrick. Over and over and over again. I missed this with Ben. Mum and Dad had to carry that particular burden. And now I am making up for it.

"He died," I say. It is all I can manage.

She nods. "I know," she says. She doesn't tell me she is sorry. She doesn't wail and moan, or say how awful, what a lovely bloke. She just looks at me, that same curious look on her face.

"Are you Maggie?" she says.

I nod.

She slides onto the bench next to me.

"He didn't tell you he was coming here," she says.

"What?"

"He told you he was in America."

It's such an odd voice. It is so calm. I have just told her about someone she really likes, that he's dead. I have turned up out of the blue and dropped that at her feet, and she just acts as if nothing has happened – but not in an unfeeling way. Most people, if they wanted to ignore this sort of thing, would be talking fast, or muttering, or ranting, or something. She doesn't do any of these things. She just keeps calmly asking me questions. And she knows about America.

"How did you know?" I say.

"Oh, the conversations we had about you," she says. "Poor boy. Felt so guilty, bless him. If anything was stopping him from moving forward, that was it. Guilt, guilt, guilt. But that's the case with so many of them."

"So many of whom?"

She smiles at my use of the word "whom." I hear myself back and I smile too. It sounds pompous and formal. Out of place in this kitchen.

"That's better," she says. "Takes a lot less effort to smile than it does to scowl like you've been doing."

"It's called grieving," I say, the scowl returning to its place.

"Oh sweetheart," she says. "I wasn't judging you. I was a bit clumsy, that's all. But it's OK to smile. It really is. It's OK to smile. Patrick has been to see me. He's all right."

"What?"

"He's being helped. His soul is being made ready to move on. But he'll be with you for a little while yet."

"What are you talking about?"

"Drink your tea, dear. And we should really feed the dog, shouldn't we?"

"What?"

"The dog in the car. M. Meg, is it? You've been worrying about her food. But you shouldn't, really. We have plenty."

I don't know what to think. I am aware that my mouth is open and my eyebrows are knitting themselves together. I must look like a guppy fish that's had its face gathered. I can't seem to think. She seems to know an awful lot, and I know I haven't told her. But then, I've been forgetting whole chunks of conversation with other people. Perhaps I told her about Meg, without realising it. Except I didn't, I know I didn't. So has she read my mind? You see it on the telly all the time, don't you? There's that illusionist man who wears red velvet waistcoats and tells people what they're thinking. I've never worked out how he does it. But that must be the explanation. She's got some clever way of mind reading and she's using it on me now to unsettle me. Except that would be unkind, and she doesn't seem like an unkind person.

"How do you know this stuff?" I say.

"Oh, dear, it isn't me. No. It's the spirits I work with. They tell me things."

"Spirits?"

"Yes. Look, this is a lot for you to take in, isn't it? I think we should fetch your things from the car, and then you can have a nice bath and some supper, or the other way around, if you prefer, and I will answer any questions you have when you're ready. Yes?"

The idea of supper is too much to stomach. But the bath sounds good. I can't go anywhere. I don't know how many miles I have left in the tank, and besides I am tired. I don't think I can drive any more. She might be a weirdo, but she doesn't appear to be a dangerous one. And I'm *tired*.

"I'm not going to harm you, dear. I promise."

That smile again. That soft face. I am trying to let my suspicion take me over and run me out of here, but it won't. Against my will, I trust this woman.

I follow her to the car. She opens the door, which I forgot to lock. I never forget to lock it. Meg jumps out. She is wagging her tail and bouncing around.

"She's OK." I am surprised.

The woman laughs. "Patrick is here."

I shiver. This is getting too spooky. I look around. I can't see him. But Meg is looking at something next to me. And she is twirling round and round and round with joy.

"What do you mean?" I say.

"His spirit is here. Standing right next to you."

I feel a buzzing on the back of my head. I shiver.

"He is stroking your head. Don't you feel it?"

"No. Look, I think I should go."

"Don't be silly. Come on in. We'll get you settled. Where are you going off to at this time of night? No. Come in, I'll run you a bath. Come along."

I find myself obeying, following her as if I am being pushed from behind. She leaps up the stairs like a much younger woman. She pushes open a door at the top and turns on a light in the room before going in. It is a guest bedroom. There are floral curtains and a matching bedspread, in blues and greens. The room has varnished floorboards under foot, with a lone rug by the bed which picks out the green from the linen. It looks soft and welcoming. Gently she lays down my handbag.

"You've brought no clothes, I see. I think my daughter has a spare pair of jeans still at home. They should fit you. And you'll have to make do with one of my husband's shirts. Not to worry. We'll sort you out. If you leave your clothes by the door, I'll pop them in the wash tonight. They'll be dry by the morning."

"It's fine. I'll be going home first thing. These will be fine."

"Oh, my dear, you're all wet and muddy. Look at you."

I look down. She's right. The clothes I have on are soaking. I hadn't noticed. I am cold, too, and I hadn't noticed that either.

She opens a door on the far side of the bed and pulls a light switch, then disappears from view. I hear running water.

"Right," she says. "That should be ready in a few minutes. There are clean towels and a bathrobe in there. Leave your clothes outside the door when you're ready. All right, dear?"

I don't know what to say. I nod.

She puts her hand on my arm. "It's a sad time for you, dear, it really is."

I wait for her to tell me that it'll all come to an end, that time's a great healer. I brace myself for my own reaction to that. She doesn't. She just smiles at me and rubs my arm. "I'll be downstairs if you need anything at all."

There is music playing. I am standing on the steps. I can't find my keys. They must be in my bag somewhere, but they just won't seem to fall into my hands. It is not one of my CDs. It's a piano solo. Clever improvisation around a tune I'm not familiar with. Patrick must be in, listening to the stereo. I knock on the door. The music carries on. Nobody answers. Perhaps he didn't hear me. I knock louder. Still no response. Perhaps it is a burglar.

I push the keyhole cover aside and peer in. I can't see any signs of a disturbance. I can't see much from this angle, but the plant is still standing, and I think it's in the burgling manual to turn that sort of thing on the side to create as much mess as possible. I may be wrong, of course. There may be clean burglars. Perhaps the ones that have broken in and are listening to my stereo can't hear me because they are wiping my kitchen surfaces. Or perhaps Patrick is doing that. That's more likely. I knock again. The piano suddenly stops. Another, dramatic chord rings out. It occurs to me that these are piano playing burglars, not CD playing burglars. And now Patrick is at the door, smiling at me. I am confused. I recover quickly.

"You didn't tell me you played the piano."

"I don't very often. Every now and again."

He pulls me into the living room, takes my bags from me and puts them on the floor, undoes my coat, gently eases it from me and drapes it over the chair. He is smiling. It is that secret smile that he wears a lot. It denotes the sharing of a private joke that all else are excluded from. I find myself smiling back.

"I've missed you," he says.

He is kissing my neck. "Woman!" he says, in his caveman voice. He lifts me up and throws me over his shoulder. I am giggling. I can't help it. "To the bedroom!"

He charges towards the bedroom door so fast that I bang my head on the doorframe.

"Oh shit!" he says. "Are you OK?"

I am not sure. I can't really think.

"Mags?" he says.

Gently, he lifts me off his shoulders until he is carrying me like you carry a child. He lays me on the bed and lies on his side next to me, touching my head.

"Mags? Can you speak?" He is touching the place where the frame hit with tender fingers. I am looking at his eyes. Those piercing blue eyes.

"God, you're beautiful," I say.

He stops looking at the side of my head and stares at my face instead. "We better get you to hospital," he says. "You're deluded."

"You're beautiful," I say.

"Not a patch on you right now," he says. He shuffles closer so that our bodies are touching all the way to the feet. Well, to my feet. His legs are a fair bit longer. He puts his arm under my head like a pillow and the other arm over my tummy. He is still looking at me. I am still looking at him.

"Don't ever leave me," I say.

"I promise," he says.

"Sorry, that was very needy of me."

"I love you," he says. It is the first time he has said it. He didn't need to tell me. I knew. I love him too. Do you say it back right away, or should you hang onto it for a time when he won't expect it?

And now we're veering away. We aren't on the bed any more. He is still holding me. My head doesn't hurt. We are standing in a dormitory with bunk beds in it. There are twelve beds, but nobody in them.

"I promised I wouldn't leave you," he says. "I haven't."

"What are you talking about?"

"I am still here."

And now I remember. I remember about the bus. I remember he has died. It doesn't make sense. Why is he standing here?

"I love you," he says.

"I love you too," I say.

"You said it back," he says.

"I don't know when I'll get another chance. Where have you been? What was all that stuff about the bus?"

"Ask about the barn."

"What?"

"Tomorrow. Ask Irene about the barn."

"What are you talking about?"

He shakes his head. He is looking deep into my eyes, as if there is another world to be seen in there. The blue of his eyes spreads throughout my vision, fading him out of it. Now I can't see him any more, but I can still feel his arms around me.

"I love you," he whispers.

And now he's gone and I'm awake and I know it was just a dream. Just a sodding dream. But it was so real. His face wasn't crumpled like it has been. It was his face. Those were his eyes. That was his touch. I felt it. I felt it like it really happened. Except it didn't, because it was just a dream. I have been sleeping in the bath and now I'm cold. And lonely. So, so lonely. I miss him. Is that allowed? I miss him so much.

There is a knocking at the door.

"Are you all right in there, love?"

"What? Yes." I hope she can't hear me crying.

"I'm sorry. I just hadn't heard you get out, and it's been such a long time. You must be cold."

I reach for the towel and climb out of the bath. I am shivering.

"Silly. I fell asleep," I say. "I'm all right. I'll be down in a second."

"No hurry. There's some clothes for you here. Whenever you're ready."

I hear her feet padding across the floorboards in the bedroom. The outer door closes. I dry myself off, wrap myself in the towel and perch on the edge of the bath.

It was "I like New York in June." That's what he was playing. He played it differently each time, improvising around the central theme and having fun with it. He always had fun with that song. I can remember that feeling, back in my flat, when I felt he was playing it again, but through me.

I don't know what's going on.

She has prepared soup.

"Thought you could do with something nice and warming. I brought some leeks in today so I thought it might be nice to do a Cockaleeky.

"Have you just made this?" I say. "For me? From scratch? Not out of a tin or anything?"

"It's no trouble," she says. "We don't have processed food here. It's all cooked from good, wholesome ingredients. Our bodies were not designed to withstand the onslaught from a processed meal."

"Wow."

"I enjoy my cooking. Brings me in closer touch with God."

I feel the fizzing on my shoulders that I often feel when people start talking about God. It's as if there are hackles there waiting to rise, but not quite managing it. Oh shit. Meg.

"I forgot about the dog," I say, pushing the bench back so that I can get out.

"Stay and eat your soup," she says. "Meg's away in the other room, stretched out by the fire. She's fine. Really."

I return to my soup. In truth I didn't really want to leave it in the first place, it is so delicious. I don't remember tasting food as good as this. It's really hard to explain it. It's as if all the other food I've ever had is black and white and this is glorious Technicolor. Which sounds bonkers. I'm going bonkers. It's official.

"You enjoying that?" she says.

"How do you get it so...?" I can't think of the word.

"I prepare it with love," she says. "Makes all the difference in the world."

Oh well. At least I'm not alone. She's bonkers too.

The living room is enormous. It is a square room with seats arranged in little groups. There is a wing back chair by the fire and a man sitting in it. Meg is lying at his feet.

"This is Glen," says the woman. I realise with some embarrassment that I don't even know her name. She smiles at me. "I'm Irene. Irene Chase. Pleased to meet you."

"I'm sorry," I say. "I've been so rude."

"We don't worry about things like that here, do we Glen?"

Glen grunts. He is deeply interested in a book that he is reading. She laughs. "Glen is my squeeze," she says.

"What?"

Glen guffaws from behind his book. "And she's my bit of stuff."

They look a bit old for that sort of thing, if I'm honest. I don't say anything.

"Do you think it finishes?" she says. "Desire? When would you have stopped desiring Patrick?"

I think of the dream, of him holding me, of his face. "Never," I say.

She chuckles. "And when would he have stopped desiring you?"

"Oh God." I hide my face. I know it has gone scarlet.

She laughs again. "It wasn't your physical body."

"Sorry?"

"That's part of it, of course. It was your soul. You two were linked at the soul level. Still are. He would have loved you when you were old and grey and covered in wrinkles, like me. He would have loved you when you put on a few pounds. It was you he loved, not your outer shell."

I have no idea what she's getting at, but I can feel tears dripping down my face.

"That's it, love. You let it out. You need to let some of this go."

"I don't know what you're telling me."

"Where he is now, he is so beautiful. He is casting off this shell we carry around with us on Earth. He is becoming his true self. And you are walking around in the shell we carry around on Earth. But he sees you. Like he always saw you. He sees you for who you really are."

"Oh for God's sake," says Glen. "Leave the poor girl be."

He smiles at me. Then he smiles at her, deep into her eyes. I am reminded again of the dream. Of how Patrick looked at me before he disappeared behind the blue of his eyes.

Irene! He said ask Irene. And she is Irene.

"Can I see the barn?" I say.

She is surprised.

"There are people sleeping now," she says. I don't know why this should make any difference. I haven't seen or heard any people, so presumably they haven't heard me. And it isn't as though we'll make much noise going outside. "In the morning," she says, "when they're all up and about. You can see the barn. But you're much better off where you are."

I look around me. The fire is crackling away in the grate. There is another wing back chair the other side of it. Meg is stretched out between the two chairs. I think she's probably right. I am much better off where I am tonight. I sit down in the empty chair and tickle Meg's chest with my feet. She groans in the way that only a Labrador can. That's what Patrick used to say, anyway. I don't know these things. She's the only Labrador I've ever known, really.

Irene disappears. I look into the fire. She reappears. I have no idea how long she has been gone. She brings me a cocoa. She smiles at me and turns to take up a seat at the table behind me, where she switches on a reading lamp and unfolds a newspaper.

I don't know what this feeling is. I am sort of enveloped in it. I think it's peace. But he's gone, and I should be feeling awful. And here I am feeling peace. Something clutches at my stomach. Does this mean I didn't care enough? Perhaps that's why he went, because I didn't care enough. The clutching feeling spreads, and now it has my heart. Perhaps this is all just showing me what I should have been like, how I should have been with him. Maybe I should have made him fresh soup and looked deep into his eyes and stuff like that. Maybe I didn't do enough.

The feeling of peace has disappeared. It is replaced with the familiar jumpy feeling, the anxiety that has followed me around since Friday. Perhaps even before. I slurp down my hot chocolate.

"I'm going to bed," I say.

Irene looks up at me. She smiles once more. "Be good to yourself," she says. "Peace go with you."

Does she know? She shows no sign of knowing. Does she think I'm a cow? Does Patrick? Has he been watching from some corner of the room and wondering how I could be so uncaring? I glance around, looking for shadows.

"Everything all right?" says Glen.

"Um. Yes. Yes, I think so."

"You sleep well now, you hear?"

He returns to his book. Irene is back at her paper. It is just them. Of course it is. What was I thinking? I let myself out of the room and head up the stairs to bed. But I'm not going to sleep. I know I won't.

Wednesday, 29th November

I open my eyes. There is a chink of light under the curtains. I roll over away from it and pull the covers up over my head. Too early. Too early.

I can hear noise outside. A door opens and bangs shut. Somebody laughs. Somebody else joins in. What time is it?

I let the cover fall back again and rub my face. I check my watch. I don't know why I always do that. It doesn't work. There is no clock in the room. I roll towards the edge of the bed and sit up. I look around. I like this room. It isn't just the prettiness of it. There is tranquillity here. I consider lying back down again but the day is clearly starting out there. I slept. I can't believe it. I slept all night.

I part the curtains enough to see outside without the outside seeing in. I am wearing one of Glen's shirts and he is not a tall man. I think the outside world could do without seeing my naked bottom half this early in the morning.

The sun is low and in my eyes. I can see the yard and the barn that I need to have a look inside. I shudder. What am I going to find? Later. After breakfast.

I can smell toast.

We are on the side of a hill. I didn't see that last night. It cuts away below us into a softly curving valley. I remember what Patrick used to say about Camberdale. How it reminded him of a woman, with its soft curves and tree lined valleys. For the first time, I think I see what he means. He was actually referring to the naughty bits. I never worked that out before. And it is beautiful. I look down at the

112

forbidden bits of my body. I have always tried to ignore them, to pretend they didn't exist. Patrick made them OK. He didn't seem to mind them. Seemed actively to like them, which was always a bit of a shock for me. He loved the parts of me that I couldn't believe anyone could love – that I was more than a little bit ashamed of. Do you know? I never realised that before. It never occurred to me that I was *ashamed* of my body. I knew I didn't *like* it all that much. But I was. Am. Have been. I don't know. Looking out over this valley, all I see is beauty. Perhaps that's what he saw when he looked at me.

People appear, out of the barn. I step back from the window and drop the curtain. I don't want to be seen. I certainly don't want to be seen looking where I've been looking. I hear laughter, and the front door opens. Someone calls, "Iree-eene!" in a high pitched voice. He is shushed. The chatter continues, but much quieter.

I must get up.

Patrick comes into my vision. Patrick how he was last night when I was asleep in the bath, how he was before all this happened. I wonder why he came to see me. Why, if he was going to take the trouble to visit, he wouldn't answer my questions about CT, or the car, or America. He wouldn't, would he? Because it was a dream. It wasn't real. It was a product of my overactive imagination. That's all. I really must get a grip.

Still, I might as well have a look in the barn.

Irene is smiling and doling out scrambled eggs to a table full of men. They are talking in hushed tones.

She sees me and smiles even more. "There you are! Sorry if we woke you. You look like you've had a good sleep."

The men have stopped talking and are all looking at me. I feel like the little girl who used to have to stand up in church and take the collection, as if I am about to mess up the ritual, and there is something I am bound to get wrong at any moment. I would quite like to turn around and go back out again. The men are smiling, though. There are twelve of them. One of them pushes another of them away from him with a soft nudge and gestures for me to climb onto the bench beside him. He grabs a white mug from a collection in front of him and puts it in front of the seat he has indicated for me to take. "Please," he says. "Sit down. Would you like tea or coffee?"

I climb into the seat, thankful that I have on Irene's daughter's jeans and not my straight skirt. "Tea."

He calls up the table. "Jack. Tea pot."

It is duly passed down, in the silence. "Thank you," I say. I want to break the silence. I can't think of anything to say. "Thanks."

"I'm Simon," he says. "That's Pete, the other side of you." I shake the hand that is offered. "This is Mikey, Stephan, John P, John S, Tom, Ahmed, Jack, Harry, Phil and William." They wave hello as he says each name. I won't remember them. I tried to, as he was going round. Pete means stone, so I looked in Pete's face for a resemblance to Stone, but couldn't see it. Archangel Michael, he's supposed to be all about courage, but this guy looks a bit thin and weedy. And now I'm miles behind him and I can't think of any ways of remembering these names that I haven't really listened to. Never mind.

Irene fetches me a plate of toast. It is the bread she made last night. She puts a jar of honey in front of me and calls up the table for the butter, which is duly delivered. "Glen Chase honey," she says. "Glen's bees. Famous. We export this to all sorts of places. Have you heard of it?"

"No."

"No. People in this country eat that rubbish from the supermarkets," she says, shaking her head.

I keep quiet. I quite like the honey I get from the supermarket. I'm not sure I'm really in a honey mood today, but I'd better have some so as not to offend. She watches me spread it thinly on my toast and take a bite.

It is quite wonderful. Tastes like honey, of course, but there is that same Technicolor quality to it that I experienced with the soup last night. It is like I never really tasted honey before, I just went through the motions. I am chewing, so I can't say anything. She seems satisfied with my reaction and moves on to fill up the coffee pot.

The men have started talking again, between themselves, louder now. Perhaps they were being quiet for my benefit before.

"Where are you from?" says Simon.

"Down South," I say. It seems strange describing it as South. To most strangers I meet it seems very far North, but this is a way on from that.

"I live in London," he says, apparently to his eggs. "This is my escape."

"What do you do here?" I say.

"Me? Oh, I'm an accountant."

"Sorry? No. No, I meant here."

He looks surprised. It clearly never occurred to him that you couldn't know about Glen Chase Hotel. Perhaps it is a reasonable assumption. After all, I have stayed the night.

"Well, there's workshops," he says. "We're all here on a meditation week."

"Meditation?"

"Yes. Isn't that why you're here?"

"No. No. I'm…" I can't think what to say.

"Sorry, I'm prying into something," he says.

"No. No. It's not that. It's…" Again, I can't put the words to it. He is looking at me, waiting for me to continue. "My boyfriend died," I say. The room is silent again.

He doesn't know what to say to me. I can see him delving into his brain, trying to come up with the words that will fix it. I am getting used to this. What will he come up with? Time is a great healer? So sorry for your loss?

I am saved by Pete. "So you've come to see Irene then? She's very good."

I am confused. I don't know what he means. I suppose I have come to see Irene in a roundabout way, but why he should know that, or assume that, I am not quite sure.

"Who would like some more eggs?" says Irene, winking at me. The men turn back to their breakfasts, relieved to have had the burden of a conversation about death removed from them in favour of more eggs. I am relieved too, although I don't want to finish my toast. I squeeze out of my seat and leave them to it. Fresh air. That's what I want.

I feel like a smoker, illicitly standing on the doorstep, stepping from one foot to the other and then back again, while the rest of the world carries on inside. Irene joins me at the front door. "Fresh air?" she says. "Doesn't come any fresher."

"What are they doing here?" I say.

"Who, the disciples?"

"What?"

"Sorry, my little joke. We always call them the disciples, because there's always twelve of them, do you see? And they're all in search of enlightenment, although some of them are further along the road than others."

"Enlightenment? They're Buddhists?"

"Some are. But mostly they're just people who have reached a crossroads, as they call it. And they want to move forwards with their lives but they can't work out which way to go. So they come here looking for answers."

"Do they find them?"

"Some do. Some find some of them. Then they go away again, and come up with a whole lot more questions."

I can see Glen over on the opposite side of the valley. He has a dog with him. "Is that Meg?"

She nods. "They've been to feed the sheep. Glen likes a walk before he gets going with his workshops." I can't see any sheep. I look up and down the valley. No sign of sheep. She laughs. "Don't worry, they're not ghost sheep. They're in the sheep sheds," she says. "Too cold for them in this weather, and we're soft, Glen and me. We like to tuck them up nice and warm. It's over on another farm, down in the next valley."

She takes my hand. "Come on. You wanted to see the barn."

We thread our way in between puddles across the farmyard. The barn is attached to the house in an L shape. There is a Dutch barn next to it with a few ancient pieces of rusty equipment. There is a tractor with no cab, from the days when cabs would not have been thought up; there is a trailer with its tow bar on a big round log. There is a spiky thing that I think is called a harrow, but don't quote me on that. The barn itself is a long low building, about the size of two buses tied together. There are four windows, evenly spaced along the

116

outside. The door is smaller than the original space for it. You can see the brickwork and the original door frame still tucked into the wall.

"Don't tell the planners about the windows," says Irene. "There'll be hell to pay. We've done three years now, and nobody's said anything. So we think we might have got away with it." She is wearing a cheeky expression, like a naughty child. Her face glows with – what is it? Joy. Yes. That's it. She has joy. For no reason, it seems to me, not the way other people have joy – when they've passed an exam, or seen an amazing film, or won a contest. Her joy is over windows, over freshly baked bread, over evenings in front of the fire. It follows her around like sunshine. What a gift to have.

She opens the door. I expected it to creak, but it doesn't. It all seems quite well kept and modern, except for the building itself.

And now we're in and the room is spinning.

"Are you all right?" Irene has my hand again. She is leading me towards one of the beds. I sit. It is a dormitory. It is the dormitory from last night, from my dream. I think I'm going to be sick.

"You saw him, didn't you?"

"What?"

"He showed you this, didn't he?"

I can't speak.

"To prove to you it wasn't just a dream. To prove he was there."

She is rubbing my back.

"Oh, Patrick, you're a monkey," she says. "She's not ready for this yet."

I shouldn't have come. I shouldn't have come. I want to be home, with Emily, with sane people. Emily! Oh, God. She doesn't know where I am. She'll be frantic.

I try to get up, to go towards the door, out of here, to air and then to safety, somewhere other than this place with its shadows and its dead people wondering round and its nutty old lady who tells them they are monkeys. My legs don't work. They don't work. What's happening to me? Has she put some sort of spell on me? Oh God, is she a witch? I didn't think there was such a thing. Oh God.

"Shhhh," she says.

"What have you done? What have you done to me?"

117

"Nothing, dear. Really."

"Why can't I move?"

"You've had a wee shock, that's all. Breathe. Breathe. You haven't been breathing properly."

Is she trying to gas me, is that it? But surely she would be suffering too. Mind you, if she's a witch, perhaps gas doesn't affect her. I hold my breath. I try to move, but my legs are wobbly. Every time I get near to upright, they just give underneath me and I end up sitting back here.

"Breathe, love. Please. You need to breathe." She is rubbing my back again. I can't hold my breath any more. I have to breathe. It's no good. Whatever she has in store for me, I'll just have to let her. I can't fight it any more. I just hope she makes it quick.

I breathe in and out a few times. The room stops spinning quite so much. She is smiling at me. "That's better," she says. "Now, shall we get you out of here and into the fresh air again?"

She helps me up. I feel silly. How could I have thought those things about her? Does she know? She knows some weird things. She seems to be able to read minds. Does she know what I was thinking about her?

"Come on, love. Come on. That's it. Oh, you've had a bad day, haven't you? And it's only breakfast time. Come on. The fellows will be away, now. They're spending the day in the woods, it's so nice out. You can come and talk to me in the kitchen. That's it. Let's get you a nice cup of something hot and you can help me with the baking."

"I need to phone."

"Sorry?"

"I didn't tell my friend where I was going. Can I use your phone?"

Barney answers.

"Mags?" he says. "Oh, thank God. Are you OK? We've been so worried. Em's out right now checking out all the... well, you know. She's got a funny mind. All that news reporting. Anyway. You OK?"

"I think so."

"Where are you?"

118

"Scotland."

"Scotland?"

"Well, not quite Scotland."

"I'm not with you."

"I found out where Patrick was last week. He was in a hotel. A sort of retreat. Near the border for Scotland."

He is quiet, which is unusual for Barney. Then: "A retreat? Wow."

"He didn't tell you, then?"

"Mags, if he had told me I would have told you. Honestly. I would."

I believe him. Barney is a lousy liar, anyway.

"Barney? Do you believe in ghosts?"

"Ghosts?"

"Yes."

"What, like headless horsemen and that sort of thing? Thumping around in the night?"

"Dead people. Being around."

"Oh. Oh, I see. Well, they've got to go somewhere, I suppose. Don't know. Haven't really thought about it. Why?"

It is on the tip of my tongue to tell him about the dream. I don't. What purpose would it serve? The rantings of a mad woman. It would just confirm what they already suspect about me. I've lost it. Gone nuts. Lost what marbles I had.

"Nothing," I say.

Barney wants to go. He needs to ring Emily and tell her to stop checking the suicide hotspots. Poor Em. Look what I put her through. I'm not sure how to make this one up to her.

Irene is stirring something with a wooden spoon in one of those brown and cream bowls that I didn't think existed any more. I didn't think people stirred things by hand, either. I thought that was what blenders and food mixers were for.

"Your friend all right?" she says.

"I don't know," I say. "She's out looking for me."

"Poor thing," she says.

"Yes."

"Can't be helped. She'll forgive you."

"You reckon?"

"She loves you, doesn't she?"

The crying has started again. This is getting ridiculous. People can't say anything to me without me showering them with tears. Irene doesn't say anything. She carries on with her stirring.

It's so quiet. The disciples are out and about chanting "Om" or whatever it is they do. There is just the sound of the stove, which is a sort of low hum, and the slapping of the spoon against the side of the bowl. Patrick arriving in his TVR would have made quite a stir. Mind you, he would have hated driving it down that muddy track that wasn't a track through the woods. No. Actually, I can't believe he would have done it. He would rather have left it at the entrance and walked. "What car was Patrick driving?" I say.

"Lord, I can't remember," she says.

"Was it a red sports car?"

"Good Lord, no. No. Nobody would bring a sports car down here. Way too difficult. I'm amazed you got yours here, to be honest. People usually bring the big ones, you know the off road thingamyjigamies. Wait a minute. No. I do remember, because it wasn't one of them. It was an estate car. Seemed an awful lot of car for just one person. Green, I think." She chuckles. "You see, the old memory still works. You just have to crank it up a little."

He had Barney's car. So perhaps Barney has his. I don't think I've asked him. Mind you, he hasn't mentioned it. You would think he might have done that. Shall I ring him? No. I'll leave it for now. I'll talk to him when I get home.

"I better get going," I say.

She looks surprised. "You're not going so soon? Stay a little longer. Just until you feel a bit stronger."

"No. The funeral's on Friday, and I need to sort some things out before then."

"What sort of things?"

I am close to saying it is none of her business, but she's been so kind. She doesn't mean any harm. I'm sure of that now, after I nearly thought she was trying to gas me to death in the dormitory. Patrick trusted her, after all. He must have done, to have told her about the lie.

"Why did he tell me he was going to America?" I say.

She is facing the oven, stirring rapidly. She stops now, pulling the pan over to the side, and looks ahead of her. She tips her head to her right, as if she is trying to decide what to say.

"He wasn't ready to tell you," she says.

"To tell me what?"

"About this. His journey. It was such a big change for him, you see. He had always been so against anything vaguely supernatural."

"You're telling me."

I think of Lottie, with her "healing" and all the mumbo jumbo she used to come out with about angels and guardians and so on. Patrick used to laugh at her if he was in a good mood. If he wasn't, he would get quite cross.

"Change is difficult, at first. It's always the way. It takes time for people to be able to let go of the beliefs they've held in the past."

"You sound like Lottie."

"Patrick said that too." She smiles at me. "He hadn't really let go of the old beliefs yet. He was on his way, but it was tentative. Fragile. He didn't want to test you out until he had tested himself. That was what this was all about."

"So he came for a meditation week?" I can hear the doubt in my voice as I'm saying it. Not Patrick. No way.

"No, as it happens, although that was what he needed. No, he came because he wanted to talk to his mother."

I can feel the breath rushing in as a gasp. "Lottie?"

"Somebody told him about me. He came to see if I could communicate with her."

"And could you?"

She smiles. "Do me a favour and breathe," she says. "You've stopped again. In through your nose, out through your mouth, like this." She demonstrates. I feel silly, but I do it.

She looks at me, assessing me. Finally, she says, "She's here now."

"Who, Lottie?"

"She says I'm to call you Thomas."

I look around me. I can't see anything. Lottie did used to call me Thomas, but Irene could have guessed that. It isn't an underused

Biblical tale, is it, that of Doubting Thomas?

"She says you're doing fine. You need to stop worrying so much and stop feeling guilty about every little thing. She says she's trying to help you, but she can only do that if you relax and let things happen."

"What are you talking about?"

Irene's eyes are fixed on something on the wall behind me. I look around, but there is nothing there. She looks as if she is listening to a conversation that I am not privy to, as if she is on the telephone.

"She says you must leave poor Mr Schofield alone. You aren't to know what his life is like, or why he has reached the places he has reached in his life."

I don't like this. How did she find this out?

"You're reading my mind," I say.

She laughs. "If only," she says. "It's such a jumble in there I'm surprised even you can read it."

I don't like this. I don't like this.

"It's all right," says Irene. "I'm sorry. That's enough for one day. You mustn't upset yourself, dear. You really mustn't. There is nothing to fear. You just need to accept. There is more to life than you and me, sitting 'neath the apple tree."

"What? Apple trees now?"

She laughs. "There is more out there than you can see. That's all I'm saying. And it is so beautiful. There is far more acceptance in the world of spirit. It's where we come from. Where we'll return to. We will see our lives reflected back at us, when we go. We will stand and watch as our choices are played out in front of us. We will have the understanding then to know and forgive ourselves. Can you imagine that, Maggie Olds? Can you imagine forgiving yourself completely? Can you imagine what your life would be like if you could do that before you took leave of it? How wonderful it could be?"

I don't know what she's talking about.

"You don't understand," she says. "But you will. You will. You just need to ask the right questions."

Irene and Glen offered to look after Meg for me. "Just until you know which way your head is screwed on," said Irene. Meg seemed happy with the suggestion, so who was I to argue? She didn't wait with them to wave goodbye, she just let herself into the house, presumably to sit by the Aga in the kitchen, which she has grown quite attached to.

I found the petrol station they suggested. It was touch and go, because it wasn't near, but I made it without having to get out and push, so now here I am pointing south and heading home. I have a map this time. I know where I am going. When I looked at it I couldn't believe the journey I made to Irene and Glen's. I took the straightest route possible. Without knowing where I was going, I drove straight there. Had I had a map, I think I would probably have got more lost.

It's been an odd couple of days.

South. Home is just a couple of hours away. Or I could keep driving. I could stay on the road until I reach another home, the home of Ben and my parents and a younger version of me. I can see it clearly, as I watch the road. I am looking at the church. I am pushing open the creaky oak door and smelling the mould in the entrance porch.

I went in to think. I didn't know the two Irises would be there cleaning the church brass.

"Oh," said the short Iris. Iris Burnsall. She had a thin face and she habitually scrunched up her features as if she was squinting in the sun, making it appear even thinner. "You've decided to show your face in here, have you?"

I tried to ignore her. I never won these battles.

The other Iris chipped in. She was taller than Iris number one, but still not very tall. "Don't you answer when people speak to you?" She dropped her voice, more to indicate that she was speaking to Iris than to stop me hearing the next part: "God takes the good ones and leaves the rest as a burden for the rest of us."

I couldn't work out the logic of this. I knew what she was implying, of course. But how did she work out that if God left the rest alive, she and her little friend weren't just as bad as me?

"The poor vicar, you have to feel for him, don't you?"

I wasn't going to get much thinking done. I got up to leave.

"Oh, are you leaving?"

They were standing in my way, staring up at me. "I didn't mean any harm," I said. "I just wanted to spend some time in here. That's all. Thinking."

"Well, you'd be better doing something to help. This carpet needs vacuuming, can't you see that? And the flowers on the altar could do with a spruce up. Something useful."

I actually thought about fetching the vacuum cleaner. But what would be the point? They would never approve of me. I was reprehensible. I was evil. I was alive. I didn't want to cry, not in front of these two. I turned around and strode towards the vestry, willing it to be unlocked, so I could let myself out through the back door. No such luck. I had to turn around and walk back around the pews and out, past the hissing snakes.

I had read the Bible. I knew what was written there. And I couldn't match it up with Christians I saw around me. All that stuff about casting the first stone, loving the Lord and then loving your fellow man, all that sort of thing. I couldn't put it together with the Christianity I saw on a daily basis. These two were definitely Old Testament. An eye for an eye. It was my fault Ben was driving that night. It was my drunken behaviour that had worried my parents for weeks beforehand. It was my being at a party I wasn't supposed to go to that brought my brother out to fetch me. That's all they saw. That's all they would ever see.

As far as they were concerned, I was a resident of Gomorrah, a harlot, a Jezebel. I was to be cast from their midst. Disposed of, like God disposed of the Egyptians. A plague of locusts would be too easy.

And they were right. Ben would still be here if it wasn't for me.

I can't remember the journey. Somehow I am standing on the steps, looking up at my flat, and I have no idea how I got here. Patrick's car is parked down the street, just like any other day. I seem to have been looking for it for ever and it's just sitting here, as if it never went away.

I am struggling to find my key. It's in my bag somewhere. The door opens. Barney takes my bag from me and beckons me into my own flat. "You better come in quietly," he says. "Maybe she won't notice."

There is a clattering noise coming from the kitchen area. Barney leads the way into the living space and looks around him for somewhere to put my bag. He is holding it out away from him, which makes me laugh. In trying to maintain his masculinity, he is managing to look camp. Sixteen stone of camp.

"Oh, I'm glad you think it's funny," says Emily. She steps over a neat pile of books on the floor. My flat has been tidied in my absence. I look around at the rest of the room, seeing the floor for the first time for some days.

"I hope you don't mind," says Barney. "I had to be here, in case you called, and there wasn't much else to do. I thought I might as well make myself useful."

"Never mind that," says Emily. "Where have you been? What were you thinking? Why didn't you phone me? Why wouldn't you? Do you know what's been going through my mind?"

I should go up to her and say I'm sorry. I should beg forgiveness. She deserves nothing less. I can't. She is standing in the gap that serves as a doorway from the kitchen part to the living part, between the work surface and the wall. She has on another short skirt. This one is grey. Her legs are so long that the skirt ends higher than the top of the oven. She looks like a giant in a tiny dolls house. It makes me giggle. Her eyes flash. It makes me laugh even more.

"So you couldn't care less, is that it? God, I feel like your mother. I had to deal with her for Christ's sake. Do you have any idea what that's been like? They're on their way here now."

If any news should stop me laughing, this is it, but I can't. I can't stop. My lungs seem to have their own ideas.

Emily's anger glows in the dim light of the living space. Now I can see twitching in her face. It is trying to smile and she is trying to stop it. The twitching gets worse. It makes my giggles worse, if that's possible.

A little laugh escapes through her nose before she can stop it.

"Oh, God," she says. She gives way to the laughter. It is hysteria more than anything else. Barney is standing in between the two of us looking confused and uncomfortable. He would very much like to escape to the safety of his own home, but he would also like to know what happens next. He stands frozen beside the sofa, the hand holding my bag lifted up, the other one by his side. He looks as if he would like to move forward, but he would also like to go back. He might be constipated, the way his knees are bent and his bottom is sticking out behind him. The sight grabs hold of my rib cage and sends it into further paroxysms.

I slow my breathing down, for some sort of control. Emily does the same. We are gulping in air together, like synchronised swimmers surfacing after a long underwater routine. I will not laugh at this thought. I can't believe I'm laughing at all. We are calmer, both of us, looking into each other's eyes, walking towards each other. She has hold of me. I have hold of her. And now we are both crying.

"Don't do that again," she says.

"I won't. I'm sorry."

Barney coughs. Then there is a big male arm around me and another around Emily. "We missed you," he says. "We can't lose both of you in the same week."

We stay like this. Time passes. It could be a minute. It could be five. Finally Barney moves away. Emily and I follow suit.

"Barney's got Patrick's car," says Emily.

"I know," I say. "I saw it."

"He thought you had his."

"What?"

She shrugs and looks at Barney, who is biting his lip. "Patrick said you wanted to see how you'd get on with it. He said you needed a bigger car. Could you borrow it while he was away? That's what he said."

"Me?"

"Yeah. And I thought, you know, that you probably had better things to worry about than giving my car back, so I didn't say anything. But the thing is I could really do with it, because I need to go to the cash and carry for Friday."

"Friday?"

I realise he means the funeral, just before he says it, and now it looks as though I have forgotten. Which of course I had, for the second running up to my saying it – but not for the thousands of seconds before that.

"The funeral," we say together.

"Sorry," I say. "Of course."

"I don't suppose you did borrow it, did you?"

"No."

"He lied to me."

"Join the club."

"Why?"

I don't know. Not really. "He was at a retreat," I say to Emily, hearing the words coming out of my mouth and feeling as though it is someone else saying them.

"A what?"

"Like vicars go to. And people who dress in orange and go around chanting stuff. It's very quiet there and they eat nothing but wholesome foods and do meditation courses. And there's this weird old lady who thinks she can talk to dead people."

As I'm saying it, I can feel myself being disloyal to Irene. She isn't a weird old lady, not in that sense. I mean, yes, she's weird, in that she's not like anybody I ever met, but why did I choose that adjective? Why couldn't I have gone with kind, or gentle, or welcoming? Or just different? Why did I plump for weird? As I'm speaking I can feel a little chasm of distance opening up between me and my new friend. Acquaintance. It is as though I could have chosen a different route, and I haven't. I have plumped for this one. This one feels familiar. That one might take me to a place that I have no idea about, and no wish to travel to.

"Can she?" says Barney.

"Can she what?"

"Talk to the dead?"

"I don't know. She seems to think so."

"And what do you think?"

"I think maybe the imagination plays tricks. Maybe she is quite clever with, you know, psychology and so on. I don't know."

"What did she say?"

I am saved from this particular frying pan by a knock on the door. Barney opens it. My mother stands there, looking forlorn and small, like a child in need of a cuddle.

"Oh, you're home! Oh, thank goodness for that. I thought we were going to have to bury you too. Your father is parking the car. Help me off with this, will you dear? Who are you?"

"Barney, nice to…"

She cuts him off. She won't remember his name. She didn't listen to it.

"It's been the most awful drive. Roadworks four times on the A1, would you believe it? Four times. And always down to 30."

"You came on the A1?"

I am surprised. If Dad is parking the car, then he is driving. But then, I suppose they were in a hurry to get here.

"I don't understand why traffic has to actually stop. But it always does, doesn't it? Always. It's been dreadful. Absolutely dreadful."

Emily comes forward to say hello, holding out her hand to shake my mother's. Mum thinks about it and slowly accepts the hand, blushing as she does so. Emily does not look surprised. She does not look hurt, or even angry. She mutters something about tea and disappears into the kitchen. My mother clutches my shoulders and stares at my face. She checks out my eyes, my hair, my forehead, my cheeks, my chin, my nose, and my eyes again.

"You're not eating," she pronounces. I start to contradict her, but she keeps talking. "Oh, darling, I can't tell you how sorry I am. It's just too, too dreadful, it really is. After all that you've been through, to now have to go through this." There is a box of tissues on the television set behind me. She reaches for one.

I am unmoved. I know this is strange. Mostly, at the moment, I will take any excuse to join in when someone is crying. But my mother's grief is inaccessible to me. It is something only she can experience. It is almost a barrier in itself, a wall of hysteria that has formed all around her. I can't push myself through it. I'm not sure I would want to, even if I could. I find myself comforting her.

"Mrs Olds," says Barney. "Why don't you sit down?" He takes her arm and guides her away from me, to the sofa. He winks at me, sadness dimming his smile as he does so.

"Sorry." This is Dad. He has just arrived. "Couldn't find a space. You've found his car I see." He kisses me on the cheek and hugs me. "You OK love?" I nod. He goes to sit on the arm of the sofa, where he puts his hand on Mum's back. "Where was it?"

Between us, we explain. I hope the others won't talk about Glen Chase. I hope Dad won't ask. I don't want to know Mum's reaction to it. I need to sort out what I think first.

They start to talk logistics. They will be here until the funeral. They will stay on Friday night if I want them to. They will stay longer if need be. The parish will understand. They want me to say yes, I want you to. I know this. I can't. They talk about the bed and breakfast down the road.

"Why don't you stay at Patrick's house?" says Barney.

"What? No," I say, before I can stop myself or come out with something slightly more tactful. Patrick's house has my clothes in it, in a closet in his bedroom. It has letters from me to Patrick. Naughty emails. I can't have my mother there, looking around in the middle of the night, knowing things.

"Actually, that's not a bad…" says my mother.

My father is looking at me. He cuts in. "I think we'd be better at the B&B love. It would feel uncomfortable there, at his house. Don't you think?"

My mother has on the face that says she doesn't see why, but she is looking at him and he is nodding very intently. She starts to nod with him. I can breathe again. Barney brushes past me on his way to the piano stool to sit down. "Sorry," he whispers.

There is a silence. My mother picks imaginary hairs off my father's trousers. My father watches. Barney picks up a music book from the piano and puts it down again. Emily is still in the kitchen. I swallow a couple of times, and wonder whether I should break the silence, but I don't know what with. The phone does it for me. I pick it up.

"Hello?"

"Yeah, hi. Ms Olds? Yeah?"

"She answers the phone when it isn't me ringing," whispers my mother, just loud enough for my hearing.

"Yes," I say, turning away from her to concentrate.

"Yeah hi. It's Asef from the Mobile Place. Listen, we've checked out that phone, but it's dead. You know what I mean?"

"I do." CT is further away than ever.

"There's just no way into it. I don't know what you did to it. Must have hit it with a hammer or something."

"Something like that."

I put the phone down. Mum wants to know what's going on. Who has upset me? I am disappointed, because I was hoping not to show them my disappointment. I tell her about the phone.

"Why on Earth are you worrying about that at a time like this?"

"I just..." What can I tell her?

Dad chips in. "You know, love," he says to her. "You remember. You fix on the little things. Don't you remember how you had to pick up Ben's jacket from the cleaners? How you took his skateboard to the shop to see if they could mend it, even though he hadn't used it for years? Don't you remember? You cling to the things you have, don't you?"

"I did no such thing," she says.

Emily brings the tea things through. Dad helps her hand everyone a cup. She has bought cake. When did she do that? I don't want any, but she has gone to the effort, and so must I.

We eat. We slurp. We make polite noises at each other. We avoid looking into each other's eyes. Barney makes an excuse to go.

"I have to try and find my car," he says.

"Of course," I say. "I'll call Ginger John."

"Ginger John?" says my mother.

"The policeman. Family Liaison Officer, he said he was. He said he'd help."

"And you call him Ginger John?"

"Well, not to his face. It's just kind of... stuck in my mind."

She is not happy. This is not respectful. Dad puts his hand on hers. Don't say anything, he is urging with his touch. Leave it be. Let it lie.

John laughs when I tell him Patrick lent his car to his friend and that they've been looking for the wrong one. "After all that," he says. "I've been driving round for days looking out for a red TVR. I've even been dreaming about them. How are you doing?"

"I'm OK."

"Yes?"

"Yep."

"OK. Well, we'll start looking for this one then. Legacy, you say?"

"Green." I give him the registration number.

"Thank you," says my mother in my ear.

I shut my eyes. The ten year old me returns to haunt my nervous system. She used to stand over me then, every time I was on the phone, telling me what to say before I said it. It used to have this uplifting effect on my shoulders then, too.

"Thank you," I say into the phone. I am trying not to sound annoyed.

"Anything I can do about the funeral?" he asks.

"I don't think so. Patrick's friend – Barney. He's doing everything. Will you come?"

"I'll be there. If that's OK with you."

"Of course. There's food and stuff afterwards. At his house."

It is reassuring that he will be there. I am not sure why. I have no idea how many people will show up, but I have seen Barney's lists and he seems to be catering for a lot. The rugby team, I suppose, the staff at the hospital. People he has treated. Strangers. It is an odd thing, to be surrounded by strangers on a day like that. I imagine. Lottie's funeral was different. I knew her and loved her, but she wasn't my whole world, not like Ben, not like Patrick. This will be the first funeral like that for me.

"Were there lots of strangers at Ben's funeral?" I say.

My mother takes a hasty breath in. Dad pats her hand. "We knew them all," he says. "Except for a couple of the kids from the Tech. They were very supportive."

I haven't ever asked before. I haven't wanted to know. I presume I was alone, in hospital. There wasn't any other way it could have been. They couldn't have stayed with me and buried my brother at the same time. Besides, I wasn't very good company. I didn't wake up for three months. I don't want to think about this. Why am I thinking about it?

Irene comes into my vision. Suddenly I am in her kitchen. I can smell the bread and feel the warmth from the stove. "Dad?" I say.

"What, love?"

"What do you think about mediums?"

There is a cooling of the air around me. It is sharp, somehow. It doesn't hurt to breathe, exactly, but it isn't the most comfortable thing in the world either. My father has hold of my mother's hand. Hers is squeezing his, because his skin is white around her fingers. He is looking at me. She is looking at her lap.

"I, er... Why do you ask?" he says.

"Do you believe they can speak to the dead?" I should be backing off, but I am pressing forward. I don't know why.

Dad brings his other hand to enclose my mother's in both of his. He glances at her. She is still studying her knees. It is not like her not to have chipped in. I don't understand.

"I believe in life after death," he says. "I'm just not sure that people who claim to be able to contact the dead are all that they, er, they claim to be."

"Why?"

Again, he looks at my mother, and back at me.

"I think that some of them prey on the weak and vulnerable," he says. "There is nothing more desolate, more desperate than grief. I think they..."

My mother snaps into action.

"There is," she says. "There is something more desolate. There is having the belief that you will be together again, one day, some day, there is having that ripped from your insides. There is the sure knowledge that you have lost for ever. For ever. If he was there, he would have come to me. He was my baby." She is crying. It never occurred to me that she would visit a medium. It was so against all the normality she tried so hard to preserve. This time her grief is not the wall it was before. This time it draws me forwards. My father has my mother's shoulders. He is hugging and rocking her. I kneel beside her feet and place my head on her knee. "I'm sorry, Mum. I'm sorry," I say.

She kind of gulps.

She strokes my hair.

We haven't done this before. I don't remember the last time I touched my mother, or she touched me, without one or the other of us recoiling.

Now they have gone to the B&B. Emily has come out of the kitchen and I am at the piano.

"Are you going to play?" she says.

I shake my head.

"Will they be all right, do you think?" she says. "It seems to be bringing things back for them."

"Yes," I say. I am not sure if I am saying yes to the question of their welfare, or to the question of their grief. Both, perhaps.

"I had some thoughts about CT," she says.

"Do you know who it is?"

"Well, not exactly. It's just a thought. But what if it isn't a person?"

"How do you mean?"

"It's just I was at the hospital trying to find out about your insurance guy. In case he went there after the crash."

Mr Schofield clouds my vision. "Did you find him?"

She shakes her head. "Still looking. But I have a plan. There's something I'm going to try tomorrow. Anyway, CT."

"Yes?"

"There's a medical procedure." She consults her notebook. "Computerised Tomography. Haven't you heard of a CT scan? It's used to check out all sorts of problems, like cancer and stuff. Was he ill?"

I don't think so. Mind you, if he thought he had cancer, maybe that would explain why he would want to get in touch with a medium. Maybe he wanted to believe that life continued after death.

"Why would you need more than one?"

"Sorry?"

"It was in his diary every Thursday for weeks. Is it a treatment?"

She looks disappointed. "No. No. It's just a diagnostic thing. I forgot it was a regular thing."

"Oh. It's probably not computerised what–do–you–call–it, then."

"Probably not, no," she says.

"What about Mr Schofield?"

"Trust me. I'll find him. Tomorrow. OK?"

Thursday, 30ᵗʰ November

Another night. Another morning.

Barney calls before my parents arrive. Ginger John has found his car. Will I go with him?

"It sounds really wet," he says. "But I don't want to go on my own."

I leave a note for Mum and Dad. An errand, I say. Well, it *is* a sort of errand. We take my car. The TVR has broken down again, and we can't be bothered to get out the jump leads.

Ginger John's directions get us straight there, no mucking about. Perhaps it is because he is a policeman. Barney's car is parked on a residential street. It is spattered in mud. There is a note tucked under the windscreen. "This car has been parked here for several days now. This is my house. I would like to be able to park my own car outside my own house. Is that too much to ask?"

Barney presses the remote control key and opens the driver door. He retrieves a pen from the side pocket and turns the note over. "Piss off," he writes. He marches up to the nearest door and pushes the note through the letter box.

"Barney!" I say. Barney is not given to anger. He explained it to me once. He said you could understand anything you wanted by looking at beer. "There is mild, there is stout and there is bitter," he said. "You can be two but not all three. "I am mild and stout."

"What about lager?" I said.

"Lager's for football players and when you're on holiday in a hot

135

country. There are no words of wisdom hidden anywhere in lager."

Patrick had come in then. "Is Barns on about his beer again? What am I Barney?"

"You're mild and bitter."

Patrick laughed. So did I. But actually, there was some truth to it. Barney is returning from the house. "What if…?" I say. "Er. What if it's a little old lady or something?"

"I've had enough," he says. "Sorry."

He presses the button that opens the boot. He waits, unsure of himself. He makes a decision and opens the boot to look inside. He releases the fabric thing that hides the contents. There is a small suitcase in there, which belongs to Patrick. Barney looks at me. He leans forward and unzips the bag.

"Clothes," he says. "Just clothes. And a book. *The Celestine Prophecy*. Do you know it?"

I shake my head. He rezips the bag and gives a short, nervous laugh. "Don't know what I was expecting," he says. The back seat is empty. There is one of those parking clock things that councils give out to limit how long you can park somewhere in the driver side door, and of course the pen came from there. There is a tube of mints in a little tray in front of the gear stick. Otherwise the car is empty.

"I thought we were going to find something," I say, leaning against the passenger door. "Something about this CT thing."

He puts an arm round me. "So did I."

I glance down the street. It is just a street, like any other. Terraced houses line it either side. There is the occasional fledgling tree, growing out of gaps in the pavement – attempts by the council to make it a more pleasant place to live. It is not unpleasant. It's just a street. I look up and down at the houses. Should we knock on these doors? Should we question everybody?

Barney is looking at me.

"We can't," he says. "It wouldn't be right."

"What was he doing here, Barns?"

"God knows."

A bus goes past at the top of the road. "Shit. Come on." I take Barney's hand and run up to the main road. Barney lags a little, as he points his key at the car. Now he is running with me, pulling me along. We are of the same mind. There is a bus stop on the other side, but the bus is pulling away.

We cross the road and examine the information signs.

Number 58. The number of Patrick's bus. We check the list of places it goes to. Morton. Bardwell. Shepley. Pitts Park. Wyverham. Sunnington. Mornvale. South Stains. Strayfield. "Do you recognise any of them?" I ask. Obviously we both know of Strayfield, but I don't think I've ever been to any of the others.

Barney shakes his head. "You?"

"No."

The number 58 comes into view. Barney reaches into his pocket for some change. "Shall we?" he says.

"I haven't brought any money."

"That's OK. Come on."

Barney counts out the correct change. The driver doesn't bother to look at us. She is chewing something and staring ahead. She is impatient. She wants to get on. I wonder if she was driving Patrick's bus. She is not the sort of person you ask.

The bus is nearly empty. We both stop and consider a seat half way down the aisle. It occurs to both of us at the same time that Patrick sat in the middle. We move on, settling on a seat near the back. The bus pulls out into the road.

"What are we looking for?" asks Barney.

"I have no idea," I say.

We go past a school, the sharp metal railings and white zig zags on the road giving it away. There is a row of shops, with parking up on the pavement outside the front. There is a hairdresser, a green grocer, one of those open-all-night mini-supermarkets, a butcher with writing all over blackboards out front, a fabric shop with lots of curtains hanging in the window. The row of shops ends, and now there are some dark terraces. They don't look very welcoming. On the other side of the road is a petrol station. "What was the fuel level like?" I say.

"I don't know. Didn't switch the engine on. Maybe he ran out."

A mental note is made, between us, to check when we get back.

The road opens out now. There is grass on the left, behind which is a residential area of larger houses. There is a car dealership on the right.

A set of traffic lights. Another school. This one proclaims itself a Catholic School for Girls.

The bus is coming to a stop again. I don't know what we're looking for. Am I seeing it and not seeing it at the same time?

There is an argument at the front. The driver is taking exception to something. A teenage boy puffs smoke in her face. She starts to push open the little door that keeps her in the driving seat. Wisely, the boy runs away, off the bus. She sits back down, muttering something to herself.

We are underway again.

This is much more industrial. There are some derelict factories on the left, their blackened out windows giving them a forlorn and neglected appearance. On the right is a bright new building in a sort of orangey red brick with white pointing up. "Coral Financial Services," it says on a sign. I will check that with Emily later. Could Mr Schofield have been going here?

We plunge on. There is an industrial estate on our left, behind some trees. We try to read the sign as we pass, but our driver is really putting her foot down. I can tell you there is a pet supply place, but that is all. There are fields on the right.

Now we are plunging down a slip-road towards a dual carriageway. We pull out into the traffic, which is fairly heavy. Someone beeps at us. Our driver makes a gesture through the window to signal her displeasure.

"She's a charmer," says Barney.

The dual carriageway is short-lived. We are off at the next junction and turning left at a roundabout. More fields on our left, some cultivated for crops, one with a horse in it. And now we are in amongst houses once again. This is quite smart, this area. The houses are large and set back from the road behind tall hedges and fences. Some have elaborate stonework on the gate posts.

"I don't recognise any of this," says Barney.

"Me neither."

At a set of traffic lights, we turn right.

We pass a church on our left. We are coming up to a major set of traffic lights. There are some more shops here. We stop at the lights. I am feeling sick. Barney takes my hand. I look around me. There is a bakery, on the corner. On the pavement outside it there is a big yellow sign. It is one of those signs the police use to ask for witnesses. I think I may choke.

"Is this it?" I say. Barney is looking at the other side of the road, across the junction. I follow his gaze. There is a metal post. There is a bunch of flowers tied to it.

"I want to get out," I say.

I run to the front of the bus. Barney follows me.

"Let me out," I say.

"Wait till the stop," says the woman.

Something grips me. I am shouting. I don't even know what I'm saying. Barney is trying to get hold of me but I won't be held. A car horn sounds behind to point out the lights have changed. The woman looks scared. She shrugs for bravado and opens the door. Barney pulls me out of the bus. He is saying things in a soothing voice. I am crying now. What happened? How did I get from shouting to crying? I don't remember. We cross the road, dodging cars that beep at us. And now we are standing in front of the metal post. It isn't even bent. There is no message on the flowers.

My legs have given way, but I don't fall. Barney has me. He is holding me up. He lifts me up and carries me back across the road to the bakery. "You're not supposed to lift," I say.

"Sod that," he says.

The baker brings a seat out from behind the counter. He has been watching us across the road. "Tea," he says. "Sweet tea." He disappears again into the kitchen.

Barney is crouching next to me, looking up at my face, holding my hand.

I am breathing a bit easier now. "Thank you," I say.

He turns away. He is crying.

The baker brings three cups of tea and presents us with one each. He is a short man with very white hair. He doesn't look old enough for it to be so white. "I'm sorry I don't have another chair," he says. "Did you know the man that died?"

We nod.

He shakes his head. "I didn't see. I was out the back, checking the ovens. The police came round and asked, but I couldn't tell them anything."

"Do you know who put the flowers there?" I say.

"It was that policeman. Tall. Red face. Ginger hair."

Barney puts his hand on my shoulder. "Is there a florist near here?" he says.

The baker points. "Just round the corner. Maybe 50 yards."

We drink our tea and thank him. Barney buys some cakes. We head for the florists. It is on another street corner. Raines Street. Same street Car Treats is on. Small world. I wonder if Amanda's wound has healed on her forehead, or if she has smacked her head again and it is a permanent fixture.

Barney buys lilies. White. Same as we put on Lottie's coffin. Patrick would approve. We place them on the road in front of the lamp post.

"Do you want to go home?" he says.

"I think we should carry on. Get to the end of the line."

"Just in case," he says.

"Yes."

"In case of what?"

"In case we see anything," I say. " In case there is anything to see. I don't know. In case. I want to know where he was going. I want to understand. Don't you?"

He puts his arm round my shoulders. "Come on, then," he says.

We wait at the bus stop for twenty minutes. Neither of us speaks. Two buses arrive together. Of course.

There are more shops on this road. There is an interior design place, a shop full of computer games, another hairdresser, a tanning place, a chemists. There is a run down bookshop, a charity shop, a bank and a newsagents. And now we are again in a residential area. The road has widened, and there are parking spaces either side, with meters. The houses have small front gardens so they are not directly on the road. I can see the centre of Strayfield up ahead. The bus station is not far away.

Barney nudges me just before the turning for the bus station and points down a little lane. It is very narrow, but there is a shop half way down it. "Look," he says. The shop is called Classy Taste. The words are written in a decidedly unclassy olde worlde script.

"I told you," says Barney. "I told you it wasn't another woman. What did I tell you?"

The bus pulls into its allotted space and Barney tows me off it. We plunge back out of the bus station, down the little street and into the shop. There are candles everywhere, many of them shaped like hearts. There are gift boxes stacked high by the counter, and all sorts of ornaments of cats or dogs or pigs or sheep in glass cases all over the place.

"You're trying to tell me he came here every Thursday evening? Why? Was he short of cash, or something? Couldn't he have got a job closer to home?" I know what I am saying doesn't make sense. So does Barney.

"I don't know yet, do I?" he says.

There is a woman behind the counter. She is wrapping something for a customer while blowing her long, straight hair out of her eyes. She is extremely pretty. Barney falters. He always does around beautiful women. I never understand why. They must get their share of jerks sniffing around. Maybe a stocky but kind man with a genuine smile would be a refreshing change. I sense him tense and breathe in, summoning his courage to speak to her.

"Excuse me," he says.

"Hold on a second." The till beeps and she hands the chip and pin machine to her customer, who duly presses the right buttons. With the steady hands of long practice, she whips the card out of the machine and hands it back to the customer while dropping the receipt and the gift into a black and white paper carrier bag with pink string handles.

As the customer is leaving, she fixes Barney with a pair of beautiful brown eyes and says, "What can I do for you?"

Barney looks uncomfortable. I wonder if his heart is thudding like mine. She is very possible. Very possible. She is really lovely. Everything about her is lovely. She has straight, dark brown, flowing hair. She has on a low cut blouse, and there is good reason to wear it. She has long legs in tight jeans. She has a gentle assured manner. If Patrick had a perfect woman list, she would tick most, if not all, of the boxes.

"Do you know Patrick?" he says. He speaks very quietly. She has to ask him to repeat it. He clears his throat and does so.

She shakes her head. "Patrick who?"

"Patrick, er, Patrick Miles."

She looks over his shoulder, as if hoping to find the answer written on a paper mobile behind him.

"Big. Tall," he says. "Curly black hair. Blue eyes. Looks like a rugby player."

She shakes her head. "No. Should I?"

"No. No reason. Er. Does anybody else work here?"

She smiles at him. "No. Just me. It's my shop."

"Oh. OK. Thanks."

We turn to leave.

"What's your name?" she says.

He blushes. "James," he says. James Rubbel."

She laughs. "Rubbel? Like the Flintstones?"

He looks at his feet and nods.

"Nice to meet you, James," she says.

We are standing at the bus station, waiting for a number 58 to take us back.

"What do you think?" he says.

"I think she liked you," I say.

He blushes again. "No. I mean, CT. Not Classy Taste."

"Definitely not. Did you see the crap in there? Not remotely classy. Or tasteful."

"You know what I mean."

"I do. I don't think he's been visiting Classy Taste every Thursday. Do you?"

"No."

"Unless he was using an assumed name and a wig."

"What? No. No way."

"I'm kidding. She certainly doesn't seem to be missing anybody."

"No."

"Well, not in that sense, anyway."

Poor Barney. I didn't know he could go so red.

"She was lovely, though, wasn't she?" he says.

The bus journey seems longer in reverse. Barney is quiet. I am thinking about how he lifted me and carried me across the street. He is not supposed to do that. The doctors would have a field day. And now I am thinking of that day two years ago, when Barney was still in hospital and Patrick was trying to help him to walk.

Barney was quiet then, too.

Patrick put the hoist thing over his wheelchair and put his arms in the slings that attach to the metal arms. Barney said nothing. His head was tipped over to the side.

"Help me out, big guy," said Patrick.

"What's the point?" said Barney.

Patrick looked at me. I didn't know what to say. This was not like Barney. Patrick stopped fiddling with the straps and crouched down into a squat, looking up at Barney's face.

"What's up?"

Barney let out a short, harsh laugh with no humour in it. "What do you think?"

"It takes time, that's all."

"There hasn't been any progress for days. Weeks."

"There has. Hasn't there, Mags?" I stepped forward, nodding, hoping he couldn't tell that I was lying.

"This is it," said Barney.

"What do you mean?"

"This is as far as I go."

"Barns, you can't do that."

"Do what?"

"You can't give up on me. You have to keep going. Keep believing. You can't stop. I won't let you."

"It isn't about you, though is it?"

Patrick stepped back, winded. I squeezed the fingers of one hand in the fingers of the other. This was only a matter of time. We knew this, surely. What was he expecting?

Barney nodded in my direction. I shrank in my seat. "She knows. Look at her. She knows the truth. You're just living in a fantasy world. It's all very well believing, Patrick, but sooner or later you have to face the facts. Sooner or later you have to say: 'Well, you know? His neck snapped. It snapped. It's amazing that he can move his arms and legs at all. But this is as far as it goes.'"

"Why are you doing this? Who have you been talking to?" Patrick looked around him, searching for inspiration somewhere, anywhere. His eyes landed on me. "Mags. Tell him. Tell him you believe."

I couldn't. I didn't. I opened my mouth, but nothing came out.

"Fuck!" shouted Patrick. "Right, listen to me." His voice sounded odd, as if it was coming from further away than where he was standing. "Both of you. Listen. This is what happens. You create your own world, all right? You are given the cards to play with, and it is up to you to accept your hand and play it. Now, you can play your hand like you're stumbling around in the dark, or you can play it like you're reaching for the light. You have no idea where reaching for the light will take you. You know damn well what will happen if you stumble around in the dark. It's the same thing that happens now. You get stuck, because you stay where you are. But if you look for the light... The light is belief. It's belief. All things are possible when you believe."

Barney looked up. It took some effort. It always did. The mending nerves and muscles and whatever else it was that had broken in there took a lot of effort to bring round. "What are you talking about, Paddy? You sound like Lottie."

Patrick laughed. His voice returned to normal. "I do, don't I?"

"Where did that come from?" Patrick looked surprised. It was a reasonable question. Barney was usually the one who kept Patrick going, not the other way around.

"I have no idea," he said.

"All right," Barney said. "Come on. Let's get going."

Patrick worked the hoist and Barney was on his feet once more, painfully edging one foot forwards.

That was the day it changed. Lottie said afterwards that the times when you're ready to give up are the most positive times of all. "Your body clings to what is familiar," she said. "It doesn't like change. So it makes you feel despair, so you won't push through and discover what it is possible to discover. It is those times you must look for the possibilities. When things are going well, it is easy. When they are going badly and it is hard, that is your chance to make a difference."

Patrick and I had laughed at her. But it was true that Barney made the most progress on the day he felt the most despair.

"What are you thinking about?" says Barney.

"Patrick," I say. "And the power of belief."

He smiles and holds my hand.

"We thought we were invincible," he says. "I broke my neck, for God's sake, and look at me now. Then this. It's such a fucked up world."

Mum and Dad are there at the flat when we get back. It is spotless. The piles of things have been sorted into one place, over in the bay window. Dad is sitting on the sofa. Mum has on a pair of rubber gloves and is emerging from the bathroom.

"Where have you been?" she says.

"They found Barney's car. How did you…?"

"Emily let us in, before she went to work," says Dad.

"Sorry," I say.

"Where was the car? Was it a long way away?"

"Um. No. Not really. Couple of miles. It's just, we wanted to visit the place where, you know."

Dad nods. Mum looks aghast. "What on Earth for? Sounds thoroughly morbid to me."

Dad smiles at me. He long ago stopped being shocked by Mum's selective memory. She used to deliver flowers weekly to the place where Ben and I crashed. She used to give me grief for not doing that. I couldn't go there. Something prevented me, a sort of invisible barrier, but not a physical one, a sort of barrier within myself. It's inadequate, but it's the best way I can describe it. I have never been back there, even now.

"How are you feeling?" he says.

I search for a description. Can't find one. "OK," I say.

The door opens. Emily is there. "Found him!" she says. She sees my father and falters. She sees my mother. "Ah. Sorry," she says. "I, er, I forgot. Oh, wow." She is looking round the flat. "You've done an amazing job, Mrs O."

Mum looks proud and uncomfortable at the same time. I wonder if she will be able to resist a response to the Mrs O label. She battles with herself, but it is a look from my father which wins out. She smiles at Emily. "Thank you," she says. "Whom have you found?"

Emily looks at me for help. I shake my head. Don't tell her.

"It's, um. It's a man that we've been wanting to trace. Um. At work."

"Well, I'm sure it's very exciting," says my mother. "But I think Margaret has bigger things to worry about at this moment in time."

Emily stares at her pink designer shoes. She apologises. I try to catch her eye to thank her, but she is not looking in my direction.

Dad is watching me. "I feel like a walk," he says. "Mags? Will you join me?"

"It's freezing out," I say.

"So we'll wrap up warm." He has on his voice of quiet authority. It is the one he uses for parishioners that are behaving unreasonably. I wonder what I have done. Mum looks at us with suspicion, Emily with desperation. She really doesn't want to be left here with my mother, but my father clearly has not invited her. When he wills it, he can make his desires very clear. It is something he has always been able to do. He doesn't have to say anything, he simply intends something, and it comes about. I wish he could intend a different outcome for Ben and me, or for Patrick, but perhaps it doesn't work for things like that.

The tide is coming in fast, so we stick with the walkway behind the sea wall. Dad doesn't say anything to begin with. We just walk. He puts his arm around me and matches his steps to mine. We walk to the end of the road, where the choice is between the high cliff path or the grassy bit where everybody takes their dogs. We opt for the cliff path.

It is cold, but it is bright and there is no wind to speak of, so it should be pleasant up there today.

"Who has Emily found?" he says.

I can't lie to my father. I never have been able to.

"Mr Schofield," I say.

"And who is that?"

I tell him about the first visit from Ginger John. I tell him about the certainty of the two police officers of this man's guilt in running a red light. I tell him of the lack of witnesses, the broken camera, and the changed story.

"He murdered Patrick," I say. "He is Patrick's murderer."

My dad squeezes my shoulders harder, and then lets go and takes my hand instead. He doesn't say anything. We walk up to the highest point on the cliff path. There is a bench here. It has an inscription. It says, "For Jean, who loved this view."

We sit down.

"Jean was right," my father says. He always says that when we sit here.

He takes in a deep breath and blows out again.

"What are you planning to do when you find this Mr Schofield?" he says.

"I don't know."

He is silent. He nods.

"He shouldn't get away with it," I say.

"He won't," says my father.

"He is doing."

Dad takes my hand. He carries on looking out to sea. "This life is so short," he says. "For some of us it is shorter than for others, but in the grand scheme of things, our souls are only on the Earth for such a very short time."

I have heard this before. I try not to roll my eyes.

"God has a plan for this man. There is balance in all things. There will be justice, even if there hasn't been already."

"So he's going to Hell then?"

He looks at me. He knows I am mocking him.

"There will be a reckoning. It is not your decision to make, baby girl."

"So what am I supposed to do?"

"Forgiveness benefits the forgiver, perhaps more than the forgiven. Forgive."

"How?"

"Faith. Ask God to help you."

"Look, Dad, I know this is your life and everything, but that doesn't work for me."

"How do you mean?"

"If God exists, he certainly doesn't listen to me. He doesn't help me."

"What makes you say that?"

"How can you even ask that?"

Dad faces out to the sea again. He nods. "Ben," he says. I don't say anything.

Eventually he says, "I struggled with that one too. It was a tremendous test of faith. Why would a loving God take my boy away? Why would he put my girl through what she went through, what she is still going through? But then I realised something. It wasn't my decision to make."

I wait for him to continue. He doesn't.

"What? Is that it?"

"It is indeed. There is more comfort in that than you can ever know until you once accept it," he says.

I don't know what he's talking about.

He tries again. "We have trials, a number of trials in life. Things that we must learn from. Loss is the greatest of these trials. It is not until you accept your trials that you begin to learn from them."

"What, so I need to see the greater good, is that what you're saying?"

"No. No, baby girl. It's not what I'm saying. I'm saying you need to accept the things that happen to you. You need to feel your grief. You need to lick your wounds. And you need to look inside of yourself. Only then will you find the peace that belongs to you."

"To me?"

"To you, to me, to Mr Schofield."

I don't accept that. I won't accept that. "But he killed somebody.

And then lied. Whatever happened to an eye for an eye? That's in the Bible, isn't it?"

"There are lots of things in the Bible. They don't necessarily mean what you think they mean. Love the Lord thy God with all thy heart, and with all thy soul, and with all thy mind. Love thy neighbour as thyself. That's in the Bible. And that's the thing that will help you through this. None of that vengeance rubbish. What happens with vengeance, anyway? Let's look at this. Some kid blows up a bomb in Middle East, breaking a peace agreement. And so a nation takes revenge against a nation. Does that make sense to you?"

"No."

"No. Because once one side takes revenge, the other side sees no other option. They take revenge. And then the first side takes revenge for the revenge, and on we go. It's a downward spiral. A bloody mess. They have to ask what is the truth?"

"The truth?"

"It's a kid. A girl or a boy who has suffered, and who thinks that the only way to alleviate his or her suffering is to cause suffering in another person. It is a child who deserves our compassion. He behaves in that way because he doesn't see another. He is caught in a cycle he doesn't understand. And the cycle will go on until we bring forgiveness into it."

"No."

"No?"

"That child caused people to die."

"Yes. But why compound it with more deaths?"

"Anyway, Mr Schofield wasn't acting according to a cycle he didn't understand. He knew about the Highway Code. He must have passed a driving test, somewhere along the way. And even if he hadn't, who doesn't know about red lights? He jumped a red light. He was being selfish. And then he lied about it."

"The circumstances of his life led him to a point where he felt he had to get somewhere fast."

"How can you say that? How can you just forgive him for this? Patrick died. Don't you care?"

"Of course I care, baby girl. Of course I do. But this doesn't help you. It's a fiction to think that vengeance means you care about somebody. It doesn't help you or the person you have lost to want to cause suffering to another human being. Trust me, this man is suffering for what he has done. You don't know what is happening to him now. You don't know if he has sleepless nights. You don't know what things run through his head. You don't know why he was rushing in the first place. You don't know these things. He has caused suffering to another human being, and whenever you do that there is a price to pay. You pay a price. The still small voice within you knows what you have done."

He often talks about the still small voice. I used to listen out for it, but I never heard it.

"What do you want me to do, Daddy?"

I haven't called him Daddy since I was six years old. I don't know what made me say it now.

"Don't inflict the disease that is unforgiveness upon yourself. Ask God to help you understand what has happened. Ask him to help you forgive this man," he says.

"God won't help. He doesn't like me," I say.

"You are one of His children."

"Yeah? Well, I'm the black sheep."

"And He is the good shepherd."

"I'm sorry, Dad. I'm sorry. I know you believe all this stuff. I know you do. But I don't. OK? I tried. I looked for help, and it didn't come. It's just a convenient thing that people believe because it's too hard to believe that we are here on our own. There is no God."

He doesn't say anything for a while. He looks at me and nods.

"And yet you say He doesn't like you," he says.

Emily and Mum are laughing, which is unexpected. Em is stirring something in the kitchen. Mum is chopping vegetables.

"We must get you some better knives," she says, when she spots me standing in the archway.

"I'm OK. I don't cook much."

"No." She casts a knowing look across at Em, who grins back. They seem actually to be comfortable with one another, which I haven't seen coming.

Shit. Danny. I have forgotten him. Presumably one of us needs to pick him up from an airport or a train station. "When's Danny arriving?" I say to Em. She looks startled.

"I forgot to tell you," she says. "He rang. He's not coming."

My brain doesn't know how to handle this information. The picture I have of Patrick's funeral features his brother, of course it does. I can't recreate it without him, that wouldn't make any sense.

"He said he thought you'd understand. He said you understood about Lottie. You helped him with Patrick."

"Lottie was different." He never spoke to Lottie. He cut her out of his life completely. He spoke to Patrick often. For hours, sometimes. They were brothers. Why wouldn't he come to his brother's funeral?

"I don't understand," I say.

"Neither do I. He just said it wasn't for him."

"What?"

"Those were his words. Not for him."

I would give anything to be able to turn back the clock and go to my brother's funeral. Doesn't he give a shit?

There is a sensation on my arm. I swat it away and realise too late that it is my father's hand.

"Sorry," I say.

"Funerals are for the living," he says. "They're for the living."

The room is moving. I don't seem able to fix my eyes on anything to steady myself. Everything is at an angle, and shifting away from me. I never met Danny. But I always liked him, when we spoke on the phone when Patrick wasn't here. He is like Patrick. I wanted… This isn't about me, though, is it? It's about Patrick. Does he not have the respect for his brother that he deserves? He was my link to Patrick. The only remaining cells of his DNA.

I am sitting. I am not sure how I got here, but there is a chair under me. Emily is crouching beside me and telling me to breathe. Mum and Dad are standing together in the kitchen area. Mum is holding Dad's hand and looking at it. Did I hit it hard? Was that me?

"Why wouldn't he come?" I say.

I can see Patrick's face. He was on the phone to his brother. She died peacefully in her sleep, which everyone said was a blessing, but

Patrick didn't think so. "I'm not ready to lose her," he kept saying.

We were expecting to pick him up from the airport in the evening. We were just about to leave to drive down to London. I suggested he got the train, and we met him at the station, but Patrick wanted to pick him up. So we borrowed Barney's car.

"Hey," he said. His face broke into a smile. It was the first one I had seen all week.

I thought it was strange. He should be on the plane by now, surely?

The thought crossed Patrick's mind at the same time. "Is your plane delayed?" he said. The smile faded. I could hear Danny's voice, chatting away. I couldn't make out what he was saying. There wasn't any space in the words for Patrick to butt in.

Eventually there was a lull, and Patrick said, "She was your mother."

More of Danny's voice, thousands of miles away.

"How can you miss this?" I put my hand on his arm. He turned away from me. The force of his next response made me jump: "You just have no fucking respect, do you?" Then he hung up. He grabbed his jacket and left the house, slamming the door as he went.

I didn't understand it then. I understood his disappointment that Danny wasn't coming over. We both wanted to see him. But I didn't understand the feeling inside, the feeling of utter, desperate loneliness, like the last person in the world who could possibly understand the scale of the loss has just declared himself out of the game. Like you are completely, totally on your own in the world, there is this big gaping hole inside you which you know you will never ever fill, and the last person who could help you to forget its presence has just told you he doesn't give a shit. I understand it now. I persuaded Patrick to forgive him. This thought makes me gag. I will never forgive him. Not for Lottie, and not for Patrick.

It is a stew. I can't eat it. Mum and Dad manage a bit, but none of us is hungry. Emily takes one bite and stops. All that effort she went to.

Our appetite for talk is similarly limited. We sip glasses of water. We push food onto forks. We think about eating it, then we take a bite, then we sip glasses of water again. We don't speak. We don't look at each other. Well, I don't. The others may be glancing at each other and passing silent comment on the state of me, but I don't see them. I don't care.

Mum and Dad say they are tired and go to their B&B. Emily is left with me. I tell her to go.

"No, love," she says.

"I am not good company," I say.

"I am well aware of that."

I try not to, but I smile.

"Danny's just a selfish little shit, you know that."

"Let's not talk about him."

We talk about Mr Schofield instead. He works for one of the main insurers in town. She is waiting for a call with his home address, but she knows how to find him at work. He is back at work already. She has seen him.

"What does he look like?"

"You sure you want to know?"

"Yes."

Her glasses slide down her nose. She pushes them back up again. "Tall. Overweight. Weird forehead. Too big, or something. Walks with a limp."

"Does he look…?"

"What?"

I know it sounds ridiculous, but I say it anyway. "Sorry?"

She is thinking about it. "Mmm. Sad. He looks sad."

That's something, I suppose.

"Do you want to go and see him?"

I don't know. I think about what Dad said, about the bombers in the Middle East. I can't quite see how that relates to my situation. I just want him to be sorry, that's all. I want him to pay for what he's done. It's the funeral tomorrow. We will be busy. I tell her I'll decide then.

"I think that's a good idea," she says.

Friday, 1st December

Barney has done a good job. The house looks spotless. The leaves are tidied up in the garden. There are platefuls of food in the fridge and the pantry, waiting for later. Mum, Dad, Emily, Barney and I are now waiting for the hearse and cars. Barney has on a black suit with a dark purple tie. Dad has on his vicar's uniform. Mum a black suit she wears a lot. Em has a black V-neck sweater, with a white shirt underneath, a long black skirt and her most sober shoes, which still have crippling heels on them. I am in my wool knit dress. He liked this dress.

We will come back here later, with all those other people. Will there be many? I don't know any more. If his brother didn't love him enough to come to his funeral, will anybody else turn up?

I can't sit here like this, saying nothing. I get up and go into his office. I shut the door. I sit at the desk, lean my head against the back of the chair, the way I saw him do a thousand times. The door opens, tentatively. Barney's head appears.

"Can I come in?" he says.

I nod.

"There were some messages on the phone," he says, pointing at it. It no longer flashes. I had forgotten about the messages when I ran out to deal with Meg. I wait for him to carry on.

He shakes his head: "Mostly just boring stuff, you know."

I nod. Of course. We aren't going to find out anything now. It seems our bus journey somehow exhausted all possible avenues.

Friday, 1st December

"I was thinking we might find this CT at the funeral," he says. I glare at him. I have thought it, but not spoken the words out loud. I do not want to chase the possibility away.

"There was this one message," he says. "From Alan. Do you know an Alan?"

"No."

"He said Patrick had his number, but of course we can't get at his numbers now. But look, he said something about a Christine. Do you know a Christine?"

I don't. "What did he say, exactly?"

"He said he wasn't sure if Patrick remembered, but Christine was having a get-together. That was the term he used. A get-together. And, as he didn't have a car, did Patrick want him to give him a lift?"

"Who didn't have a car?"

"Patrick."

"Patrick didn't have a car?"

"That's what he said."

"But he did have a car. He had your car."

"I know. I don't get it either."

"Alan who?"

"He just said Alan."

"Christine?"

"Yes."

It is something. I have no idea how to take it forward, but at least it is something more than we had a few moments ago.

There is a knock on the door. I feel myself shiver. The undertakers have arrived.

There are two of them and they are very tall and thin. The man has a slight bend to his shoulders and knees, as if he is always being weighed down by an imaginary coffin. The lady is very rigid and upright. Her clothes look odd. She seems to have a very long back and it is out of proportion with her legs. The black jacket comes down a long way, and then the A-line black skirt starts. I wonder whether God ran out of matching legs when he made her body, and gave her a set from a short person instead. How can I be thinking such cruel thoughts now? She walks forward when she sees me and takes my hand. "You must be Maggie," she says. She has warm eyes.

I nod. She tells me she is called Sandra, but that I'm not to worry if I can't remember it. I have better things to think about, she says. She says she will answer to "Oi you," if necessary. I find myself smiling. She squeezes my hand. She says not to worry about a thing. They are there to make sure it goes smoothly. She guides us to the car behind the hearse. I don't know if I'm supposed to look at it or not. I can't not. Lilies. Barney has gone for lilies. Just one arrangement. Beautiful. Not over the top. The way he would have liked. I feel my eyes filling up. Sandra squeezes my arm and helps me into the car, followed by my mother, Emily, Barney and Dad.

The drive is slow. I am aware that I want it to be over, but I don't want the time to pass. I want to get out. Emily leans forward and tells me to breathe.

I wonder for a moment if there will be a seat for us in the Crematorium, there are so many people here. There are quite a few standing at the back. Ginger John is there, with his colleague whose name I still can't remember. Other people. Lots of other people. I know a few of the faces, but many of them are a mystery to me. Is there a Christine amongst them?

Dad has my right arm, Barney has my left. They are practically carrying me to my seat. The coffin goes ahead of us. I don't know where to look, but not straight at it. I keep my eyes on the floor a few feet ahead of us.

Barney asked me if I wanted to say a few words. I didn't. I don't. He has spoken at length to the man who is conducting the service. He is a humanist. That's what Patrick wanted. Mum is shifting uncomfortably in her seat, but Dad doesn't seem to mind. His hand is on mine throughout.

Barney checked the music with me, but I wasn't really listening. So I am surprised when I hear a song by Queen ringing out around the chapel. It is the one they used to sing a lot when Barney was recovering. I nod. It is too ridiculous for words. There are no tears, because this is not real. That coffin doesn't house Patrick. He isn't there. These people didn't know him, who are they? This is all a dream, a mad irrational product of a deranged mind. I will wake up soon and find I just had too much gin last night. I am not sitting here, looking at a wooden box with Patrick in it and tapping my feet to Freddie Mercury. I am not doing it.

Then Barney gets up to speak.

People stir, as he moves towards the lectern. There are a few coughs. He clears his throat as well.

"Patrick was my best friend," he says. His voice cracks. And now I know it is real. It is not a dream. This is actually happening, and there is nothing I can do to slow it down or stop it, it will continue on, piling forward until it has driven a swathe through our lives. This is it. This is the moment I never thought would come. This is goodbye. Here are the tears. Here is the shaking. Why do I have to be surrounded by people? I want the floor to open and take me away. I want death to swallow me whole. I want out. I want out. I want out.

Dad grabs my shoulders. "Shhhh," he says. "Shhhh."

Barney has stopped speaking and is looking at me. I see the pain in his eyes, to match my own. I feel a breath whipping in through my body. I swallow. I nod at him to carry on.

And now somehow we are at Patrick's house. Jed is here, helping himself to sausage rolls and listening as January talks. Shy Miles, who would always rather fade into the background but instead has taken over my show in my absence, is helping Emily carry around plates of food. Spell FM summed up in two little tableaux. None of the others are here, but I think I saw them at the church.

There are a lot of walking wounded: people on crutches and people in slings, people who wince when they move. Patrick's patients, I presume. I should go round and ask them if they are Christine or Alan, or if they know them. I don't. I can't. I can't even speak to them. I am wandering around his house looking for peace and finding only people. People with stories to tell about Patrick. Keeping him alive in their conversations, but their portrayals are different to mine, and I'm not sure I want to hear them. I turn away from a group of people in the dining room and find myself in Lottie's drawing room. Patrick never came in here, not after she had gone. It felt too like an invasion of her space. There is a giant in here, on his own, sitting in Lottie's chair and looking out of the window. He stands when he sees me.

"Sorry," he says. "I was looking for some quiet. Sorry."

"It's OK. Stay."

He must be six foot six, at the very least. He has vast shoulders. He might be even bigger than Patrick. He is blond. He carries his head sweetly to the side. He can't be older than eighteen, and it must be difficult being so big when you're going through puberty and so on. That might explain the shyness.

It occurs to me I have seen him somewhere before.

"Have we met?" I say.

He looks towards his feet. "Not really," he says. "I think you came to watch a training session once."

Now I remember. I know who it is. I had wanted to see Patrick in action. He had been training the under eighteens side every spare moment he had, and I wanted to know what went on, how he handled it, what he looked like when he was teaching the game that he loved. I had never been quite that close to the action before. When you see it on the telly or from the stands, you can tell it is a physical game, but when you're standing on a rugby pitch and watching someone only a few feet away biff into a mat that somebody else is holding up, you get a real sense of just how brutal it is, just how committed its players must be to winning the ball, over and above their personal safety.

He put them through it for about forty minutes, and then he stopped them for a little pep talk. They seemed to like this bit. They all huddled round him, linked in a circle with their arms around the men to either side. I moved forward, to see if I could hear what he was saying. I loved hearing him talk about rugby. It lit him up. "Rugby teams don't win without it," he was saying. "You have to know that the man standing next to you will step up and take a hit for you, and that you will do the same for him. That he will put in that crucial tackle to stop the other team scoring. That you will do the same. You must inspire belief and you must commit to believing. Understand?"

They all nodded.

"It doesn't happen overnight," he said. "If you don't work on it, you can't just expect it to be there. You have to practise. Every training session, every friendly match, you have to practise believing, every bit as much as you practise passing the ball, making the tackles, perfecting the ruck. You practise believing. Trust me, it will pay off."

They made some funny grunting noises and leapt in the air, some sort of tribal firing up. Then he let them go to the changing rooms. Session over. He came over to talk to me. "I saw you looking at all those thighs," he said.

"Mmm." I responded. "But there was one stand-out pair, put all the others in the shade…"

And now I am thinking of something I should not be thinking about while talking to this young innocent before me. He does look ever so familiar, though. I don't think it was just the training session. I don't really remember seeing him there, although he must have been there, for him to remember me. But there is another reason I am remembering him. It's another occasion. A match. I can't quite grasp it from my memory.

"I'm really sorry, Mrs Miles," he says. I don't correct him. I can hear the chatter building in the other rooms. It sounds quite a party. I sit in the other chair, the partner to the one that the young colossus occupied when I came in. "Sit down," I say. "What's your name?"

"Angus," he says.

"Angus." I remember the name too. Angus. God, this is annoying. Why do I remember him?

"I don't suppose," I say, "that you have any idea what the initials CT stand for, do you?"

He looks puzzled. "I had a CT scan once, is that what you mean? Not sure what it stands for, though. Maybe cardio something. I think it was to look at my heart."

The worried look on his face as he searches for the answer, the attempt to shrink back into the chair, the head tilted onto the side, it's all so familiar. And the name. "It isn't just the training day," I say. "Where have I met you before?"

He shuffles uncomfortably. He can't look at me. He coughs a little and says, "I don't know. I, er…. Would you like another drink?"

"No, thanks."

"I think I'll… er… yes."

He makes a hurried exit. And now the memory slams itself into my brain. Patrick lost his temper, and it was an impressive sight to see. It was a match. The under eighteens had got through to the semi-finals of some big tournament, I forget which. Angus Brown was sent off. Angus Brown. I remember, because there was quite a bit of talk about it afterwards. Patrick absolutely flew at him, and the poor kid looked dejected enough at the sight of the red card. He had done something called a spear tackle. I think that's when you pick somebody up and ram them into the ground, head first. Rugby is a brutal game, you're allowed to do all sorts of things to other people, including stamping on them if they are in your way, but they draw the line at ramming a person's head into the soil, it seems.

"What if you had caused serious injury?" Patrick had said. "Finished the poor kid's career? Or worse? What then? How would you live with yourself?"

I wondered then if somebody had spear tackled Patrick; if that was what happened to his playing. I had tried to ask Barney, but he was always very evasive about Patrick's rugby career. They had a pact not to talk about it. Lottie was in on it too, because she always changed the subject if rugby made an appearance in a conversation, even when Barney was doing really well with the Kestrels.

Angus the spear tackler. Patrick dropped him from the team, and didn't reinstate him for months. I remember, because he used to ring up a lot, and leave messages. Of course. That's why the name is so familiar. He was desperate to get back on the team. I wonder if he ever relented? He must have done, because Angus stopped calling. Yes. He must have relented. Poor kid. You have to be so committed, it must be hard to remember sometimes that you're not actually out to kill your opponent, just incapacitate him. It must be easy to overstep the mark.

Dad arrives. "How you doing, baby girl?"

I nod, then I shake my head. I am running out of answers to that question.

He nods and sits down in the chair that Angus vacated. "I've met some really nice people from his work. They're talking about a memorial. Apparently they've raised quite a bit of money. Had you thought about that at all?"

"No."

"No. Well, there's plenty of time. There's a lady called Erica, she's his boss, is that right? She said to say she's sorry she hasn't been to see you but she thought you'd rather be left alone."

She is right, of course, but that's not why she hasn't been to see me. I understand that. It's because she wouldn't know what to say. Dad squeezes my hand.

"Is Ginny there?" I say.

"Yes, I think so."

"And the Kestrels?"

"There's a group of very well built men, if that's what you mean. I felt rather small in their company."

I laugh. "That's better," he says. "Are you going to come out and talk to anybody?"

I look at the door. I can't. Dad nods. "No. That's OK. You don't have to go anywhere if you don't want to."

I can hear my mother's voice in the other room. She is asking where I am. "Am I being rude?" I say.

"I don't think anyone is thinking about that," he says.

"Dad?"

"Yes."

"Have you come across anybody called Christine?"

He thinks about it. "No. Why?"

"Nothing."

"Still trying to find CT?"

I nod.

He doesn't say anything. The door opens. My mother is here.

"What are you doing in here? You really must come and talk to your guests, dear. It is terribly rude."

Dad smiles at me and squeezes my hand. We stand together. "They all loved him," he whispers. "Remember that. They all miss him too."

The noise level is growing throughout the house. As we walk back through the dining room, we can hear a chant beginning. "Barney, Barney," they shout. We reach the door to the living room just as that familiar tenor voice starts up:

"I like New York in June."

There is a cheer, followed by a chorus of: "How 'bout you?". Dad squeezes my arm. "You all right, love?"

I nod. I push open the door.

"I like a Gershwin tune," sings Barney. The rugby team and assorted injured people sing, "How about you?"

Barney sees me and falters. Everyone turns to look, guilty expressions on their faces.

I walk through them and sit at the piano. I play a chord, and the swirly bits, as Patrick used to call them. It is the introduction to the song, as he used to play it.

I reach the end of the introduction and take my hands off the keys, turning to look at Barney. He seems unable to move. I nod at him. Shakily, he starts the song again. I let the accompaniment play itself. It's a no brainer, this song, you just follow the singer, then in the gaps you get to have some fun, improvising around the main theme and getting grander and grander with the chords as you go. Patrick always did that. I find my own hands playing the song the way he would have done.

The room is getting more crowded; the choruses of "How about you?" are getting louder. We reach the bit about holding hands in the movie show and I see my parents, over by the door to my left. Dad has his arm around Mum. There are tears in both their eyes, but they are smiling. Everyone is smiling. I think I might be too.

What now? The house is back together. We have locked it up and come back to the flat. Mum and Dad are talking about going back to the B&B. I have suggested they go home, but they say they will stay another day. The parish can survive without them for one more day.

Emily is exhausted. She is asleep on my bed. Barney is sitting in the window looking out at the moonlit sea.

"What now?" I say.

Dad looks surprised. He has just answered that, in that he has just suggested that he and Mum head off for the night. The realisation dawns, I was not referring to the logistics of the evening.

"One step at a time," he says. "The journey of a thousand miles…"

It is one of his favourite sayings. It is a quote, from Confucius, I think, although I can never remember who says what. The journey of a thousand miles starts with the first step.

"Rest," he says. "Tackle tomorrow when tomorrow comes."

They kiss me goodnight. Mum squeezes my fingers in hers, and has a long look at my face. She is older than I remember. Perhaps I haven't looked at her properly for a while.

"Goodbye, Barney," my father calls across the room. Barney doesn't appear to notice. Then he waves his hand vaguely, but he doesn't take his eyes off the sea. Mum starts to look cross, but Dad shrugs his shoulders and rubs hers. "Bye, love."

They are gone.

I join Barney at the window. We say nothing. The sea chops and stutters its way up the beach. A gull swoops and rises again, stretching out its wings at the sheer joy of living.

"Did he mind, do you think?" says Barney.

"Mind what?"

"That we laughed at his funeral?"

"I think he was laughing too," I say. I have no idea where it came from, I just said it. But now I come to think of it, my memory of this afternoon contains Patrick's voice. As I played the piano, his voice was amongst the singers. His presence was in the room. Is it a fancy? Probably. Something my mind concocts to comfort me in my hour of need. But so what? It *is* comforting. I glance at Barney's face. The furrows that were there when I joined him have lessened. Perhaps it is comforting to him too.

"I don't think there were any Christines there," he says. "I asked everyone I could, but…"

"It's OK," I say. "I think we are going to have to live with the mystery."

"He loved you, though. I know he did."

I nod. "I know he did too."

163

"So you're going to let this CT thing go?"

"I don't see any other options, do you?"

"No. Not really, no."

I shall just have to live with my memories of him, and try very hard not to taint them with this little scrap of doubt that lingers in the back of my mind. He never gave me reason to doubt him. Not until he died. So somehow I must find a way to trust the dead Patrick, the same way that I trusted the living one.

There is the sound of a collision, down below. We look to our right. We can just make out a car parked at a strange angle across the road. "Better go and help," says Barney. "You call the police."

He is mediating when I get there. A grey haired man in a Porsche is refusing to show his insurance details to a middle aged woman in a hatchback. She is grimacing and holding her neck. Barney is trying his best to keep the peace.

"If you looked where you were going…" says the man.

"I was driving along a straight road. How could I predict that you would just pull out in front of me?" says the woman.

"You were dithering. Kept slowing down. I thought you were letting me out."

"You were just being impatient. I was travelling at the speed limit."

"I don't think this is very productive," says Barney.

"It's 30, not bloody 15," says the man.

"Yes. 30. That's right."

"I'm sure it was just one of those misunderstandings. But the point is…" says Barney.

"Women drivers," says the man.

The woman jumps back into her car, turns on the engine, puts it into gear and rams it into the side of the Porsche that doesn't have a dent.

Barney stares, nonplussed.

The man shouts and jumps up and down.

The woman reverses and rams it again. Then she stops and gets out, wiping her hands together in that gesture that says, job done.

"What are you doing?" says Barney.

She folds her arms and looks at the man. "Women drivers," she says. "Shame about your car."

I think for a second the man is going to hit her, but he doesn't. He actually looks as if he might cry.

"I'm really sorry," says Barney. "But I'm a witness. And that wasn't an accident, that bit."

"No," she says. "But it was so worth it."

"But what if you go to prison?"

"I won't go to prison," she says. "My husband works for the CPS."

The police arrive. We each give a statement. Both the man and the woman are looking smug, although what they have to look smug about, I am at a loss to understand. I don't want to see what happens. I don't care if she goes to prison or not, they are both as bad as each other. Selfish people, using their cars to try to prove a point about themselves to people who really couldn't care less about them. But even so, there they are, proving a point, and putting the rest of the world out at the same time.

Like running a red light.

"Come on, I'll walk you home," says Barney.

"I think I want to track down Mr Schofield," I say.

He stops and looks at me. "Not tonight, though?"

"No. Not tonight. Tomorrow. You coming?"

He thinks about it. He walks on a bit. He stops again. "Do you know? I think I'll miss this one out, if you don't mind."

Why? I don't say that. I say, "OK."

"OK. It's just that I'd rather forget how it happened now. I need to forget. I need to… I don't know. I just don't want to chase round after some bloke."

"Patrick's killer."

"Even so. I don't know what purpose it would serve. It won't bring him back."

I hate that. It won't bring him back. People say that all the time, as if you thought it would. It won't bring him back, no, I know that. I'm not completely stupid. But it will make him pay. He must pay. I try to move on from that thought, but I always come back to my

165

image of him, sitting on his sofa, watching a football match and eating crisps, having got away with it. And I don't even know what I'm going to do when I find him. I don't even know how I think he should pay. But he should pay. That's fair enough, isn't it?

There is no way for sleep to claim me. I am too full of thoughts about cars and lights and crashes. I lie there. I get up. I sit down in the window. I pace. It is a good job Emily has gone home. I wouldn't want to keep her awake. I sit in the window. I think of Patrick: his arms, the solidity of his presence. I shut my eyes. There is the faintest hint of blue across my vision. I feel a buzzing on the back of my head, and now I see him, faint, it is almost as if I am imagining him, but not. If I was imagining him I would have some control over his actions. He is acting apart from me, separate and free. I am seeing him. I am certain of it. Here, with my eyes closed, I am looking at the man I love.

"Hi," he says. It is his voice, but it is coming from inside my head. "Do you remember our third date?"

I am trying to hear more, but I can't. Any words that come into my head now arrive in my own voice. There is a jumble of them. They make no sense. The sight of him has gone too. He's gone. I see blue once more. Now I see black.

Our third date. I hadn't invited him into the flat on the previous two. Part of me had longed to, but another part won out. And now he was here and I was frightened. He kept coming to sit next to me and I kept moving away from him. I ended up on the window seat, clutching my glass of wine and shaking.

"What's the matter?" he said.

I couldn't say it. I had never said it out loud. How could I?

He came and sat next to me again. He took my wine and placed it on the piano, then saw my face and stood up to place it on the coffee table. He took both my hands. He looked at me. I tried not to look at him. I lost my reason when I looked into the blue of his eyes.

"It's OK," he said.

I didn't say anything.

"Are you cold?" he said.

I was trembling, but it wasn't cold. I had never felt quite this on edge before. My senses had never been quite this alert.

He leaned forward and kissed me. I began to go with it but I couldn't. The sense of desire was so all consuming, it met with the nervous fizzing in my tummy and became unbearable. I drew back.

"I can't," I said.

"Can't what?"

And now I was in the position of having to say that I couldn't have sex, when for all I knew he may not have wanted to. What if he didn't want to, and here I was assuming he did?

He laughed. "Mags, it's OK. We can go slow. We don't have to have sex or anything. We could just…" He kissed me again. It was soft, tender. I felt a rush of electricity running through me and I so wanted to dive forwards, but I couldn't.

"I can't." I pushed away from him and moved over to the piano. I would be safe on the piano stool.

"Mags," he said. "What's the matter?"

I didn't know what to say to him. I didn't really know what to say at all. I couldn't control this feeling. I was on a fairground ride and I would not be able to get off if I went any further.

"Shall I go?" he said.

A lurch of disappointment whistled through my frame. "No. No, don't go."

"But you keep moving away from me…. Do I repel you?"

"Oh, God, how can you think that?"

"What am I supposed to think? Tell me. Talk to me. For God's sake, tell me what's the matter."

He didn't raise his voice. It wasn't a device. He wasn't trying to manipulate me. Others had done that. He just wanted to know. The soft force of his voice and the hurt he was trying to conceal made their way through to my guts. I felt a sharp pain, deep in my belly.

"I can't have sex," I said.

"What?"

"I can't have sex."

"OK. We don't have to. We can go as slow as you want, I've said that."

"No, you don't understand. I can't."

"Can't ever?"

"I'm not… very good at it."

I could hear the words as they came out of my mouth. They seemed ridiculous, even to me. He smiled. "It's not a competition," he said.

"Don't laugh at me." I could feel tears of humiliation rising to my face. I tried to get up and run to the bedroom. I had trusted him and he had laughed. He caught me. He held me so I couldn't get away. He was much stronger than me. I could feel the power in his arms. I could feel something else, as well, but I didn't want to think about that. Oh God, was he going to force me?

"Shhhh," he said. "Maggie, I'm not laughing at you. I'm not. Talk to me. Please. Why can't you have sex?"

"It's always…"

"What?"

"It's always such a big disappointment."

He was still holding me, standing behind me with his arms around mine, holding me firm so I couldn't get away. I couldn't see his face. I didn't know what he was thinking. The words were out there. He now knew my deficiencies, my greatest shame. The thing I never admitted to anybody. I was frigid; those horrible words that the boys at school chased the girls around with, and it would have been all right if it hadn't been true, but it was true about me. I would laugh along with them, but deep down my insides were tearing down the middle. I carried it with me to college. Lost my virginity much later than everybody else. And failed, when I did. I couldn't reach orgasm. The word itself made me recoil. I couldn't get pleasure out of sex, and because of that, how could I possibly give pleasure? And besides, if it is always a disappointment, there comes a time when you start to loathe the person in front of you, the cause of all the frustration. I didn't want to loathe Patrick. I was starting to love him. That in itself made me laugh, because how could I love somebody I hardly knew, and how could it go any further if I couldn't have sex with him?

He loosened his hold on me and turned me round to face him. He locked his fingers together in the small of my back. I still couldn't get away, but the hold was less firm than it had been, and now I was forced to look at him, to see the effect of my confession.

"You're lovely," he said. I wasn't quite expecting that. I blushed. He kissed me. "Is this disappointing?" he said.

"No."

He unlocked his hands and stepped back. "Do me a favour and stand there for me," he said.

I nodded.

"If you want me to stop, just say and I'll stop," he said.

He kissed me again. "I am your obedient slave," he said. I laughed.

"There it is," he said. "I knew I could amuse you somehow. Stop looking so worried."

He kissed my neck. I felt my body want to crumple and melt. "Is this disappointing?" he said.

"No."

He moved along my arm to my hand. Kissed the palm of my hand. "Is this disappointing?"

He lifted me up and took me to the bedroom, and lay me down really gently on the bed. He carried on with his exploration, not letting me kiss him back although I was desperate to do just that, instructing me to stay there, lie there, relax, don't move. Is this disappointing?

He kept going, all over my body, teasing me with that question, over and over again, until I was at such a point of arousal I couldn't take it any more. Then we reached the bit I had been dreading. Then. And I think I may have screamed with the release of it all. With that pulsing sense of electricity on every nerve ending, there came a release of all that had gone before. All those bad experiences, all that pent up hatred, all the fears about my body not quite making the grade, they all rose up and exploded together.

"So," he said. "Was that a disappointment, then?"

I started to laugh and I couldn't stop. I pulled a pillow from the floor where it had dropped and hit him over the head with it. He grabbed it and threw it over the other side of the bed, and then caught my arms and rolled me onto my back. He nestled his head on my shoulder and rested his arm across my middle. It was amazing, this feeling of our bodies touching each other. It's hard to describe. There was more intimacy in him lying next to me after the act, more of a feeling of being known and of knowing, than I had ever experienced before. I never grew tired of being close to his body. It was me. I was him. This sounds ridiculous. I don't know what I'm saying.

We lay like that for a long time. I have no idea how long, except that the sun was coming up by the time we moved, so it must have been a while. I came to a number of realisations, lying there. I realised what nonsense it was to carry around all that shame about my sexuality. I realised that sex wasn't about being someone or something. It wasn't about being good at it. It was about each moment: the enjoyment of each individual moment, not an end result that you don't know how to reach and besides you can't reach without all the moments that lead up to it.

And I realised with a force that would never let me go and still hasn't let me go, that I loved this man and never wanted to be without him.

Saturday, 2nd December

And now it is morning and I can't see Patrick any more. I have a vision of Mr Schofield where Patrick should be.

Emily's "Hello?" is not the usual lively sing-song that habit has led me to expect. It is more questioning, less sure of itself. It is also filled with sleep.

"It's me," I say.

"What time is it?"

I don't know. Early. I can't sleep.

"It isn't even light yet."

"Sorry. I need Schofield's address."

She is quiet. I can hear the sound of the telephone wire, but nothing else. Not even breathing. Has she put the phone down and gone to find it?

"Hello?" I say.

"I'm here. Look, about that…"

"What?"

"The Schofield thing. I'm not sure…"

"Just give me the address."

"Give me a couple of hours."

"No."

"No?"

"I can't wait another couple of hours. I have to go now. I can't sit here, thinking. It's too hard. There is too much time. I can't deal with all the time. I have to see. That's all I want to do. See his house. See his life. I'm not going to do anything. I just need to find out."

I can hear the words running away from me. I know I am not making sense, I can hear it. There is still silence on the other end of the line.

"He killed a man, Emily. And he lied about it. Don't you want to do something? Don't you think he should pay? You know, maybe we could find out some stuff about him and do an exposé or something on the radio. Or something."

I know this will get her. She's big on retribution. She was all for the local paper printing the names of paedophiles in that row last year.

She sighs. "OK," she says. "Wait there. I'll come and get you."

She has hung up before I can say no.

The street has large detached houses set back from the road behind tall fences, walls and hedges. The houses are not particularly old, but designed to look as though they came from an earlier age. This one owes its lineage to the Tudor period, but the conservatory on the side looks decidedly post-plastic. We couldn't park near the house, because the road has double yellow lines all along it on both sides, and we don't want to draw into the drive, for obvious reasons. So we have parked on a side street and walked, and now we are standing next to a large evergreen hedge, looking up at the many curtain clad windows.

"Big house," says Emily.

I nod.

"He's doing all right for himself, then."

I nod again.

"He'd be all right for a bit of compensation, if you wanted to take him to court."

"What?"

"Compensation. Look. He's obviously got money."

I can't believe she's said this.

"I'm only saying, if you want to hurt him, that's how you'll do it, through his wallet. He clearly treasures his wallet. That's all I'm saying."

"How would you put a price on Patrick?" I say.

"Oh, God, that's not what I meant."

The idea of some clinical courtroom where lots of calm, well educated people who for all I know have never lost anything in their lives make decisions about mine, about Patrick's, ours, about how much each of us was worth before we lost it, fills me with disgust. It isn't about money. It has never been about money.

"I just want to see this man say he's sorry."

"And then it'll all be all right, will it?"

"No."

"So what's the point?"

"The point is he won't haunt my thoughts. He won't be there to taint my memories, I won't have him sitting there on his giant sofa, filling his face with crisps, demanding things from his long suffering wife, his legs splayed out all over the place in a kind of self satisfied, smug sprawl, because he's got away with it and he knows he has and now he is invincible because nobody is going to ever haul him up and make him look at what he's done, when I want to be thinking about Patrick. I won't see him everywhere on the streets, driving through red lights and turning right when he's signalling left, and ramming his well insured car into other people's just because he can, because he is the sort of person that gets away with it. I won't imagine that when eventually someone sees fit to put me out of my misery and I step out of the road and into the path of an oncoming car, I won't imagine that the car I step in front of is his."

Emily looks at me, shock carving out some future wrinkles on her face. "Wow," she says.

I am a little surprised at myself.

"Sorry," I say. "But he should be made to look at what he's done. That's all. He shouldn't just get away with it."

We look again at the house. There is a blue-grey hue to the sky up above us. Daylight is beginning its competition with the streetlights. The house slumbers on, its curtains a testament to the soundless, dreamless sleep of the inhabitants.

"So what do you want to do?" says Emily.

And I don't know. I don't know. I have that small child feeling again. I don't know what I'm doing. I want someone to show me the way.

Emily looks around her, and fixes her gaze on several large white stones which have been laid in a circle to mark the edge of the lawn.

"Come on," she says. She picks one of the stones up, carefully avoiding damage to the graphic design on her nails.

She hands it to me. "Go on, then," she says.

I pick the window closest to me. I hurl the brick with all the force I can muster, which isn't great, to be honest, because I still feel a little like a small child. The stone bounces off the glass and lands back down in the border in front of the window. Emily sighs. "Oh, God," she says. She picks up another stone and hurls it herself. The glass breaks with a loud clatter. She grabs my wrist and pulls me out of the front garden and behind the hedge.

There is no sound. Nobody stirs. No curtains twitch, no lights come on, nobody shouts, "Oi," or whatever it is you shout in this situation. Nobody is home.

I don't know if I am disappointed or relieved.

There isn't much to say, so we aren't saying anything. Emily has been to get food, and now we are both looking at bacon sandwiches and thinking how hard it would be to eat them.

The stairs make a clattering noise, as somebody makes a tentative way up them. I must have a look at the fixings, they really don't sound safe at all.

There is a knock on the door.

Emily goes to answer it.

The tall lady from the funeral place is standing there. Sandra. I remember her name.

She smiles and asks me how I am. I tell her fine. She smiles and nods. She knows I am not, her eyes are saying, but she will play along if that's the game.

"I am sorry to disturb you," she says. "But James asked me to drop the list off this morning. I am going on holiday this afternoon, and I wanted to leave everything in order for you."

"List?" I say.

"The people who attended the funeral. James seemed to think it might be important for you to have it, sooner, rather than later."

I feel numb. I am not sure what to say. She didn't need to do this. She is going on holiday. I should ask her in, but I want to look at that list.

Emily offers her a cup of tea. "Oh, I'm so sorry," she says. "I would love to normally, but I have so much to do before I go. Do call my colleagues if you want anything."

She wobbles down the stairs, leaving Emily and me standing in the doorway, staring at the piece of paper.

"Is there a Christine?" says Emily.

I cast my eyes down the columns of names. My toes have gone cold. Just my toes. Christine. Here it is.

"Christine Thornhill," I say.

She doesn't say, "CT," and neither do I. I show her the page. There, between a Mark Sewell and a Sophie Frith, is one Christine Thornhill.

My head starts to prickle, right on the top, as if someone is holding a very mild electric fence against it.

Emily gets out the telephone directory. "Thornhill. One, two, three….. five of them."

"Any in Strayfield?"

"Don't know, just the street names. Hang on." She turns on my computer and opens up the Multimap page. She starts typing in the postcodes. "This one. Thornhill, C," she says. "So either it's in her name or hubby is a C as well."

"Or she lives alone," I say.

She pauses in her search. Perhaps she considers whether it is a good idea to follow this up or not, but it is too late now. We are on a downhill slope and our brakes have gone. We will find out who Christine Thornhill is. We must.

"9 Highwood Avenue," says Emily. She prints off the map.

Barney arrives, looking tired. "What's up?" he says.

"We've found Christine," I say.

"What? Where? How?"

"Funeral list." I kiss him. It was his idea to get the list. I didn't even know there would be one.

"9 Highwood Avenue," says Emily, handing him the map.

"That's only about two or three stops on from where he…" Barney nods to punctuate this sentence without saying the word, then adds, "On the bus route."

It is a good job he came. It just looks like a map to me. How he knows where the bus stops are is beyond me.

Barney is gathering his car keys. I don't know.

"Come on," says Emily.

"I don't know," I say.

Barney shuts the door he has just opened and walks towards me. "Mags," he says.

"I know," I say.

"You wanted the answers," he says.

"I know," I say.

"Do you want to wait, until you're ready? We don't have to go now."

"We do," I say.

Emily fetches my coat and helps me on with it. We wobble our way down the stairs.

"This does not feel safe," says Emily. "Is there a screw loose or something?"

Highwood Avenue is a row of terraced houses. There is not much space for parking, but Barney manages to squeeze the car in at the end of the street. We walk back to number 9. The door has a little stained glass window, and you can make out a lightly painted hall with stairs going up straight off it on the right hand side and a couple of doors to the left. We ring twice.

"Won't be long," says a woman's voice. We hear shuffling around.

"So sorry," she says, as she fiddles with the handle on the other side. "I've been trying to sort out my loft, and it took me a while to get down. The ladder's stuck, I'm afraid. And now I can't find the key. Where is it?" We hear her disappearing off. It goes quiet, then she returns again, jangling a key.

She looks as if she hasn't seen daylight for a while, the way she is blinking. The day is not that bright. She is quite a bit older than us. She is perhaps in her mid-fifties, perhaps older. Slim, tall, green eyes, brown hair flecked with grey. She has a very welcoming smile.

"Patrick's friend," she says to Barney. He looks confused, as if he recognises her but can't remember. "I thought you spoke beautifully," she says, smiling at him.

She doesn't seem surprised that three virtual strangers have arrived on her doorstep.

"And you're Maggie," she says to me. "I'm sorry, I don't know your name," turning to Emily.

Emily fills her in.

She leads us past a bicycle in the hall, round to the left of the staircase, and then stands back and gestures for us to go through a door that she has opened at the back of the house. This doesn't quite feel real. She hasn't asked what we're doing here, and we are being shepherded through to a sitting room, our coats are being taken, we are being invited to sit.

The sitting room has a large squashy red sofa and a couple of red armchairs. They have all seen better days. There is evidence that cats have pulled holes and runs in the arms of the chairs, and there is a patch of white hair where Barney is about to sit. I start to stop him, but Christine catches his arm and suggests he go for one of the chairs.

"I'll sit here," she says. "Next to Maggie. I'm already covered in fluff, but you look rather smart."

He does. I hadn't noticed. He has on a pair of dark trousers that aren't jeans and aren't part of a tracksuit. How had I not spotted that?

She offers tea. We accept. She disappears through a door which presumably takes her to a kitchen. We don't speak. We just look around the room. There is a picture of a very fluffy cat stretched out in the sun, hanging on the wall over a Victorian black fireplace, in which there are thick cream candles. There are some photos of people on a bookshelf to the right, behind Barney. There is a photo of a young man next to me. I pick it up and look at it. He is covered in mud, and wearing a striped shirt and shorts. He holds a rugby ball.

"Small world," I say to Barney.

"How do you mean?" he says. I pass him the photo.

He seems to breathe in rapidly. "Is there something wrong?" I say. He looks up at me. "Thornhill," he says. "Christine Thornhill?"

"What about it?" says Emily. She takes the photo from Barney.

Barney seems unable to speak. As Christine returns, he seems to sort of shrink into his chair.

She is a very thoughtful host. She has put biscuits onto a plate, and she hands each of us a napkin before passing out the tea and asking me to take a biscuit and pass it on. I am not hungry, but I take one anyway. I do not wish to appear rude.

Barney doesn't take a biscuit. Neither does he take the tea that is offered to him. He seems to have retreated into a little world of his own.

"Now," says Christine. "What can I do for you?" Her accent is mild, but clearly she grew up near here. Her voice is the voice on the answer phone: the one that told him not to come and see her. I am hit by the certainty of that fact and I find myself unable to speak. I thought he was having an affair. When I heard that voice, with its slight, almost sexy lilt, I couldn't see any alternative. And yes, he was visiting this woman, but she is just about old enough to be his mother, so I can't believe it is for the sorts of reasons I have been thinking, which is sort of a relief. But then why was he visiting her every week? And what is wrong with Barney? All these things I need to say, and none will come out of my mouth.

Emily comes to my rescue.

"We were wondering how you know Patrick?" she said.

"You were?" Christine glances across at Barney. He looks away, discomfort clouding his face. She smiles at him, but he doesn't see it.

"Gosh," she says. "I really don't know where to start." She looks at each one of us in turn, considering how to proceed. Just tell us, I want to shout, but I don't. She is too charming, too in control of herself and the situation. I feel more than a little intimidated.

"I better put James here out of his misery," she says. She takes hold of my hand and squeezes it as she looks into my eyes to deliver her bombshell. "The short answer is that Patrick killed my son."

I am not sure what is happening.

There is talking. I can hear that. Arguing. One voice is Emily's. The other is less familiar, and yet it is stuck in my head on a loop. Patrick killed my son. Over and over and over again, one version of it clattering into another and echoing throughout my brain.

Patrick killed my son. The short answer. And now my head is coming into balance again and thinking is beginning to be possible. I don't believe it. I don't believe that Patrick killed anybody. Perhaps that's what Emily is saying.

Barney left.

He left.

Why would he leave?

"It isn't true." Those words form in my head. Do I say them? There is a hand on my back. Someone is telling me to put my head between my legs.

"Why would you do this to her?" I think that is Emily speaking. "Why would you put her through this now? Or ever? Have you got some kind of illness? Some psychiatric disease, makes you stick your oar into other people's lives and want to poison people's memories? Is that it?"

Her voice is galloping on. Perhaps she is afflicted with the same disease of the brain as me, where thoughts are jumbled but still going round in a loop. Nothing makes sense. None of what she is saying makes sense. We came here. This woman didn't come to us. So it's not as if she tracked us down to torture us. Although she came to the funeral. And Patrick was coming here. On a bus. And for weeks beforehand. And why would he do that, if he did what she said he did? And why would he do what she said he did?

"I need you both to calm down." The voice is stern, firm and hard to describe. Powerful. That's it. Powerful. My head stops whizzing around. Emily stops speaking.

"Emily," says Christine, and it occurs to me that it isn't unkind, the way she's doing it. "Emily. Sit down, would you dear?"

Emily does as she's told, coming to sit next to me, gripping my hand.

"The best thing to do at this point would be to listen. Then you can make your minds up, can't you, about whether or not what I say is true? But when you are not in possession of the information I have to tell you, how can you possibly decide? So. Are you going to listen?"

We nod. I am transported back to the primary school classroom, being told off by Mrs Wise. We haven't listened. Of course. This is our fault. When we listen, we will discover that she didn't say what we think she said, and even if she did, that it didn't mean what we think it meant.

She moves over to the fireplace, touching a picture as if composing herself, although she doesn't appear to be discomposed. "My son, Edward, played rugby. He was very good. He was what they call a flanker. We lived here, but there was another really good flanker who played for the Kestrels at the time, and so Edward moved away to play for the Bisons."

I know the Bisons. Based down South. Good team.

"The boy who kept Edward out of the team here was called Patrick Miles."

I find my mind racing ahead of what she is going to say. She is going to suggest that Patrick was jealous of this Edward. She is going to say that he poisoned him, or followed him home from a pub and stabbed him, or something. She can't make that allegation. That isn't Patrick. Patrick wouldn't do that. "Hang on a minute," I say.

"Let me finish. Please."

It is not the words that stop me. It is the tears in her eyes. I know those tears – I have seen them before. This woman lost her son.

I stop my assault on her story. She sits down and looks directly at me, no shame in those tears, and no apology for them.

"He was living down South, playing for a different team. He was doing well. He scored a try in his first match, and kept going from there. More tries. He was particularly good at spoiling the line-out – do you know that expression? Well, he was very competitive, and he was getting a name for that. Meanwhile, for the Kestrels, Patrick was doing very well and making a name for himself. Edward's team came up for a match. The England scouts were coming. The press were speculating about the competition between the two. There was a rumour that the England coach was coming himself, although he didn't in the end. But the boys were very excited, as you can imagine. They knew each other. They were friends."

There is a growing feeling of discomfort in my gut. I am finding it hard to stay here and listen to this. I don't want to hear what she is saying, but I can't move, and her words are finding their way through the morass of thoughts that I can't shut up. When I want to hear something, the morass stops me from listening, but now that I don't want to hear it, I can't do anything else. She stands again. She keeps on sitting and standing.

"The high ball went up, Edward jumped to catch it. Patrick tackled him in the air."

That's illegal. Patrick didn't approve of anything even vaguely illegal.

"He wanted to win that ball. So he pulled Edward's legs away from him when he was jumping to catch the ball. Edward kept hold of the ball instead of softening his landing. He landed on his head. His neck snapped."

I am suddenly very aware of how quiet it is in here. There is not even the sound of a clock ticking. There is muffled traffic outside, and there is breathing. I think it might be mine. Christine turns and looks out of the window again.

"There wasn't anything they could do."

She has stopped talking. She is standing by the window, looking out. I can't seem to move. I can't even swallow. I can see the picture she is painting with these words, but I can't put Patrick in it.

Emily moves first.

"Patrick did that?"

Christine is still looking out of the window. She nods.

"But he was always so straight. So…" Her words peter out.

"Tackled someone in the air?" I watch the words come out of my mouth but it doesn't feel like it's me speaking.

"It doesn't make sense," says Emily.

"What doesn't?" says Christine.

Emily looks at me. The confusion that is rattling around my system is written there on her face.

Christine sighs. "Did you never wonder why he stopped playing?"

"Injury," says Emily.

"What else have his injuries stopped him from doing?" She looks at me when she says this. Emily starts to say something but stops. I have to look away. I discounted injury a long time ago. I used to wonder about it. I used to watch him when a rugby match was on. Every muscle tensed. He lived every tackle, sidestepped past every defender, shouldered every charge, all while sitting on the sidelines, watching and twitching. His face was alight and yet he didn't play. I wondered if perhaps he wasn't good enough. I thought he must have failed at a trial for something or other and, being the perfectionist that he was, just not wanted to play in a minor league. I never brought it up because I didn't want to upset him. If that was the reason, and I was sure it was, what good would it do to make him say so?

"I should have asked him," I say.

"You don't believe this, do you?" says Emily.

"I thought he just didn't get into the team," I say.

And now I'm wondering about Christine again. What is her motive in all this? If this is true, (and I'm starting to see that it must be – after all, Barney spooked at something, and Barney would have known this) then why is the mother of the dead player showing an interest in Patrick? Did she somehow engineer this? Did she take her revenge? Was Mr Schofield in her employ? Have I thrown a stone at the window of an innocent man? Well, not innocent. He still did it. But maybe he was paid to do it. Maybe the repayments on the mortgage were too high and he had to find some dodgy work to cover it. What am I thinking? If she was going to kill him, wouldn't she have found a more predictable way than this? How can you guarantee a death, only one death, by causing a bus to crash? Or perhaps she didn't mean to kill him. Perhaps she only wanted to make him pay, like I wanted Mr Schofield to pay. But why would she want the bus driver to pay as well, and all the other people who might potentially have been on the bus?

My head hurts.

"Maggie, please, breathe," she says.

I am numb. All I can do is look at her.

"Breathe. In through the nose, out over the tongue, like this." She shows me. I try to copy her. My brain starts to slow down.

"People are always telling me to breathe," I say.

"That's because you hold your breath."

"I do?"

Emily laughs, next to me. "You go a funny colour," she says.

"What is your interest in us?" I say.

I hear Emily take in a quick breath, as if she is surprised by my question. Christine pauses as she considers her answer.

"I don't have an interest in you," she says. "Other than that you are my very welcome visitors."

"OK, Patrick. What was your interest in Patrick?"

"I was helping him."

"How?"

There is another pause, and Christine looks as if she is listening to something I can't hear. "I am a spiritual teacher," she says eventually.

"What?"

"Patrick came to me to find some answers."

"What?"

"There comes a stage in life when we all look around us and wonder what it's all about, why we are here, that sort of question. Patrick was looking ahead at his future and seeing more of the same and wondering. Is that all there is? It's a very interesting question."

"And he thought you knew the answers?"

"He was looking for them. As soon as you start to look for them, people appear in your life to help you find them."

"New Age bollocks," says Emily.

Christine smiles. "I thought so too, once," she says. "Then I lost my son and realised that the way I had seen things up to that point would simply not suffice. There was no explanation that my brain could give me as to why my son should be taken away at that age. There was no academic answer to this. I had to let go of my reliance on my intellectual mind, the thing I felt had served me for so long, but which I now see was actually holding me back."

"But if you let go of your mind," says Emily, "what is left? You have to think with something."

"Indeed," says Christine. "But we have a lot more to our brains than the bit we are aware of. There is a whole miracle of engineering that is our subconscious mind. It is our subconscious mind, working in conjunction with our heart and our soul, that leads us to the answers we seek."

"Mindless drivel," says Emily. She seems distressed, though. Her eyes pop as she says this. I have the feeling that she is ashamed of herself even as the words come out of her mouth, but still she has no power to stop them. Again, Christine laughs.

"Tell me," she says, "do you ever stop thinking?"

Emily looks at me, the skin around her eyes scrunched inwards in concentration. "When you stop thinking you're dead," she says.

"I want you to try something for me," says Christine. "I want you to observe your thoughts. Let them come into your head, look at them, and then let them out again, as if you have opened up a funnel in the top of your head, there," she touches the top of Emily's head, "and you are just releasing them into the Universe."

"What would be the point in that?" says Emily.

"Interesting experiment, that's all," says Christine. "Just a few minutes. That's all. A minute, even. Just to see what happens."

She won't do it. I know she won't. The expression on her face says it all. I might, though. Later. Might as well give it a try. I think it might be a relief not to have quite so many thoughts as this, because now my mind is whizzing and whirring again and concocting other situations. How did she find Patrick? Did she track him down? What was her purpose in doing that? I can see her watching me. She is looking at me, but through me, the way Lottie used to sometimes.

"I was visiting Edward," she says. "I often go out there to the graveyard, just to chat to him, especially if I have a particularly challenging client. I find it clears my head, and more often than not, he finds me the answer."

"Who does?"

"Edward."

"Oh."

"Patrick had the same idea. He came to see Edward too. I found him at the graveside one day, oh, about six months ago. He was pacing. He was distraught. I think that would be the best description."

"Lottie died six months ago," I say.

"Yes."

I manage to look into her eyes again. There doesn't seem to be animosity there. That's what I don't understand. Perhaps Patrick's death has cleared her need to have him pay for it.

"He saw me and wanted to leave, he was very embarrassed. He seemed to think that I was going to beat him up. I persuaded him to stay and we talked about Edward. He told me about his mother's death. About you."

"Me?"

"Yes."

"What about me?"

"He was suffering with bouts of depression. He said he had started taking it out on you. He didn't want that. He wanted to know what to do about it."

"He was depressed?"

"Sometimes."

I feel that sensation again, the one where an abyss starts to open up in my stomach, and if I'm not careful I shall plunge into it and never find my way out. The man that I love was depressed and didn't confide in me. Why not? Was I not sympathetic to him? Was I too wrapped up in my own life, and my own troubles, such as they were?

"Oh God," I say.

"It isn't your fault," she says.

"Patrick was depressed?" says Emily. "Patrick?"

"He was ashamed of it. He liked to pretend to the world that all was well, but he was very low."

"I like New York in June, that Patrick?" says Emily.

"He had grief to contend with, and guilt. He suffered a lot of guilt."

I remember thinking that he seemed fine very quickly after Lottie died. I remember thinking how good it was, that he was coping really well. A lot better than I had managed after Ben. A lot better than I am managing now.

"He never forgave himself for what happened to Edward," she says.

"Well, you wouldn't, would you?" I say.

"Why not?"

She is looking straight at me, and I know there is an answer, but I don't know what to say to this. The situation is all wrong. I'm having to explain to a wronged mother about why you would always feel guilty for snuffing out her son's life? Is this the right way round?

"He was a young man, who believed with all his heart that he had to win that ball," she says. "He made a silly mistake in the heat of the moment. It was the sort of mistake that ninety-nine times out of a hundred would not have resulted in a death. He was unlucky. So was Edward. That's all."

Now I am finding it difficult to follow what she is saying. She is very earnest, I can see that. She is nodding as she speaks, and shaking her head and nodding again.

"Edward could have let go of the ball. He could have put his hands out to save himself. He didn't. He wanted to win."

"Are you saying Patrick was not responsible?" I say.

"Oh, he was responsible. But he knew that. He would never have done it again. If he had continued with his playing career he would have been the most sporting person on the pitch. But there really is no point in allowing a mistake to swallow you whole."

"A mistake?"

"Yes."

"But your son died."

"Yes."

"How can you...? How do you...? How can you just, what, smile and say, ah well? Is that what you're doing?"

"No, lovey. No. I miss my boy. I still miss him. But it does nobody any good for me to be ranting and raving about another boy who rashly made a tackle he wasn't supposed to make. Had the tables been turned, had it been Edward making that tackle, would I have wanted Patrick's mother to curse him, or him to stop living his life? No."

"So, what, you just shrug your shoulders?" says Emily. Her glasses are all the way down her nose. She notices and shoves them back up again with her index finger.

"No. No. I grieved. I felt as though my life had ended. I spent long hours crying and shouting and screaming, and I may even have stuck pins into a picture of Patrick at one stage."

"I didn't think of that," I say. They both turn to me, looking for an explanation. "Sorry. I, er, I interrupted you. Carry on."

"But then I separated the grief from everything else. This feeling of being wronged. I took that out and had a good look at it. I was doing it to avoid feeling the pain of the loss. I was shutting that out and focusing on this other stimulus. It gave me some relief from the misery, I suppose. Gave me something else to think about. And I decided that it benefited nobody for me to feel a grievance towards the other boy."

"You decided?" I say.

"Yes."

"Just like that? You just decided?"

"I did."

"And what happened?"

"I was healed."

"Just like that?"

"No. No, it took a little while."

"How long?"

"Time is an illusion, Maggie. It is just an illusion. Things take as long as they need to take. A balance needed to be restored. That began with my decision. Then the world had to shake itself up a little bit to restore the balance. That's where time comes into it."

"What are you going on about?"

"Patrick was here and now he's not. Does the fact that he is not here mean that he no longer exists?"

I have no idea what answer she wants me to give. I look at Emily for support, but she is as open-mouthed as I am.

"Think about it," says Christine. "Understand it. Then come and see me again."

And now we are on the street outside. I have no idea what just happened. She seemed to decide the visit was over and we're here. And I have questions flooding into my head again.

Why was Patrick coming to see her? What did they talk about? Does she know about me, and if so how much does she know? Does

187

she know about Ben? Why are there so many healers and weird people entering my life right now? What's going on? Am I just surrounded by nutcases? How could she just forgive Patrick like that, didn't she love her son? No. That's not the right question. She clearly loved her son. But how could she do that? Does she know about me and Mr Schofield? What does she know? And does she think that I'm a rubbish person for succumbing to ideas of getting even? Should I just forgive and forget? How do you do that?

And on, and on. They keep on coming, I can't seem to stop them. And here is Barney's car, but there is no sign of Barney.

Emily tries the door. It won't open. She slaps the flat of her hand on the window in anger and squints up and down the street. There is no sign of him. We could shout his name, but we have just left this hushed room with all its dampened atmosphere of calm quiet, and I don't think I could raise my voice, even if I wanted to.

"Come on," whispers Emily. "Let's see if he's found a coffee shop, or something."

She takes my arm and we walk up towards the main road, matching steps as closely as we can, but Emily's legs start at the same height as my waist, so soon we disengage our arms and carry on in a more comfortable fashion. Neither of us speaks. I wonder what is happening in that brain of hers. Patrick used to say it was like a missile launcher. The missiles she fired today didn't seem to hit their target with Christine Thornhill. She just didn't rise to anything.

I have a picture of Patrick pulling at someone's legs in the air. I can see Barney, emerging from a scrum and looking up, running towards him, shouting no. I'm sure that's not how it happened. I know it isn't. If the ball was in the air, then there was no scrum going on. They would all have been chasing the ball, or preparing to defend or attack. Barney would have been on the run, so perhaps he and all the team mates were shouting no at the same time. Perhaps they were cursing the slowness of their legs, and willing themselves closer to the action, closer to the awful accident they could see unfolding in front of them. No. They wouldn't have seen it. They would have just seen the two boys competing for that ball. There is never time on the rugby pitch to see and stop these things. All the same, I know that

Barney was there that day. He must have been. Barney has played for the Kestrels for years. So Barney knew about Edward Thornhill. Barney knew all this time and never said a word. Did they talk about it, I wonder? When Patrick met me, did he sit Barney down and make him swear never to breathe a word of it to me? Didn't he trust me? That question again. It seems that the story I concocted for myself, this partnership that was oh so perfect, well, it wasn't all that I imagined. Christine Thornhill, aka CT, is not the person I imagined, her involvement is not the affair I have been observing in my imagination at every moment that Mr Schofield has been absent from it. Even so, what she represents is still the same. No trust. He didn't trust me, and so does that mean that I shouldn't trust him?

There is a church at the end of the road, opposite the junction of Highwood Avenue and the main street, metal gates under a stone archway set in a high wall its contact with the outside world. Emily looks left and right, searching for Barney, or for clues to his whereabouts. I am looking through that archway above the gate, feeling myself drawn in its direction. I start to cross the road. She pulls me back as a car whizzes past. "What are you doing?" she says. I remember that comment I made before, about stepping in front of a car. I remember her face. I wish I hadn't mentioned it. I don't think I'm going to do it, but sometimes it's comforting to have in reserve.

"Church," I say. "Churchyard."

She notices the church for the first time, pushing her glasses back up her nose to peer at it. We allow some more cars to pass us and we cross. The gate sticks. Its hinges have dropped from their original position, and we have to lift the gate a little in order to open it. Emily lets me do this, then sweeps past me into the graveyard, slipping slightly on the greasy stone flags. The church is up ahead. It is one of those squat square ones with a little tower. The oak doors are firmly shut in their arched door frame. I think about trying the cast iron rings that function as door handles, but something stops me. I don't want to go in. Instead, I follow the path round to the side of the building. Emily is following me, but she is having to move more slowly because of her high heels and the slippery stones of the path.

"It's easier here," I say. "This bit's gravel."

The graveyard is a big one for the size of the church. It surprises me that it has survived the centuries of house building around it. Barney stands over in the corner furthest from the road, looking down at a small headstone. I walk over to join him, Emily following some distance behind.

He is crying. He doesn't look around when I get there. I stand next to him. "She told you then?" he says.

I nod. He doesn't say anything for a moment, just stands there nodding as if he is agreeing with somebody that it was a good thing to tell me, after all. When he speaks, the words come out slowly to begin with, but building in speed until they are tripping over each other.

"It was the worst day of our lives," he says. "Thorny was a mate. We used to call him "Phone Home". They were joking around about what the papers were saying and everything. Had a bet on. Patrick was favourite, you know, with the journalists and so on, and Thorny bet him that he'd win them over to his side in that match. Said he'd make him look like a numpty. Kept winding him up. Paddy didn't seem bothered by it, in the changing room. He was there, you know, singing, the way he always did, and he had this little ritual for luck, he used to put his toes into the wrong boot before switching them both at the same time to the right boots, and all that, and he was doing that, and singing and laughing with the lads. Then we got out on the pitch and he played like a demon, you know? Played great, man. He was winning the ball at lineout, and making loads of ground beyond the gain line, and just everything he did seemed to work, we were ahead, you know? We had three tries and they had a couple of penalties, but no tries. And he came up in the last ten minutes and said, "Let's make sure they don't score. Whatever we do now." I remember it because he was so determined. And someone put the ball up and it happened to be Thorny who got there first, and I don't know how Patrick was where he was. Must have wanted to prove a point, and he took him out. Just took him out. None of us could believe it. I don't think even Pads could believe he'd done it. And Thorny was just lying there, not moving. Paddy was red carded, but I don't think he would have played on anyway. He looked like someone had taken a great big slice out of his middle, like he could barely stand up.

"We didn't understand it, because there wasn't any need for it. We'd won the game. There was no way they were coming back from that. But it happened. It just happened. Pads himself didn't seem to know why. I asked him about it, but he used to just say he didn't know. He didn't know what happened. It just came over him that he had to have that ball. Said he saw black. That was the phrase he used. He saw black."

The words crash to a halt, and I am left remembering that he said that to me recently, about seeing black. It was after a row. I think I had annoyed him about something. I was getting good at that towards the end. He went for a walk and then came back in and said he was sorry. So sorry, he said, but he just saw black. I didn't really know what he meant. I still don't, not really.

Emily arrives and reads the inscription on the gravestone: "Edward Ivan Thornhill, 1974 – 1993. Beloved son".

I put my hand on Barney's back. I don't know what else to do. I can see Patrick standing here, pacing around, talking to Edward Thornhill, telling him he was sorry, wishing himself back to the start of the game, longing for it to be different. Christine said time was an illusion, well, if that's the case, let's all rewind, shall we? Let's all buzz back to that illusion that was time before all this happened. Let's undo my wrongdoings, and bring back my brother, let's undo Patrick's and bring back this Thorny guy, let's undo Mr Schofield's and bring back Patrick. Why can't we do that? If she's right, and time is an illusion, why are we all living here with all this bloody misery? Why aren't we surrounding ourselves with only good things and creating happiness in our worlds?

We can't. That's why. Emily was right. Christine was talking bollocks. How much of it was bollocks, I wonder? Did she really forgive Patrick, or was she just living in this enormous well of denial? Were Patrick's visits actually about getting even with him? Was she putting him through all kinds of hell, trying to make him understand the errors of his ways, and dressing it up as being for his own good? And why did he buy it? Why would he? I keep asking questions, and

I'm not finding any answers, just more questions.

My mother was in denial, as they called it. She repainted the house and set up a church fund and redesigned the garden and started volunteering at the local hospital, all the time telling everyone she was OK, she didn't need their help; she just needed to be left to get on with things.

I didn't see that with CT. I saw something else, something I didn't understand. It was as if she just accepted what had happened. She had the tears, she had the emotions, but she wasn't fighting. If you love someone, how do you not fight the situation that takes them away from you? And yet there was this sense around her, something about the way the air was around her, that didn't have that feeling of fight about it. Instead it had peace – an extravagant fund of peace which permeated her entire house and her entire being. Should I be like that? Should I be peaceful about all of this? No. It's wrong. If you love somebody and lose them, I don't see how you can just have peace. I don't see it at all. That's selfish, to just be all right about it, when your loved one is rotting in the ground, or in an urn. I shudder. I don't want to think about the urn. No. You have to rail against it. What was it Dylan Thomas said? "Rage, rage, against the dying of the light." He said it about old people, but still. That's what you have to do. Because otherwise you're not valuing the light very highly, are you?

We aren't saying much now. Each of us is churning over the latest events in our own private little worlds. Emily keeps twitching her glasses down her nose and then pushing them back up again. Barney is driving, so at least he has the distraction of being able to change gear every so often, which he does with more violence than usual. I don't know what to think. It occurs to me that if I don't know what to think, then maybe thinking nothing at all might not be such a bad plan. What did she say? Let the thoughts come in, and then let them go out again, out of the top of your head. OK. Well, I don't think it's going to do anything, and I don't have to let Emily know that's what I'm doing, so why not?

I nestle into my seat, pulling the seat belt away from my shoulder where it has begun to burrow in. I shut my eyes. Thoughts. I can feel my eyeballs trying to twist round in my head to see what I'm doing. They begin to ache. I relax them back, which is odd. There is a sort of bright red all the way across my vision. Don't need that thought, so there's the funnel, I'll let it go. The funnel is a sort of pale yellow, that's interesting. I let that go too. This is a ridiculous exercise, what on earth is it going to achieve? Is Christine sitting laughing at me in her living room? Ah, but this is a thought too. I let it go. I feel myself shudder a little as that one leaves. Odd. I keep going. Some thoughts are harder to let go of than others. Some demand attention. I find myself giving it, then I remember myself, and I let it go. My eyeballs are twisting around again in my head. I feel tired. I decide to stop.

I open my eyes. I see Emily in the rear view mirror. She has her arms crossed and she is watching the world as we pass it.

"You're awake," says Barney.

I nod. I feel strange. Different. I can't describe it. It's as if I'm further away, somehow, experiencing the world through a soft fabric.

The stairs have actually fallen off the side of the house. We can't get up them. There doesn't appear to be an injured person here, just a set of stairs tipped over on its side like one of those paintings where the stairs go at all sorts of angles into scenes that don't make sense if you think about them as part of reality: the sort of paintings that are designed to mess with your mind. My mind is certainly being messed with. Why would they just fall off, without a person on them? But here they are. We are going to struggle to get in.

I look up at the door. The piece of stone that was at the top of the stairs is sticking out from the wall of the house, so it must have been built into it. If I can get to it, I can stand on the ledge and we can get in. There is a high fence to the right of it, separating my patch of garden from the lady downstairs. I pull on it to see how strong it is. It holds firm.

"What are you doing?" says Barney.

"Getting in," I say.

I heave myself up the fence, but my arms aren't strong enough. I can't seem to get as far as sitting on it. The highest I can reach has my chest in line with the top of the fence.

"Let's go to Barney's," says Emily.

"Give me a leg up, will you?" I say.

Barney looks reluctant, but he steps forward anyway. It is much easier with his help, and now I am sitting on the fence, pondering my next move. If I shuffle along a bit, I will be able to use the wall of the house to help me balance on my feet. I shift myself the three feet I need to cover, and put my hand against the stone. It is warm, which surprises me. I had expected it to be cold.

"Don't look," I say.

"I need to catch you if you fall," says Barney.

"I have to hitch up my skirt."

"It's nothing he hasn't seen before," says Emily.

I feel my skin prickle on the back of my neck, remembering that day in Patrick's house when I was cooking breakfast, waiting for him to come back from a workout with Barney, wearing nothing but the briefest of aprons. I remember the feeling of shock as Barney came in too. It was the first time we met. I can feel my face heating up. I want to avoid looking at Barney, but something makes me do just that. He is blushing too. That hadn't occurred to me, that he would have been embarrassed to see, when I thought it was the being seen that was the embarrassing bit.

"You told her?" he says.

"You'll have told all your buddies." The words come out with a harsh edge to them. I have thought this before. I have seen them in my mind's eye, in the changing room at the game, laughing and joking about my various attributes and non-attributes.

"I never told a soul," says Barney.

"What? Why?" says Emily. "It's funny."

"Because she wouldn't want me to."

Emily's mouth is open. She realises and closes it. She glances at me. I don't know what to say.

"There are some decent men in the world, you know," says Barney. "You want to think the worst, but if you're always looking for it, that's what you'll always see."

"You sound like Lottie," says Emily.

"Well Lottie knew what she was talking about."

"She was barking mad," says Emily. "Like that Christine woman."

I don't want to go into this now. I know Barney is annoyed that I doubted Patrick's loyalty to me. To be honest, I am annoyed with myself. But I am more annoyed with Patrick for not trusting me with secrets that were important to him, and I don't really want to think about it right now. I wobble a bit, getting to my feet, but I manage it. The wall is helping. I can just about get the tips of my fingers to the ledge by the door, but if I couldn't get onto the fence, I am not sure how I am going to get up here. I reach a little further, and get my hand to the ledge, but I can't bring myself to let my legs go.

"How are you going to lift yourself up there?" says Barney. "I can't reach to give you a push. Come down. Let me do it."

"No. You'll break your neck." It was Patrick's joke with Barney. It was what he always said. I thought it would make him laugh, but it doesn't.

"Shut up," he says. He turns away and I can't see him. I am sorry. I want to say it, but perhaps he has left.

"What are you doing?" says Emily.

There is a scraping sound of metal on stone.

"Stop it, you'll hurt yourself," she says.

"What's going on?" I say. I can't see.

"Barney's trying to cause himself an injury."

"Oh shut up, I'm fine," he says.

I push myself off the ledge, back towards the fence, using the wall again to balance. I sit back down on the fence, conceding defeat. Now I can see what's going on. Barney is lifting the stairs, by himself. Emily keeps going forwards to touch them, as if to help, and then stepping back again, rubbing the dirt off her hands.

"Barney," I say.

"It's fine. They're not heavy," he says, but he is grunting, so I don't believe him. He heaves the steps up and leans them against the wall. "There," he says "Now, I've wedged it there, but we need to fix it. I could probably do with a drill and some screws. Any ideas?"

"Patrick's house," says Emily.

"OK then," he says. He pulls me down off the fence in such a hurry that I can't resist being tipped over his shoulder. "Stop it, Barney, you don't have anything to prove to me."

"Oh, but I do," he says. "Look. I'm fine. I'm fine."

"But..."

"If you don't agree with me that I am fine, you can just stay up there," he says.

"But..."

"Fine."

He starts walking towards the car.

"Put me down," I say. He ignores me. Emily giggles. "He looks fine to me," she says.

"OK, OK. You're fine," I say.

"Mean it," he says.

For God's sake.

"Well?" he says.

"I mean it."

He puts me down. "I don't believe you," he says. His hair is ruffled and tipped over to one side.

"I'm sorry," I say.

He shakes his head. There is no need, he is implying.

"For telling Emily," I say. "And for Patrick."

His eyebrows move together. "What do you mean, for Patrick?"

I don't know what I want to say. There are so many competing threads to this particular line of thought, and I can't find an end. I go with the middle of the knot. Perhaps I will be able to pick it apart. "He couldn't tell me about Edward Thornhill. He lied. He made you lie. I wasn't good enough. I should have... I don't know. I should have been someone he told. I wasn't. And you had to conceal it from me. I don't know. I'm sorry."

I don't think I have pulled anything apart. The knot seems more firmly tied than ever.

Barney puts his arms around my back and hugs me to him. "You didn't do anything wrong," he says. "Paddy felt guilty. That's all. He didn't want to tell you because he loved you."

"He didn't trust me."

"He didn't trust himself."

Apparently this house is mine. It doesn't feel like mine. It feels very much like Patrick's, and I'm not sure what to do with it. I can't live in it. That would be too strange. But I can't sell it. Selling it would be selling off what is left of Lottie, what is left of Patrick. I don't need to think about this now.

Barney is in the cupboard under the stairs, moving things around, looking for Patrick's tools. There is an old feminist shadow in my brain that tells me I ought to fix my own stairs, that I shouldn't be relying on a man to do it for me, that I'm perfectly capable and all the rest of it. There is another part of me that says, "Who cares?" I'm afraid the second one is winning out today. If Barney wants to play with drills and so on, I am happy to let him. It is giving him something to do.

Emily has gone straight for the kettle. I am beginning to think she is obsessed with tea.

I am in Patrick's study. I always seem to end up in here these days. I run my hands along the books in the bookshelves. Motivational stuff, a lot of it. Books by past rugby players, books by coaches, books by psychologists, they all line up one by one, waiting for their time to be read. He read them all. He was always reading.

His smell is in here. Perhaps that is why I like it so much. I can almost feel his presence, because I can smell his smell.

I sit down at the desk and breathe in deeply through my nose. I find myself breathing out over my tongue, as Christine suggested. It feels nice. I carry on. Emily arrives with tea.

"There you are," she says.

"His smell is here," I say.

"His smell?"

"Yes."

"What, did he fart a lot in here, or something?"

I shouldn't have said anything. I turn away. She has gone, anyway. She is looking for Barney.

I hear them talking, through the closed door. It is a muffled, distant sound. I shut my eyes. I listen to that sound, and then something shifts, and it is as if I am listening beyond it. I am reaching beyond the noise of them talking, beyond the traffic noise in the road outside, beyond the slight hum from the electric light, beyond the creek of the chair. I am tuning in to silence: the silence that lies behind the noise. I suddenly feel a part of something vast, but I am not an insignificant part. I am integral. It is part of me and I am part of it. I am silence. I am nothing. But I am everything at the same time.

I see a blinding flash of white light, and suddenly the noise piles in. The silence has gone. And Emily and Barney are standing in the doorway, looking at me.

"Are you ready?" says Barney.

"Have you had a good sleep?" says Emily.

Was I asleep? I don't think I was. But my tea has gone cold, and it feels as if no time has passed at all. I must have been. It was a dream. Just a dream.

"Come on," says Barney. "It'll be dark soon."

"In a minute," I say. "You go. I'll be right with you."

I hear them going out through the kitchen and out of the back door. I look around the room. It is the same, and yet it feels different. I can't describe it. I am not sure there are words to do so. The phone sits in front of me, the answer phone light red and steady. No new messages. The memory of Christine's message comes back to me. I press play, hoping that Barney hasn't wiped anything.

The messages play through. All the clicks and beeps, all the missed appointments. Here it is.

"Patrick. Don't come today. I'll tell you about it later. Don't come."

It is. It's her. The voice sounds younger than she looks, but it is definitely Christine.

Sunday, 3rd December

It took longer than any of us expected to fix the stairs last night. Emily and I stood pointing torches in the direction of the wall, while Barney took his life in his hands on the stairs, fixing them back in place.

When we finished, it was too late to call Christine. Emily stayed and slept on the sofa, and Barney left. I lay awake for a long time. I don't remember what I thought about. I just remember that my brain did seem quite busy. And now it's six, and I'm wide awake and looking out over the sea. There is still a bit of moon over there, and the water is a beautiful midnight blue colour. A lone jogger in bare feet mooches across the beach. Brave man. Or stupid. It must be freezing out there.

I will go today. I will see Christine, and I will ask her some things. That's what I'll do. I'll go on my own. Yes. That's what I'll do.

It is a very narrow street, with cars on both sides, which makes it difficult to park. Every time you swing the nose out to get the back end into a space, you worry that you're hitting the car on the other side. It takes me a couple of goes. I look around to make sure nobody is looking. I hate it when people think I'm no good at parking. Although why on Earth I should care what complete strangers think about my parking ability, I have no idea. Even so, it seems I do.

I look at my watch. She said 11.15. It's 11. I'd better wait. It's not fair to turn up early, especially when she works from home. I close my eyes and find myself doing that breathing thing again. I remember yesterday, and the experience of the silence beyond the noise. Might as well try it again. I listen hard to the sounds all around me. There is traffic up the road. There is a school playground somewhere near, because I can hear children shouting and playing. Someone is hammering a nail in a wall somewhere, over and over again. Or perhaps he is hammering lots of nails, one after the other. I try to reach behind all this, focusing hard. My eyeballs turn around again inside my head. I wish that bloke would stop with his hammering. And those kids, how loud do they have to be?

Nothing. I can't reach the silence. All I can hear is noise, crowding in on me. No good. I check my watch. A minute, maybe two have passed since I started. It must have been a dream yesterday. Emily was right. I was just asleep.

There is no answer when I ring the doorbell. I know it made a sound in the house, because I heard it. I think about pressing it again, but my mother was always very strict on that: you shouldn't hassle people by ringing twice, you should give them the chance to answer the first one. I wait. There is no movement, no sign of life. Feeling the same rebellion against my mother that I always feel in this situation, I reach forward a tentative finger and press the doorbell again. Again it chimes inside the house. Again there is no movement.

She said 11.15. It was only two hours ago that I spoke to her. It is now 11.15. Well, 11.18 now. I will try once more. Sorry, Mum.

A window opens above me. "Let yourself in, my love. I will be with you as soon as I can." The tone is short, but cheerful. I am not sure whether I have been told off or not. I think I probably have.

I turn the handle and let myself inside. The bicycle is still in the hall. There is the soft hum of central heating and as I brush past the radiator in the space left by the bicycle, I can feel that it is hot. I go past the stairs and stop. Should I wait here, or let myself into the living room? I don't want her to feel that I am invading her privacy, but then she did say I should just come in. I also don't want her to think I am being nosy or that I have assumed I will be welcome in her living room. Perhaps I should just wait here in the hall. There aren't any chairs though. If this was the waiting area, she would presumably have provided chairs. I'll have a quick look in the living room, and see if it looks like she uses it for people waiting, and if it's all pristine and smart and unwelcoming, I'll come back and sit on the stairs.

I push the door open, slowly, so that I can change my mind and close it again at any moment. The room is as it was the other day, except there is a folder on the coffee table. On the folder is a note. "Treating one of my regulars. If I get held up, why don't you have a look through these? You know where the kitchen is. CT."

I pick up the folder and open it. There is a picture of some boys in striped shirts and white shorts. One of them is clearly Patrick. It is a story about an under 14 side. It describes the precocious talents of a young winger, Edward Thornhill, third from the left. He looks very little compared to the others.

So he and Patrick were on the same side. They did know each other well.

It is talking about a match where they beat the Craythorne Crimsons (a team I haven't heard of) 3-0. Then it talks about three tries, so maybe they score the juniors differently.

I leaf through. Press cutting after press cutting, it follows Edward's progress through the years of playing in junior leagues. I can see this boy growing and growing, switching around to different places on the side as his size alters and his shape changes. And now here are some descriptions of his senior play, finding a home in a new team. Here are rave reviews of try-making and try scoring. Here is the first mention in a national newspaper. Here are more. And here is the speculation about the big match against the Kestrels.

It stops here. She hasn't collected any more cuttings. I can't say I blame her.

"What do you think?" she says from the door, making me start.

"He must have been very good," I say.

"He was. You see Patrick?"

"Yes."

"He was a good boy. Sweet. Kind to his mother. He always impressed me, you know. Every time I saw him."

I arrived with questions. I wanted to ask so many things, about what happened yesterday, about her, about what was happening, and I can't seem to find any of them in my head. All I can find is this confusion. I can't seem to get past it. He killed her son and here she is talking about how lovely he was.

"Are you for real?" I say.

She laughs. "You must talk about him. You must remember all the things you loved about him. It's so important. There is a terrible sorrow to grief, but there is a flip side to it as well. There is the joy of having known, of having loved."

I have tears in my eyes again, but so does she.

"I don't understand how you can be so nice about him," I say.

She walks towards me and takes the folder out of my hand, turning and placing it in its home on the shelf between two similar looking folders. "Come," she says.

I follow her out of the room and up the stairs, turning at the top and walking along a landing, past three closed doors to a large open room which takes up the full width of the front of the house. The December sun is streaming in at a low angle through the two windows. There is a fireplace over at the far end of the room, and a fire crackles away within it. Two straight backed chairs sit facing it either side. There is a massage couch set up in the middle, covered in white towels, and sitting on top of a cream rug. Two more chairs, matching the ones by the fire, are placed near the couch, one at each end. A wooden box sits on a table which is tucked into the corner to the right of the fire. It is open and contains a number of small glass bottles with screw tops on them. There is a ramekin dish sitting beside the box, and another one over on top of a bookshelf on the wall opposite the windows.

"What is this?" I say.

"This is my treatment room. Come. Sit. Let's have a chat."

Warily I walk past the couch. Lottie had one of these. Patrick didn't know what to do with it when she died. In fact, thinking about it, I have no idea what he did in the end. Did he sell it? I can't remember.

"Sit," says Christine.

"I thought you said you were a spiritual teacher," I say.

"I am."

"So what's the couch thing for?"

"That's for healing."

She watches me as she says this. I know she is checking for a reaction. I try not to give one.

"You don't like the thought of healing," she says.

"What?"

"Patrick told me. He said you and he had very similar views on the subject. Before he came here, that is."

Again, she stops talking and waits, watching me.

"His mother…" I say. She doesn't fill the silence left by my not finishing my sentence, so I am forced to continue. "She… Well, she thought she had these magical powers, like she could put a spell on people and they would be well."

"Really?" she says, smiling. "Is that how she described it?"

I think back. I can't remember. No. Actually. Probably not. "She said something about changing people's beliefs."

"And what did you think about that?"

"I thought it was unbelievably arrogant."

She nods. She waits for me to say something else, but I am getting wise to this. I will not tip any more of my thoughts into the silence.

"Why?" she says.

"Why what?"

"Why did you think it was arrogant?"

There is another silence, but not because I have decided not to speak. I am looking for the answer to her question, and I can't find it. It's obvious, isn't it?

"Go on," she says. "It's your mind. These are your thoughts. What's the answer?"

I can feel a little wave of crossness rising up my spine. "If you think you have the power to make people well by changing their beliefs, which by implication means you think your beliefs are more valid than theirs, then that's arrogant, isn't it?"

She nods again, but her nods aren't agreement, they are a signal that she has heard what I said.

"What is truth?" she says.

"Sorry, what?"

"Simple enough question. What is truth?"

I am not sure what she wants me to say.

She waits.

"OK," she says, after a pause which I get the feeling is far more awkward for me than it is for her. "What is *the* truth?"

I don't know why that's supposed to make it any easier, but I have a go anyway. "It's what really happened. If you're telling the truth, you're talking about things that are real, as opposed to stories you make up to make yourself look better, or to get you out of trouble."

"Right. So what is truth?"

"I don't know what you're asking me."

"How many truths are there?"

I don't really get what she's saying to me. "What is the truth to one person might be something totally different to somebody else. So I suppose there are as many truths as there are people."

"Really?"

This is too general for me. I need to find an example, something tangible, specific. "OK. Emily once wore a yellow mini-dress to an awards thing, which I thought looked hideous. But there was a fashion journalist there, and she was raving about it. So the truth for me was that it was horrible, and the truth for the other person was that it was nice. Either way, we probably both said the same thing."

"Which is?"

"That she looked nice. No point hurting her feelings."

"OK. So you lied."

"Yes."

"So was the journalist's opinion the truth?"

"Not for me."

"All right. What is perception?"

"Oh," I say. It is what I have just described.

"Is truth the same as perception?" she says.

My head is starting to hurt. I wasn't expecting the conversation to be such hard work. I don't know what I *was* expecting.

"What is the truth of the Emily yellow dress scenario?" she says.

A glimmer of understanding flashes across my head. "The truth is that I see it one way and another person sees it another."

"And which one is right?"

The glimmer of understanding fades again.

"Sorry?"

"Which perception is right? Which is the truth?"

"The expert in fashion, I suppose."

"So her opinion is more valid than yours?"

"Well, it's based on learning and knowledge, rather than just... I don't know."

"But fashion changes, doesn't it? One expert in the 1920s might have a different attitude to the yellow dress than another expert in 2007."

"I suppose."

"So which one of those is true?"

There is an answer here, I know there is, and I don't want to get it wrong. I don't want her to think I'm stupid. I stare numbly back at her, a sculpture of stupidity no doubt carved into my features.

She laughs. "It's all right, my love," she says. "I'm being hard on you. I want to get you to think, to challenge your perceptions, that's all."

"So what is the answer? What is the truth?"

"The truth is that truth is truth and perception is perception."

I'm not sure I'm any further along.

"Occasionally, you will perceive truth, but only if you are open to doing so. Far more likely, you will perceive perception. The intellectual mind can only cope with perception. There is more to us, so much more, than our intellectual minds."

"You see, this is where I have a problem," I say.

"Why?"

"Because it's all very well saying there's more to us than our intellectual minds, but isn't that how we understand the world? So aren't you asking me to have faith in something I will never understand, because you're saying my intellectual mind isn't up to the job? And isn't that a bit of a hopeless place to be?"

"Why do you assume you will never understand it?"

"I don't. You do. You say the human mind isn't up to the job."

"The human mind is. It's the 3% of the brain that we use that isn't."

I am shaking my head. "This is how they get you, isn't it? By telling you you're not good enough."

"I haven't said you're not good enough."

"You did."

"No. *You* did."

She stands up and goes over to the table. There is a jug of water there that I didn't notice when I came in, and two glasses. She fills the glasses and comes back to her seat, handing me one of them. I am a lot thirstier than I realised.

"Thirsty work, breaking old patterns of thought," she says.

We drink. I feel unsettled and I am cross with myself for it. Why should I let her rattle me?

"How do you think our minds learn new things?" she says.

I ponder this, taking my time over my next sip of water. "By repetition. If you say something over and over it goes in. Or if you write it down."

"So you're saying our minds learn by words?"

"Yes."

"What if there is a world of wisdom, a universe of wisdom, beyond our understanding, which is not borne of words?"

"I don't follow." I'm not sure how you think without words, for a start.

"Tell me," she says, "have you tried meditating?"

I nod.

"And what happened?"

"My brain quietened down a bit. But then it got noisy again."

"And when it was quiet, was that pleasant?"

"I suppose."

"Did you see any colours?"

"No."

"Ah. Well. Don't look for them. But notice if you are shown them. The trick is to notice the experiences you are given, and not to judge them. That way you will begin to understand wisdom without words. There is so much more to life than we can express with words, you know. They limit us, because they come from our past. They are designed to communicate a level of experience that we have had, but they are not yet adapted to the experience that we *will* have. How can they, if we invent language, and we haven't had it yet?"

I feel that sensation of the eyeballs trying to turn around inside my brain again. I can't seem to think properly.

"Dwell upon it," she says. "In your meditation. Let your subconscious lead you to the answers."

The session is over. I can tell by the finality she has in her voice. I want to ask her something else, but I can't think of anything. I just don't want to leave. She leads me to the door, along the landing and down the stairs.

She opens the door. Soon I will be out there again. But there is no comfort out there. The only comfort I have found is in here. I don't want to go. I need to find something to keep her talking, just so I can stay a little longer. Is this how Patrick felt?

"What is the truth?" I say.

"Sorry?"

"The truth about Emily's yellow dress? You said that liking it and not liking it were perceptions, not the truth. So what's the truth? Is it good, bad, or indifferent?"

"Yes," she says.

"Sorry?"

"It is yellow," she says. "And that's the truth."

Mr Schofield's house has a board in the window, but there are still no signs of life here. There is no car outside, there are no voices. The windows all look dark. I have thrown caution to the wind and parked in the drive. I didn't want to go home. I didn't know *what* I wanted so I drove around a bit and somehow I am here, looking at this place of wealth and soullessness. Wow. Where did that come from? Was that truth, or perception, I wonder?

I am thinking of the funeral, when we sang. Was that wrong? Is that why the stairs came off my home, as a punishment? I should surely be relentlessly miserable. I am, most of the time. I certainly don't need to try. But that was a burst of something akin to happiness, which we all had together, and perhaps that is not what should be happening. It doesn't show a lot of respect for Patrick, does it, to be imitating him and smiling, now he's dead?

What is the truth?

Oh, God, I don't know. The truth is the stairs fell off. I suppose that's all I can say with any certainty.

What was it she said? She said something about learning, but not with the intellectual mind. Learning without words. I have nothing better to do, do I? I close my eyes. I try to block the thoughts out of my head. But instead I am left with an amplified thought, "I will not think. I will not think. Am I thinking? I am. Stop it." I play it over and over again, bashing other thoughts out with it as soon as they arise.

This does not feel good. It carries the familiar pains of stress into my body. My shoulders start to hurt a little bit, my mouth goes dry and I seem to be tensing my legs for some reason. I don't get it. Isn't this what I did yesterday? That felt relaxing, and this feels horrible.

There is a knock on the window, right next to my head. I jump, and open my eyes.

A large man with a wide neck and deep runnels along his brow which make his skin look like plastic is standing there, looking at me.

"Can I help you?" he says, through the glass.

I open the door and get out, facing him in the driveway.

"Are you Mr Schofield?" I say. My legs are shaking.

"Yes." He is looking at me with suspicion. Perhaps he thinks I intend to sell him something.

"My name is Maggie Olds."

He steps back. Shock first, and then fury spread across his face.

"Piss off," he says. "Piss off and leave me alone." He turns and marches back towards the house.

Is that it?

"I just wanted to hear you say sorry," I shout after him. "That's not a lot, is it, for a man's life?"

"Fuck off."

"Where've you been?" says Emily, as I let myself back into the flat. She is draped across the sofa reading a book.

I am still bristling from my conversation with Mr Schofield. Her question has the effect of raising my hackles further. "You don't have to be here all the time," I say.

"Oh. Thanks." She slams the book shut and swings her legs off the sofa, sitting up and folding her arms to glare at me over the top of her specs.

"Look, I'm grateful, OK? It's just, you have a life to lead as well, don't you?"

She pushes her glasses back up her nose and recrosses her arms. "What's happened?" she says.

I don't want to tell her. I don't want to admit I've been to see Christine, and I don't want her to know about Mr Schofield. I don't want reproof for either of those two things. As I see it, there was no choice for me. I had to do them both. I don't want her telling me I didn't, or asking questions that I can't answer. I know she will think I've done wrong, and I don't want to have to hear it.

"Nothing," I say.

She sighs. "OK," she says. "If that's how you want it." She gets up and starts to pack her bag. "I'll be at home," she says.

"Sorry," I say.

"Look, you want to be left alone, just say so. All right? I don't have to be here if you don't want me to be. Let me know when you feel like being friends, and I'll think about it, OK?"

She will be cross with herself for that, I know she will. But she shouldn't be. I deserve it.

She slams the door as she leaves. I am left in the empty silence of my flat.

I sit on the piano stool, facing out to the sea. I can hear her high heels clanking down the road. I can hear a car door open and slam shut. I can hear the engine start. I can hear the car set off, accelerating hard, the gear change much higher than it needs to be. I can hear the gulls, gassing to each other. I can hear people laughing on the pavement outside. I can hear life, I suppose. Everyone else's life. Mine has stopped, but theirs carries on, as normal. They can laugh and joke and feel. I am condemned to this place of no feeling, where numbness overrides all things. Except anger, of course. I seem to manage anger all right.

I remember Christine describing that as a distraction. How is anger a distraction? Surely what I feel about that horrible, rude, selfish man, Mr Schofield, is the main event, not the distraction. After all, he did cause the accident. So how can this be a distraction?

What is true? The words weave their way into my brain, making me stop. What is true? I think about the feeling I had when I was sitting in Christine's treatment room. It was peace; that is the only way I can describe it. I certainly don't have it now.

Now I am angry. And that's his fault, isn't it? He had no right to do what he did. What was he thinking, jumping a red light? He would have known what the consequences might be, but he decided it was worth taking the risk, and then he told me, the person who loved Patrick more than anything in the world, he told me to piss off. And worse. He is just a reprehensible human being. He doesn't deserve the life he's got. He deserves to be made to pay. It's his fault. He had no right. People like that, they love taking risks at others' expense.

I seem to be on a rollercoaster of thought, and I can't seem to step off it. I must stop thinking. I must get that peace back. I need it.

Bastard. What was he thinking?

What is true? Again those words in my head, uninvited.

Is it not his fault but mine that I am angry?

There is a shockwave rippling through my stomach at the question. It seems to bite through the loop of thoughts and images about Schofield that are still churning around in my head. I want to say, of course it's his fault, but I am angry and Christine is not. And Dad is not.

Is my father right? Should I forgive and forget? What was it he said? "Forgiveness benefits the forgiver more than the forgiven." I'm not sure I heard him properly at the time. I thought he meant some kind of celestial reward after death, the way most rewards seem to come in the Christian church. But perhaps he means in life. After all, I don't want to be Mrs Angry. I just don't.

So perhaps I should forgive the bastard.

Yes. OK.

I will.

Easy. It's just a decision, after all.

I have now forgiven Mr Schofield for snuffing out the life of the man I love. Even though he was in the wrong and hasn't had to pay for it. I will forgive him. There.

What now?

I am looking for a difference. But I don't feel different. Except possibly I feel a little more agitated. I close my eyes.

Empty. Empty brain. Come on. You can do it.

But the thoughts rise up in waves. My head is drowning in thoughts that I can't stop. The same ones, over and over and round and around. IT'S NOT FAIR!

It's not bloody fair. It isn't. He shouldn't be dead. I shouldn't be here on my own. This is not right. Is there just no way of rewinding the clock and bringing him back? And if not, why not?

Round and around and around.

"Patrick!" I shout. "Patrick!" But he doesn't answer me. How can he? He's dead.

And there is Mr Schofield's face, in my mind's eye. The plastic set of his brow. The turned down mouth, as if he expects hostility at any moment. Piss off.

I feel a surge of emotion, frightening in its force, well up from somewhere deep within me and rip through my body until my ears are blocked by a roaring noise and I know I am shouting because I can feel my mouth moving and the muscles in my throat contracting, but I can't hear what I'm saying and I don't know. I don't know.

Is this it?

Am I loony bin material?

I can't stop.

And here is Barney, squeezing me in his big arms. "Shhh," he is saying. "Shhh."

I am not sure when he arrived. I am not sure how long I was in that state. I am not sure when I stopped shouting, if indeed I was shouting. I am sure of nothing any more.

"What happened?" he says.

I don't know. I shake my head at him.

He nods. He understands. How does he understand, when I don't? He hugs me again. I love him. Not in that way. Oh God. I didn't mean that. Patrick, if you can hear my thoughts, I didn't mean that.

Monday, 4th December

I didn't tell Barney anything. He didn't ask, after that. He just kept being there, making cups of tea, heating up soup, touching my arm or my back or the top of my head every so often, just to remind me I wasn't on my own.

I sleepwalked through yesterday. And now here I am in front of the fire in Christine's treatment room and she has asked me a question, and I can't remember what it was. I look at my glass of water, avoiding her gaze.

"It wasn't rhetorical," she says. "What do you think happened?"

I shake my head. There are no answers appearing within it. I don't know.

"Will you consent to a treatment?" she says, nodding towards the massage couch in the middle of the room.

"Massage?" I say.

"Probably not, no. Not today."

"Then what?"

"You have a lot of thoughts tripping around in your head. They are mostly dark. They are blocking you from seeing the truth. I would like to take them out."

"You're going to play with my thoughts?"

She laughs. "Not play, no. Just take out the rubbish that you don't need."

I look at the table again. If I lie down, aren't I putting myself at a disadvantage? In most interactions with human beings, if one person is lying down, isn't that person usually in trouble? Unless of course it's in a bedroom between two consenting adults. But then I certainly don't want that scenario to apply here.

"You can stay in the chair if you like," she says. Did she read my thoughts?

She smiles at me. "I can't read your thoughts," she says. "I can just pick up an impression of what they might be."

"How does that work?"

"Well, just then I had a fairly strong sense of fear about my own massage table. Now, I know that I don't fear my table, so I have to assume I am picking it up from you."

"I'm not afraid," I say. I don't want anyone telling me what I think.

"All right," she says.

I move towards the couch. "What do I do?" I say.

"You can lie on your back, if you like, or on your front and we'll take the hole out for your face so you can breathe. Whichever you prefer."

I would rather be able to see what's going on. I lie face up.

She pulls up the chair behind me and sits down. She places her hands either side of my head.

"Goodness me," she says. "You dwell on things, don't you?"

She takes one hand away from my head and I can hear her joints cracking. "Don't worry about the clicks," she says. "That's just negative energy being earthed."

I feel uncomfortable. Frightened. I am not sure I want anyone tinkering with my thoughts. Why have I agreed to this? Her other hand comes away from my head and I hear her arm cracking, as before.

Now it feels like her fingers are actually inside my head, and I know that isn't possible.

"Shut your eyes," she says. "And tell me what you can see."

How ridiculous. Oh well. In for a penny. I shut my eyes.

"Nothing," I say.

"Nothing?"

"Yes."

"Not dark, not light, not black, not blue, just nothing?"

What's she going on about? It's just the stuff you see when you shut your eyes. "It's dark," I say. In the middle it's dark, and round the outside it's sort of yellowish.

"OK. Watch," she says.

I keep watching.

And now everything has changed. I don't know how that happened. My head has calmed down, my thoughts are slower, and I am looking at pale yellow, all the way across my vision. Pale yellow. Not dark. Not what I would expect to be looking at with my eyes shut. I open them to see if the sun is shining through the window all of a sudden, but it is a grey day. Nothing has altered that.

"What did you do?" I say.

"I took the darkness out. That's all. Feel all right?"

"I do. I feel – um – lighter. Sounds mad, but I do."

She nods. She has heard this before.

"Right," she says. "Come on. Let's talk about why your attempt to forgive Mr Schofield went so spectacularly wrong." She stands and walks back over to the chairs by the fire, taking up her position on the right. I follow her and sit in the other chair.

"What happened?" she says.

I think back.

"Well, first I made the decision. To forgive him."

"Did you ask for help?"

"From whom?"

"God."

If she knew what I was thinking about the couch, she must know my thoughts about God.

"All right. You don't want to believe in God," she says. "What about the Universe? Do you believe in that?"

"How can you not believe in that? It's all around us."

"Indeed."

That's very pointed. I'm not sure what she's saying, but it is clearly significant.

"No. I didn't ask the Universe for help."

"Why not?"

"Because this is my problem. And how do you ask an inert set of atoms and molecules and systems and vacuums, and whatever else, how do you ask that for help?"

"OK. So you have trouble comprehending the Universe as a conscious entity?"

This stops me in my tracks. Shouldn't I? I know what the scientists say. I understand the scientific effects of gravity and so on. Things that appear to be supernatural can always be explained away scientifically. So the sense that I have always felt, that of being watched by something all seeing, that's just my fancy. I have written it off as that anyway. What is it? Is it real? Is it my imagination? Is it God?

"No," I say.

"No what?"

"No. I have trouble comprehending the Universe as a *non*-conscious entity."

"So why try?"

"Because it isn't scientific."

"Mmmm." She goes to the water jug and refills our glasses.

She sits back down again.

"What is science?" she says.

"It's a way of understanding how the world really works."

"So it's a quest for the truth, would you say?"

"Yes."

"Are scientists human?"

"Yes."

"So are they always open to the truth?"

I think about Galileo and his assertion that the world was round, against the best understandings of all the scientists of the time. Clearly, they were not open to the truth.

"No," I say.

"And why is that?"

"Well, sometimes the truth is just too far out of people's current understanding. Like the Earth being round, when they all understood it to be flat. They couldn't understand, because it was against everything they had been taught. Everything they believed."

"So is it fair to say that belief gets in the way of truth?"

"It depends on the belief."

"Go on."

"Well, Galileo believed that the Earth was round. So that didn't get in the way of it. It was just all the people who wouldn't listen to him."

"So how do you find the truth?"

I think about this. She is big on truth.

"I suppose you have to be open to all ideas, no matter how much they differ from your belief, until you are convinced one way or another."

She nods. "Perhaps not even then," she says.

"Sorry?"

"Truth will prove itself, over and over again, as long as you are open to see it. In practice, yes, experience teaches you to be convinced, but truth doesn't require conviction, simply openness."

She's lost me a bit.

"What does this have to do with my flip out yesterday?" I say.

"What do you believe about Mr Schofield?"

"That he did wrong."

"And?"

"And that he should pay for it."

"Why?"

"What?"

"Why?"

"Because then maybe he'll learn from it. Maybe he won't do it again."

"How do you know he hasn't learnt from it?"

"Because he told me to piss off."

Her gaze is steady, and straight through me. I want to look away, but I can't. Now she breaks it to prod the fire.

"Why do you think he did that?" she says.

"Because he's a bad man."

"So he frightens you? His badness? It frightens you?"

"Yes."

"And your presence? Might that not be frightening to him?"

"No."

Her voice shifts, as if it is coming from another place, even though it is still her voice and she hasn't moved.

"Is there anything you have done in life that you are ashamed of?" She is looking straight at me again. I don't know how much Patrick has told her. My hands have started to sweat. Of course Ben pops into my head. Of course he does. And she seems to be able to read my mind, so is there any point in my not telling her?

She waits. I don't know what to say. I am very aware of time passing, and this abyss of silence in the middle of the room that I so badly want to fill, but if I do, there will be no turning back. She will know, once and for all, how awful I am. How guilty. I feel unable to say it and unable not to say it. The result is this intolerable silence and her gaze, steady and unwavering.

"I killed my brother." The words are out. I've said them. And I can't quite believe I've done it.

"How?" she says.

I tell her about my rebellious phase, about the party I went to. I tell her about the cannabis, and about getting myself into that stupid situation with Martin Elksley. I tell her about calling Ben in tears. I tell her about him arriving to pick me up and me not saying thank you, just snapping at him when he asked me what happened. I tell her that I don't remember the journey or anything for three months after that. I tell her that he wouldn't be dead if it wasn't for me.

She nods.

"Sounds like you had a difficult time."

"Yes."

"Have you paid for it, do you think?"

Another question I wasn't expecting. I thought she'd do the usual oh you poor thing type response. Oh, but it wasn't your fault. All that. But she doesn't. Have I paid for it? Well, I haven't done jail time, and maybe I should have. But then it has altered everything about my life since then. It has cast a shadow over everything. Everything good, and everything bad. Have I paid for it?

"Yes, I suppose," I say. "But not enough."

"Why not?"

"It was his life. I'm still alive."

"Mmmm. And why have you been granted life, do you think?"

"To pay for it?"

"Or…"

"Or what?"

"Or to live it?"

I don't know what to say to that. I stare dumbly back at her.

"You have to learn to understand yourself. As you do that, as you see what drives your actions and what has led you to behave in certain ways that you don't like, you will let go of the beliefs that drove you to act in those ways. You will start to act from a place of truth, rather than in a way that you believe you must act in order to preserve things as you currently see them. You will start to understand all things, including the actions of others. And then you will be able to forgive, because you will see that there is nothing to forgive. Do you understand?"

"I'm not sure."

"OK."

She puts her glass down on the table.

"I see perception as a knot," she says. "Let's take your situation as an example. You were a rebellious teenager, and you got yourself into an unfortunate situation. That situation led eventually to an appalling circumstance that you couldn't possibly have foreseen. But it froze you in time. So let's look at the beliefs that led you to behave in that rebellious way, first of all. A lot of teenagers think that they are not taken seriously, or not loved, or not noticed, or something similar. Am I right?"

"I thought they loved Ben more."

"Yes. So this thing happens, and suddenly you are confronted with that belief, and you take it to be set in stone. Yes? It has to be the case now, doesn't it?"

I can feel the pin pricks at the back of my eyes, and I try to hold the tears back.

"Of course. He was more worth loving."

"So your perception is now that you were unloved because you deserved it, yes?"

"Yes."

"And then you listen to the perceptions of other people around you, and you gather from them that you are disapproved of, yes?"

"Exactly. So it must be right."

"Why?"

"Because it isn't just me thinking it."

"Mmm. But did you listen to all opinions? Did you give equal weight to all perceptions of you, or did you only buy the ones you wanted to hear?"

Again, she has stopped my thoughts before they could get going. I am not even sure that my heart is beating. I am thinking of Dad. He has always said he didn't blame me. But I have never believed him.

"Do you see how it works now? You see the world through filters of your own making. Your beliefs put a block on what you see, so that you only see the things that you expect to see. This is why scientists have such a problem understanding how spiritual teachers can see things they can't. It isn't because they are not real, it is because they lie outside of their experience. That's all."

"Do you have problems with scientists?"

"No, not really. There are more and more enlightened scientists out there. And the others'll get there in the end." She is smiling when she says this. "Besides, there are plenty of people on the spiritual path who are just as closed to science as some scientists are to spirituality. But that misses the point too. We must be open to truth. That's all. Zealously guarded beliefs have a tendency to get in the way of that. They put a filter up that makes people perceive their beliefs as the truth, rather than seeing through them."

"So when Lottie said she could cure illness by changing people's beliefs, she actually meant to take away these filters? To change their perceptions?"

"What do you think?"

"I don't know."

My brain is working hard, I can feel it, but it is different to the way it was overworking before. Before, the thoughts that I had were the same thoughts, rehashed and inescapable. Now it feels as if my head is wide open and anything might be possible. Occasionally words that she says find a home here, and I start to feel like I'm understanding something greater than myself. But then it moves out of my reach and I don't feel able to touch it.

"We're making you work hard now, aren't we?" she says.

"Why did I freak out yesterday?" I say.

"I can give you some of the answers, but others you must discover for yourself."

The session is over. I know it is. She doesn't have to tell me. I get up to leave.

"Thank you," I say. She just smiles. "Send my next victim up, will you?" she says.

I am sitting in the car. I am driving south, away from my flat and Patrick's house, and everything. I can see a woman walking a little white dog on the other side of a fence that runs beside the road. The woman has her coat done up to under her chin, and she looks chilled to the bone. The dog has on a red tartan coat and is trotting along impervious to the cold. I wonder how Meg's getting on in a meditation retreat. Having the time of her life, I should think.

My mother once asked me if I was lonely, living alone. She didn't know Patrick was practically living there, of course. I told her I am never lonely, unless I'm in a crowded room. I meant it. The loneliness of crowds is something I find very hard to deal with. It is the knowledge that everybody else is so much more interesting than me, and is finding fault with how dull I am. I'm not good at it.

I never really thought I was lonely otherwise, except that suddenly there was Patrick filling a void that I wasn't even aware I had. And now I know what it is to have it filled, I do have awareness of it. I can feel it gaping and yawning in my heart.

Christine has brought a break from it. I feel filled, somehow, in a way that I hadn't anticipated. It is strange. I went there looking for something, and I didn't know what it was. I'm not sure what I've found, but I'm pretty sure it is what I was looking for.

I see the teenager that I was. I see the constant comparison with my older brother, who was much more academic than me and much more popular. I can look at that girl now, as if I am looking at somebody else. I can understand why she went a bit off the rails. I know what pain she was in, thinking she would never measure up.

And all she was doing, really, when you think about it, was going to a party that her friends were allowed to go to, and she couldn't understand why they should go and she shouldn't. It was naughty, but not evil. She couldn't have known what the consequences would be. The trouble she got into there was not her fault. An outsider can see that. I seem to be able to step back now and see what happened from an outsider's viewpoint. I have never been able to do that before.

She called her brother for help. Of course she did. Who else would she call?

I am crying, watching that teenager in my mind's eye and feeling the guilty feelings as the news is broken to her about her brother. My father told me. He never said it was my fault. He never gave me a harsh word. He held me as I cried. He brushed the tears off my cheeks. He said I mustn't blame myself.

I believed my mother. It wasn't anything she said – she didn't say anything. Not for months. She wouldn't talk to me about Ben. She made it very clear that I was to blame.

Of course. She was grieving for the loss of her boy. Of course she wanted to lash out at somebody. And I was the obvious target.

I can see that now. I can see how my reaction to Mr Schofield is my mother's reaction to me.

Mr Schofield, who had to preserve his big house and his lifestyle and everything. Mr Schofield, who felt he was in a hurry and had to be somewhere and so took a risk, not thinking, in the heat of that moment, what the consequences might be. Mr Schofield, who missed whatever it was he was in a hurry to get to. Mr Schofield, who has now got to live with a death on his conscience, the way that I lived with one on mine.

Wow.

I don't hate Mr Schofield.

I should probably let him know, or something. I should turn the car around and go back to his house. But I don't turn the car around. I keep going, heading south, driving the long journey home for the first time for several years. Long in English terms, anyway. An American would think it was just a short hop. Now why did I do that? Why did I assess the thing I was thinking and reassess it in the

221

light of what someone else's response might be? It was just a thought, after all, just in my head. I didn't share it with anybody. Good God, I don't think anything straight, do I? I turn things around and around, checking them for flaws that might be found in them. I judge every word that I think, every word that I say. No wonder my brain feels too busy.

This must be what she means by the perception knot. I have my perception, and then I get very aware of what other people's perceptions might be, even though I have no way of knowing, really: it is all just guess work. And anyway, does it matter what other people's perceptions are? Sometimes it does. I don't like it when people think I'm rude, or loud, or whatever. But it seems to have become a habit. A habit of thought. And, because it is the way I think, I've never challenged it, because to challenge it I have to see it from outside of how I think, and that is how I think, I think. It sort of makes sense, but not quite. I just don't seem to be able to grasp it.

Stop thinking. The words are in my voice, in my head, but I am not aware of having generated them.

She said let the thoughts go, out through the top of the head. I didn't do that yesterday when I tried. I just tried to stop the thoughts altogether. But that's not what she said. She said let them go, which implies let them come in as well.

How do you do this and drive? Let that go. Am I doing it right? Let that go. Is this a thought? Let that go. I haven't thought anything. Oh. Yes. Let that go. Head feels different. Let that go. Bigger. Like it's expanding. How could the head be expanding? Well, it could only do that if there was more space, and so it must be a perception. Is this just a perception? Oops. I'm supposed to be letting thoughts go. Let that go. Is he cutting me up? Let that go. Bubbles. Let that go. Silence. Is this right? Shhh.

I am not sure I ever reached a place where my mind was completely still, but the thoughts certainly slowed down a lot. The difficulty seemed to be when I got on a train of thought I wanted to follow. Then I kept going with it longer than the others. Then it became harder to remember to let them go. It certainly changed things.

Because I was just observing the thoughts, and not getting involved with them, there was no way to judge them, or to write a story around them in my head. They were just there, and then they were gone. And yet I was still there, aware of things. Possibly even too aware, because it felt a bit scary on occasion. So the whole "I think therefore I am" thing – is that not right? Am I still here, even when I'm not thinking?

Who am I, if I'm not the person who thinks the way I think I think?

This is getting too difficult. I'm tired. I can't figure it out. Every time I think I grasp the meaning in all this, it moves beyond my reach again.

The journey has gone quickly, though. Here is the exit from the motorway, just up ahead.

The church is set back from the road, behind a lych gate with a heavy round handle which I have always struggled to open, and a graveyard. The handle gives me no trouble today. Perhaps I have forgotten how not to open the gate after all this time. I slip slightly on the flagstones, before finding my balance again on the gravelled track that threads its way between the graves and up to the door of the church, which is locked.

It never used to be locked.

I was hoping to gather myself a little in here before going round the corner to surprise Mum and Dad. I rattle the door, just in case I am mistaken and the heavy oak is just sticking, but no, it is locked.

"Hello?"

The voice comes from round the side of the church. It is Dad's. I can hear his footsteps scrunching in the gravel as he gets closer. I feel guilty, suddenly, as if I shouldn't be here. I don't know whether to smile at him or to sort of shrug in apology. I can't decide how to play it. But I don't have to play it, do I? I can just be, rather than being something. So I stand and watch as he comes round the corner, no attempt at an assumed expression on my face. Which is easier than I considered it might be.

He sees me and a smile appears, his and mine together, a genuine response. And now I am crying. Have I never shown anyone a genuine response to anything before? I must have done, surely.

"Baby girl!" he says. He takes my head in his hands and kisses my forehead, then turns and opens the door to the church with a long key he has tied to his belt. "It's a sad thing, this," he says. "People think they can steal from churches so we have to keep it locked. But I keep my ear out, just in case there is a lost soul in search of comfort."

"Dad."

"Well, OK, then. A lost soul in search of... what?"

I don't know. I stare at him. Why have I come?

He simply looks at me, waiting, all the time in the world.

"Forgiveness," I say.

He touches my face again, and smiles. He nods. He takes my hand and leads me to a pew near the front of the church. The sun shines through the window behind the altar, casting light on a stained glass picture of Adam and Eve with their fig leaves in place to preserve their modesty. He nods towards it.

"Tell me about Adam and Eve," he says.

"What about them?"

"Tell me the story."

I think back. That's the one about living in the Garden of Eden, and Eve being tempted by the snake to eat an apple. I never quite understood why it was such a bad thing to eat the apple, but there you go. God was cross, and punished them by making them ashamed to be naked, so the poor things were left having to cover up their bits with a few bits of leaf, and they wouldn't even have had Sellotape back then. Although, thinking about it, that might be a blessing because it might hurt to take the tape off that particular part. What am I thinking? Oh, and God made Eve pay by making all women for ever after have a horrible time in childbirth. I thought that was a particularly nice touch. And all for an apple.

"What is the significance of the apple?" he says.

"What do you mean?"

"Spiritual texts make use of symbols, because the themes they cover are so difficult to describe in words. So they use symbols that are easy to understand at the time of writing, and perhaps become less so as time passes. What is the meaning of the apple?"

I don't know what he wants me to say. I just shake my head.

"Where are they?" he says.

"The Garden of Eden."

"Which is also known as…?"

"Paradise."

"OK. So they're in Paradise. What are they doing there?"

"How do you mean?"

"What do people do in Paradise?"

"I don't know."

"They live in a state of innocence and bliss, don't they?"

"I suppose."

"What is innocence?"

"Um. Well, I suppose it's not having ever done anything wrong."

"And?"

"And not knowing. A state of not knowing."

"So they ate the apple and suddenly they knew everything?"

"They knew something they weren't supposed to know."

"And why were they not supposed to know it?"

"I don't understand."

"What was it they weren't supposed to know? What became of them?"

"They were thrown out of Paradise."

"Is Paradise a place, or a state of being?"

"Well, I suppose, if you look at it like that, it's a state of being."

"So why, after they have done this thing which they deem to be wrong, because they've been told not to do it, why is it so hard for them then to return to Paradise?"

"Because God kicked them out."

"Of a state of being?"

"Yes."

"Why was it so hard for them to return to it, if it is merely a state of being?"

I can feel my mind working, I just can't bring any coherent thoughts out of it to answer his question. It's as if I'm talking to Christine.

He smiles.

"Is it because they feel guilty, do you suppose?"

"I don't know."

"Well, think about it."

"So what are you saying? Are you saying that I shouldn't be feeling guilty, because it keeps me out of Paradise?"

"That's up to you. It depends what you want. But God doesn't want you to live in darkness. He wants you to find your way to the light."

"How do you know?"

"Because you are one of his children, my love. You are one of his children."

"So we should never feel guilty? So what? We can get away with all sorts of horrible actions against others, and that's OK? We just move on? What about bombers?"

"In my experience, bombers are not living in a state of bliss, they are driven by fear and loathing. Not innocence. So whether or not they feel guilty, they are still a long way from Paradise. The only way to innocence, to this elevated state of being, is through understanding darkness, and choosing light."

"Enlightenment?"

"Exactly."

"But the church doesn't teach that."

"Well, Jesus did, baby girl. Jesus taught us something that is already there. It is a unity of things that we have misunderstood. He taught something true. It's in most religions. This underlying thing. This possibility that is within us all. He came to help us find it. Spiritual development did not begin with Christianity. And it does not end there. Jesus taught a way of being. I think the rest of us then misinterpreted what he said a little bit. But don't tell the Bishop I said that."

"But what about all the guilty stuff?"

"Sorry?"

"You know. Be good. Be humble. If you're not humble you're evil, all that sort of stuff?"

He shakes his head. He sighs. "It took me a long time to work this one out. But I couldn't understand Ben's death in those terms. Were we being punished? What for? So I prayed. I prayed for help with understanding, and the understanding gradually came. What is the Bible for?"

"Sorry?"

"What is it for?"

"It's the story of the Jews, and then the Christians. It's to show us where we go wrong."

"Aha. So you are looking at it as a way of beating yourself and everyone around you over the head?"

"Well, it is a thick book. It would be quite an effective head basher."

He chuckles. "That it would." He takes my hand. "What if it isn't about how bad we are, but about how we could be? What if, instead of a self flagellation device, it was, in fact, a manual?"

"A manual? Like a car manual?"

He grins. "Exactly! It shows you how to work your engine! Exactly that!"

"But all those killings and things. What's that all about?"

"It tells us of our inner turmoil. The conflicts it describes are our own. They are within us. It just so happens that, at the time of writing the Bible, these inner conflicts were being played out. And they still are, to a certain extent. We are not free of wars, after all."

"I'm not following, Dad. I don't understand what you're saying."

"Our inner world creates our outer world. We all of us contribute to it. So the conflicts we see around us are in fact conflicts that exist within us, as a collective of people. If we understand these conflicts, we can move on from them. But we are so determined to look without ourselves, we don't observe what is really going on. We don't see that we cause so much of what we see out there, simply by allowing upset to continue within our own selves. It isn't an easy concept to communicate, baby girl. Not easy at all."

"So you're saying we have to be better people to stop everything horrible happening out there?"

"Not really, no. I'm saying we need to understand ourselves. It is only through understanding that we change. If we don't understand, we are stuck with our old ways of being. When we understand illusion, we will be able to see truth."

I smile.

"What?" he says.

"You sound like someone else," I say.

"Shall we go and see your mother?"

"In a minute. Dad?"

"Yes?"

"How do we understand?"

He thinks for a moment. Then: "What was it you said? Be good, be humble. Yes?"

"Yes."

"These are not things we are. They are things that we can learn. They are the reward in themselves. "On Earth as it is in Heaven." That is what we were being taught. Heaven can be here on Earth. Today. This minute. This moment. We just need to make the decision to build beauty within ourselves. And beauty is grace, humility, understanding, forgiveness, patience, joy, love. It is all these things. If we want to live in heaven, we must want to build these things within us. I think where so many of us go wrong is that we assume these things should already be there, and if they are not, that we are somehow evil. But that's because we ate of that apple. It is not the truth. Do you understand? We bought into a concept of evil."

"But it isn't possible to just change, just like that. You can't just say, I want to be like this. I want to forgive. It doesn't happen that way."

"That's where patience comes in."

I sigh. "I suppose."

"What is a false idol?" he says.

I think back to those early books of the Bible. All that stuff about Moses slaying whole nations for worshipping the wrong thing. "A golden calf," I say.

"But what does that mean?"

"It's something you worship."

"Exactly. Something you worship that isn't God. So why would you worship can't?"

"Sorry?"

"Why worship can't? Why worship my life is bad? Why worship it shouldn't be this way? Worst of all, why worship I am evil? Why give that dominion over you? Why eat of that particular apple? When instead you can worship what might be? What is possible? What beauty? Why not worship these things, these open ended things that God has given us, rather than can't and won't?"

He is animated. He has stood up and is pacing across in front of the altar. He looks young again. He has joy back, and I am glad of it. I find myself smiling.

"The world is such a wonderful place, if we can only accept the things that happen to us," he says.

"Even Ben?" I say.

He picks up the candlestick on the altar and puts it back down again. "Even Ben," he says. He looks at me. "Love is a gift, baby girl. And a gift isn't a gift with conditions. I love Ben. Even though he is no longer with me. I haven't taken that gift back. And yet I still have it to give. Nothing can change that. We miss his presence, yes, of course we do. But we have the experience of something not many people in this world have. We have known Ben. And we have known Patrick. And loved them. Do you understand? Your love carries on."

I don't understand. I miss them both. I want them both to be here. How can love carry on without them?

Dad is looking at me, but he is miles away. He is nodding. He is always nodding.

I didn't go back to the house with Dad. He nodded. He said to come and find him when I'm ready. He said we should pretend to Mum that I have only just arrived when I get there. She would be hurt, he said, if she knew I'd been home for a while and not sought her out. He didn't say "after all these years," but I knew what he meant.

The Bluebell Woods were Ben's favourite place in the world and today he would have described them as a little bare of leaf and muddy under foot. That's how he talked, as if he was standing at arms' length from the words he was using. I am not sure what he thought about God. He wanted to be a vicar at one point. He used to sit for hours watching Dad writing or practising his sermons, and he always wanted to know what was said when Dad was visiting people in the parish. He would write it all down in a big red book which he kept in a shoebox with a rubber band around it. Dad just smiled when he talked about being a vicar and told him to live a bit of life and then decide. Then he discovered biology and he stopped talking about sermons and suchlike. I don't know what happened to the red book. It must still be around somewhere. I don't know what he would have made of Adam and Eve or the truth about yellow. I'm not sure what I make of them really.

There are no leaves on the trees and the weeds have all died back for the winter, so you can see quite a long way through the wood. There is a pheasant pen on my right, but I don't think they've kept pheasants in here for years. The pen looks rather sorry for itself, and it would struggle to contain any birds, or to keep out any predators, because there are long gaps where the fence posts have toppled and been trodden under foot, twisting the wires and netting out of shape. In my memory it isn't a sad place, but today, here, with the muffled grey of the atmosphere and the cold wind and the dilapidated pheasant pen, and no Ben of course, it is just that. Sad. Forlorn. I didn't realise just how much he brought it to life.

Here is the tree he liked to climb. Here is my lookout stump. He used to make me stand on it and hoot if I saw an adult while he and Kevin Masters lit fires where they weren't supposed to and smoked illicit cigarettes. That wasn't often though. More often he came here alone, or just with me, and he pointed out a bird's nest, and taught me what foxes smelt like. He went through a naughty phase more because he seemed to think it was expected than that he actually wanted to be naughty, and I remember thinking how his voice was unnaturally loud when he was here with Kevin, and how unlike him it was to boss me about the way he did, as if I didn't matter to him at all and I know I did. I knew it then, and I know it now, with all the years lying there in between us. When we came here on our own he talked in gentle, hushed tones, as if he was trying not to disturb the wildlife all about us.

This has never struck me before, but my beloved brother acted a part for Kevin's benefit. If anyone had asked me if he would have ever done that I would have said no, but he did. He did. Not often, but he did. He used to tease Mum about it. I remember him laughing at her when she said something about how she wished she could afford better clothes for us, or how she wished we would behave in a more – God, what was the word she used? Seemly, that's it. A more seemly manner. He laughed at seeming anything. But there he was, with Kevin Masters, seeming to be a rebel, when he wasn't. And here I am in this cold wood, seeing my brother for perhaps the first time. He was human. I didn't have to worship him. In worshiping him I feel I missed seeing who he was. I think I missed knowing him.

I wonder if the old hut is still there. It's odd, the cushion of time. I would have thought I would remember every inch of these woods, but I don't. It's familiar, this little bit that I'm in, but the path to get here wasn't. I think the hut was that way, over to the right, but it doesn't look at all as I remember it. The track is wide when it used to be narrow. The trees are thinned out when they used to be tightly packed in on each other, and occasionally toppling over. In my memory there is not this much mud. But then, in my memory it is always spring here. There are always bluebells.

The hut isn't there. Of course it isn't. It was falling down when we played here. If they left it like that and some child hurt himself while trespassing, the owners could be sued. Of course there is no hut. There is a pile of logs where the hut once was. They are wet, but I don't mind. I need to think. I pick off a couple from the top of the pile and sit on the next layer down.

The irony is he would have been a great vicar. In a lot of ways he was like Dad. He knew how to listen and he knew how to make people laugh. But maybe he was a bit too shy to stand up in front of a church full of people every week. He was happier out here, with his camera, keeping quiet and watching the wildlife. I can see him now, kneeling on the wet ground with the Fuji whatsit that Dad bought him for Christmas to catch some creepy crawly or other. He is so clear in my mind; it is as if he's still there. I haven't thought of him like this for years. For years I have only thought of his death, of his absence. I haven't thought about his life.

I must be careful not to do that with Patrick. I must be careful not to turn him into a fictional version of himself, one that he would never have been able to live up to. I must remember him as he was.

And now I am back to thinking of Patrick and missing Patrick and there is a hole in my middle that I can't seem to fill and I can't seem to bear. How do I do tomorrow? That's the thing. It's all very well standing here and saying, oh yes, I did my grieving all wrong last time. I must do it better in future. The thing is, grieving involves a loss. There isn't just a hole in my middle; there is a hole in my life. I had no plans without him. I had no idea of carrying on without him. Why would I? How can you begin to conceive of a way forward, in this situation? How do people do it? I'm supposed to accept that he's dead and move on. I think everyone around me would find that a whole lot easier. But I can't. I can't. He isn't there and he is supposed to be and why should I accept that he's dead when he shouldn't be?

Why?

He was 32. He wanted to sell a design for a silent lawn mower. He had someone in Germany very interested in his idea. He wanted to get married and have children. Just two, he said. He didn't want to be greedy. He would wait until I was ready. He would have been an amazing Dad. He wanted to go to Ecuador because nobody that he knew had ever been there. He wanted to learn to abseil because he wasn't good with heights and he wanted to face it head on. He wanted to set up a charity thing in Lottie's name, although he couldn't decide what, but maybe something to do with spinal injuries because he knew a bit about that. He wanted to spend time getting to know his brother, just to see if they could last for more than three days without killing each other. He wanted to learn to speed read. He had a secret weighing him down that he needed to tell me. Would have told me. He wanted to visit the Louvre and look at the Mona Lisa, but not before he improved his French so he could talk in the right language when he got there. He wanted to write to his old geography teacher and thank her, but he always found a reason not to do it. He would have, though. One day. He would have done it.

He had so much still to do.

Why? Why has this happened?

Is this Karma? Is it punishment for the high tackle? Is it the natural order of things? Nature, restoring a balance? But why? What purpose does it serve? Grief is not balance. The gap a life leaves behind is not balance. Two deaths don't put anything right, any more than one. How is this right? I don't get it. I don't understand. Surely if he was going to learn from the high tackle thing, he should have been given the chance to live his life.

And what about me? I know it's selfish, but I can't help it. How am I supposed to just move on? We have to accept what happens to us, that's what Dad said. But there is no next. Not without him. How can I accept that? I can't be what he said. I can't be one of God's children, because I can't accept God's plan. I think it's cruel. I don't want any part of it.

I am standing now, and picking the logs, one by one, off the pile and throwing them down with all my strength, thud, at a poor old tree stump that probably doesn't deserve this. I can hear yelling, every time a log leaves my hands, so perhaps that is me. The tears are back, of course, rivulets forming down my face. Thud. What use is this? Thud. Can this be part of a plan, this utter despair? And when the despair passes, it'll all just go back to that dull numb feeling again, the emptiness still there, waiting for another attack like this one, but numbness, thud, filling its place. How can this be meant? What is there to learn from it? Thud. If God is there, and he loves his children, what the fuck is this about?

There is the shrill squeak of a small dog barking, close by. I stop throwing logs and turn around to face the sound. It is a Jack Russell. It is half wagging its tail, and half growling. Its owner is calling it from the footpath, perhaps fifty yards away: a high pitched cry that must pierce its way through the countryside for miles around. God, if he's there, has a very bizarre sense of humour. It is one of the two people on this earth that I would least like to bump into when I have tears streaking my face. It is the shorter of the two Irises.

"What are you doing?" she shouts, marching towards me, her little legs bouncing her forwards through the mulch of fallen leaves that have not yet rotted away.

I wipe my face with the back of my hand and square up to face her. She has covered half the distance between us and now there is less purpose to her stride. She pauses mid-bounce and peers at me through her pinched together eyes. The years have deepened her frown lines. The effect of that and the grey hat pulled down over her ears gives her a gargoyle-like quality. She is staring at me now, trying to piece together the scene in her mind. No doubt she is seeking the pithy comment that will send me running for home. I wait. I don't know what to say.

"It's you," she says.

I don't answer. I have the same paralysis I did at fourteen, caught in this stare.

She averts her eyes. Looks at her dog, who is sniffing my feet. "Bitzy," she says. "Bitzy, come on. Let's leave Margaret in peace." She can't wait to get away. She seems frightened, as if I might bite her or something.

She turns to go. I can't quite believe my luck. She is walking away, her dog reluctantly following. No. She is turning. I haven't escaped yet.

"I was sorry," she says. She is not looking at me. She is looking at the ground. "To hear about your..." She doesn't finish the sentence. She doesn't look at me. She doesn't wait for a response. She taps her legs to signal to her dog to walk with her, and she walks away, the bounces as she takes each step still there but damped down.

All those years I have carried her and her slightly less little friend around in my head. She's just a miserable old lady with a bitter look on her face and a correspondingly bitter outlook on the world. She couldn't show me compassion when we lost Ben, because it wasn't within her to do so. And yet I let what she thought about me govern what I thought about myself.

I feel strange. This blister of hatred that I have carried around has been pierced with a needle and is draining away into nothing. There is a warmth, a space there in my heart where before there was a fury. I turn for home. I am laughing, and I don't know why; it just seems to be the right response, somehow.

Dad's thing about the disease of unforgiveness comes into my thoughts. I am freed from it now. That particular version of it, anyway. Unforgiveness of the two Irises no longer sits solidly in my heart. I feel a surge of energy that I haven't felt before. The numbness is still there. The emptiness too. But here is something else, a new feeling. Life. It is life.

Tuesday, 5ᵗʰ December

I am surprised to see that it is after nine. I didn't think I would sleep that long. There was a stage, last night, when I didn't think I would ever sleep again.

I stayed in my old room. Mum huffed and puffed a little because she would rather have been given some warning. It isn't easy when people just turn up out of the blue. And maybe she didn't want me to see that my bedroom is now her sewing room, when Ben's has been preserved as it ever was. Our two rooms are separate from Mum and Dad's. You go up the narrow stairs in the kitchen to reach them. Ben's is on the left at the top, mine is on the right: the servants' quarters, from the days when vicarages had a certain amount of wealth about them.

I waited until I heard no more movement, which wasn't until at least two in the morning. I wonder if my mother sleeps at all any more. She seemed to spend a lot of time putting things away, and yet Dad and I had done the washing up and drying up and replacing. I crept out of my room and crossed the tiny square of landing, turning the brass handle on Ben's door as quietly as I could. I felt guilty, as if I was breaking in and snooping on something I wasn't allowed to see.

Thinking about it now, I can see it all in two dimensions, like a snapshot of a life. His photo albums still sit on his desk, one of them is open at a grey squirrel with some sort of nut in its paws. The lamp that he had as a small boy, with a smiling Thomas the Tank Engine on the shade, still sits on a faded white bedside table, under which is still an old sock. The carpet still has old tea stains on it. The wallpaper still has geometric shapes, although it is peeling away from the walls in a way that Ben would not have tolerated. Some clothes hang in the pine wardrobe. Some more lie scrunched and twisted in the drawers. He didn't have patience for folding. A few pointers to Ben and his life are there, it's true. But Ben isn't.

Dad came in when I was looking under the bed, trying to find the red book in the shoe box.

"Some things don't change," he said.

I bumped my head on the bed. I hadn't heard him come in.

"You're looking for his diary," he said. "Your mother has it. She still has it."

He sat next to me on the floor and looked around him. "I shouldn't have let this continue," he said. "It doesn't do her any good. She's got herself stuck. Had he lived, this room would not be like this now."

"But he didn't," I said.

He nodded. His eyes were sad. "No. No. He didn't."

There she is again, downstairs, moving things. I pull on my clothes from yesterday. I must stop staying in places without luggage. I hope I don't smell. The stairs are steep and you have to duck just before you reach the bottom to avoid a low beam. Ben used to say that either the vicar in olden times didn't mind his servants being struck on the head or he only employed really short servants.

"Hi Mum," I say, as my foot touches the kitchen floor. She is folding dusters. She looks surprised, as if she had forgotten I was here. A cloud of crossness passes over her features, but she recovers quickly to give me a strained smile.

"Toast?"

"No thanks. I'm not really hungry."

She has faded out again, back in her own duster-folding world. Eventually she pulls herself back and says, "Oh. You must eat something."

I pull a box of cereal out of the pantry and wave it at her. She nods. She is back with her dusters once more.

I didn't notice this when they came up to my flat. Not as bad as

236

this, anyway. But then, I had other things on my mind. Perhaps I wasn't looking for it. It is as if the numbness that I feel so keenly inside, she wears on the outside. She has surrounded herself in it. It makes the air thick, and difficult to breathe.

I don't know how Dad stands it.

He understands when I tell him I must go back. He is in the vestry, checking the communion wafers. He thinks a mouse has been at them.

"Not sure about mouse traps," he says. "After all, we are supposed to be bringing in a new Heaven and a new Earth, where the lion shall sit down with the lamb. Whacking a poor mouse over the head with a piece of metal, just for gnawing on a few wafers, doesn't seem entirely consistent with that, does it?"

"What does the Bishop say?" I ask.

"What? Oh. He's all for the traps."

I help him look for the gaps in the walls where the mouse might be getting in, but it is a bit of a futile exercise. It could be anywhere.

"She never allowed herself to grieve, you know," he says, out of nowhere.

"Sorry?"

"Your mother. She never grieved."

I don't know what he's talking about. She always grieved. She ranted and raved and threw things. She grieved. He sees my doubtful look.

"She blamed," he says. "She found all sorts of people to blame. You included, I'm sorry to say. But she never made that first step on the path to recovery. She never accepted the need to feel the loss in her heart. And I didn't help her. I think now it may be too late."

This is a very different man to the one who told me about Adam and Eve yesterday. He seems beaten.

My voice speaks, but I wasn't aware I had put the words there. "Why worship can't?" it says. He stops what he was doing, coming out from the back of the wafer cabinet and sitting back on his haunches. He looks at me, his head on one side. "Good lord, you're right," he says. "What a blind spot! You never can see these things for yourself, can you?"

Wednesday, 6th December

I am sitting on the bench at the top of the cliff, agreeing with Jean about the view, and trying to understand faith. Mum and Dad both believe in God. But whereas Dad seems to just accept all the circumstances of his life, my mother rails against them, which means that Dad seems to find comfort from his faith, while Mum's just stirs her up.

I always wanted to be more like my Dad, but it seems that the more I tried, the more like Mum I became.

That list that Dad spoke about. I'm not sure I can remember them all, but he talked about patience, acceptance, humility, and understanding, didn't he? It was like a description of him. Not me. Not Mum. So I am left with this horrible thought that I don't have any of those things, so I must after all be a bad person. I look at Patrick's death, and I can't accept it. I don't want to sit this grief thing out patiently, I don't want to humble myself before God, and say, yes, take everything away from me. I don't want to understand it, because if I understand it, that means accepting it, doesn't it? I don't want these things. I want him back. Still, even now. So perhaps I shouldn't be talking to anybody spiritual because they'll just see right through me to the horrors that lie underneath the surface. Perhaps I shouldn't see Christine any more. I am weak and pathetic, and I don't need her to tell me that.

Even so, I am now walking back towards my car, and I know full well where I am going.

The door is locked this time. I can't just open it and walk in. I can hear her fumbling around inside, looking for the key. Now the lock is clicking back. Now the door is open.

She sees me and smiles. There are circles under her eyes, but she seems alert all the same.

"I can't do it," I say.

"Oh dear," she says. "Cup of tea?"

We don't go up to the treatment room this time – the fire isn't lit and it will be too cold. "I'm a bit late this morning," she says. "Went out to the hospital for an emergency visit last night, and I'm afraid I didn't get to bed until about 6. So you'll have to bear with me a little bit."

We sit in the living room. She hums as she makes the tea things. I don't recognise the tune. I am more occupied with a long haired cat who has draped himself over my lap and is purring loudly.

"Ah, Dougal," she says. "You really should ask before you take up residence on people's knees. Are you all right with him?"

"Yes." I stroke the top of his head, and he stretches out with great enjoyment. I find my ailing spirits lifted, just a tiny bit. He rolls over and shows me his tummy.

"Touch that with great caution," says Christine, smiling indulgently at him, as if he is a beloved spoilt child.

I stroke his tummy and find my hand caught up between his front paws, his back paws kicking it away at the same time.

"Dougal!" she says. "Are his claws out?"

"No." I manage to disentangle my hand and resolve to steer clear of stroking that fluffy tummy. He rolls over again, stretches, to show me he couldn't care less what I think, and then marches off in a huff.

"Oh dear," I say. "I think I've just made an enemy."

"Dougal? Oh no. He doesn't hold grudges. Now what can I do for you?"

"I don't think I should do any more work with you," I say.

"Why ever not?"

"Because I'm not very spiritual. You're supposed to be patient, and humble, and all these things. And I'm not. I'm just not. Some people are and some people aren't. And I'm not." The words have come out a little louder than I anticipated. They reverberate around my head, even when I have stopped speaking.

"Mmmm," she says. She says that a lot. She puts her tea down. She holds one hand in the other, making a sort of O shape with her thumbs and fingers. "Why are we here, do you think?" she says.

"I don't know, I don't know, I don't know."

"Three times? We are in a muddle. All right, who is judging you, Maggie?"

She is asking me questions. I didn't want this. I just wanted to tell her and leave.

"I don't know."

"You do."

"You, my Dad, everybody."

"Are we, though?"

I don't know what to say. She looks at me as though through me, the same as before. I feel my skin growing more and more prickly.

"It's funny how people assume, when spiritual teachers talk about things like humility, that they are being judged, rather than helped."

"How do you mean?"

"We tell you that you need to develop humility, compassion, patience, and so on. You take it to mean that we think you are deficient in those things. It's very natural. People are so used to being told that they should be this and they should be that, they start to believe that they are being assessed at all times and found wanting. Especially by teachers of spiritual truth. Patrick suffered from it too."

"What do you mean?"

"Why do you think he came to me on the bus?"

"I don't know. We couldn't work it out."

"He knew that I cycle everywhere and don't own a car. When I told him that, he took it to mean that people shouldn't have a car. That he shouldn't have a car. Of course, I meant nothing of the sort."

"That was why he came on the bus?"

"People think you judge them, because they don't understand the nature of what you are teaching them. Until they understand it of course."

"And how long does that take?"

"As long as it takes," she says.

"Patience," I say.

She smiles at me, and takes my cup to pour more tea. We sit and sip in silence. I am thinking of Patrick parking his car on the bus route so that he didn't have to arrive in it and give himself away. I think I understand it. I haven't wanted to give myself away either. I didn't want her to know my guilt over Ben's death. I didn't want anybody to know that. Patrick didn't want anyone to think badly of him. He was always very careful about the impression he made upon other people. Why wouldn't he hide his filthy car-driving habit, if he believed that's how she saw it? Perception. I am starting to see what she means by a knot.

"What is faith?" she says, out of nowhere.

Funny, that's what I was thinking about only this morning, sitting on that bench overlooking the sea.

"I don't know. Belief. Some people have it, some people don't."

"So for you it is a switch? It's either on or off?"

"Yes."

"What if it is not a switch?"

"Sorry?"

"What if it is a continuum? First of all, you intend to have some faith in something outside of yourself – whether that is God, the Tao, the Universe, whatever. A small amount of faith blossoms into your system. Then your faith undergoes a number of challenges, to help it flourish and grow. It grows and grows, until you establish a link that you can feel to this Other. A link that is returned, in a two way process, so each time you meditate, or pray, or simply contemplate, your faith is strengthened, and your link to an energy you can't yet see or feel or imagine, is fully established and you can experience it. What if that were the case? What if the same were the case for patience, for humility, for all of those things you mentioned? What if all of those keys to truth were things that you could build, slowly but surely, by intending to build them? With help from a source more powerful than you yourself? What if they aren't, in fact, things that you either have or you don't have, but instead are things that you can reach towards? What if that were the case?"

"If that were the case, I would have to want them, and I don't."

"Well, you do and you don't."

"Sorry?"

"Your heart wants them. Your head is still having trouble with the whole idea of relinquishing that much control. Your heart knows that here is where your power lies, your head thinks it holds all the cards."

"Well, I'm asking my heart, and I'm getting that I don't want Patrick to be gone. That's not acceptance, is it?"

"Maggie, you just have to ask for patience, my love. That's all. Your heart is in fact telling you something very important. You simply have to learn to listen to it."

"What's that then?"

"What is it telling you about acceptance?"

"I don't know. That I don't want Patrick to be dead."

"And what else?"

"I don't know."

"Might it be telling you that it's all right to grieve?"

I can't believe it, I'm crying again. I promised myself I wouldn't.

She stands up and reaches behind me, where there is a box of tissues. She sits down again, across from me, watching and waiting. She doesn't say a word, just lets me cry.

The first wave of emotion passes, and the tears slow.

"I sometimes think that acceptance is the hardest," she says, "because before we can accept anything in our lives, we must accept ourselves. We must look within and accept our pain, accept our emotions, accept our darkness. Until we do that, what happens is that we squash it down into ourselves, and it prevents us from seeing the truth, because there it is, within us, altering how we see everything. You are grieving. Accept your grief. Experience it. Allow it to express itself. Ben too. That's what you are being given to do at this moment in time. That is all. The rest will come in due course, when you are ready."

"Accept my darkness? Am I not supposed to be avoiding darkness?"

"You can never avoid darkness by refusing to look at it. Only by shining a light upon it. What happens to darkness when you shine a light upon it?"

"It disappears."

"Precisely."

"Is grief darkness?"

"Grief is an emotion. It will only become darkness if you refuse to allow it to play out. If you are afraid of it and don't face it, darkness follows."

"So you want me to sit and feel sorry for myself?"

"I want you to listen to your heart. Literally. Listen to it beating. If then you feel sorry for yourself, feel sorry for yourself. If then you feel desperate, feel desperate. If then you feel you want him back, want him back. If then you feel joy, feel joy."

I think back to the singing at the funeral.

"Is it OK to feel joy?"

"Of course."

"But that isn't grief."

"Grief takes whatever form it takes. The point is, you must allow it to play out."

I am reminded once again of my Dad. He didn't wail and moan like my mother, he just went off and spent hours on his own. His wasn't a public grief, but perhaps it was a truer experience of it. Perhaps the acceptance he came to, the thing that has escaped both Mum and me, is no accident.

Listen to your heart beating. It's an odd piece of advice. But then, maybe my heart *does* have something to say to me. Something I have avoided hearing. And I can't think how else I will hear it.

Thursday, 7th December

I pull into that now familiar drive. The many windows of the mock
Tudor house seem to wink at me. All except the one with the
boarding in it. I stop the car and get out. I have no idea what I'm
doing here.

I ring the doorbell. There is no sound from within. I ring it again.

"What?"

The voice comes from above me. I step back and look up. Mr
Schofield's plastic face is scrunched up, squinting at me as if I am the
bright sun, from a first floor window.

"It's you," he says.

"Mr Schofield," I say.

"Look, I don't know what you want, but whatever it is, you can
have it, OK? I just want to be left alone."

"I don't want anything, Mr Schofield. I just want to talk to you."

"I haven't got anything to say."

"Please?"

He scowls at me, and pulls himself back out of the window,
shutting it as he does so.

I wait.

There is the sound of a door opening inside, then I hear shoes on
a wooden staircase, followed by shoes on a tiled floor.

He opens the door. He has on a tracksuit with brown loafers. He
looks as if he hasn't slept very much. I didn't notice this about him
before. The air of hostility still hangs heavy on his shoulders.

"What?" he says.

Now I am faced with him, I don't know how to proceed. What did I come here for? There are no words in my head, and yet I know I must say something. He looks increasingly cross as we stare at each other across the doorstep. When the words come, they come in a rush, as if I have just taken a lid off a steaming geyser. "I came to say I know you didn't mean to do it. I know it was an accident. Just a... thoughtless... accident. I know that now. And I'm sorry."

He looks at me, incredulous. There is another long pause as the words sink in.

"You're sorry?" he says.

"Yes. I blamed you, and I shouldn't have done. I'll, er... I'll pay for the window."

"You did that?"

I bite my lip.

"I'm sorry," I say.

He stands there, speechless, in his hall. I can't think of anything else to say, so I turn back to my car. I am nearly there when he calls from the doorway.

"You don't have to do that," he says.

"What?"

"Pay for the window."

"Oh. Right. Thank you." I unlock the car.

"Please," he says. I turn and face him. "Won't you come in? Talk to me?" he says.

I can feel my heart race a bit. I hadn't anticipated this. I'm not sure what I did anticipate, if I'm honest, but not this.

"Mr Schofield, I..." I say.

"Of course," he says. "Of course. Better things to do. Yes."

I relock the car and return to the doorstep. "How about we talk on neutral ground?" I say.

"Where?"

"What about the café on the main road?"

He nods. He goes back inside to pick up a coat and reset his alarm.

Now I am sitting drinking coffee with a man with a plastic face, in a café with yellow plastic tables and brown plastic chairs.

Neither of us is saying very much. I am waiting for him to start.

"I'm sorry," he says.

"You are?"

"Yes."

That was all I wanted the other day.

"Why are you being so nice to me?" he says.

"I don't know." He has a wounded look about him. I didn't notice that before. He stares at me, stirring his coffee until it attracts the attention of a woman at the next table who is trying to type into a laptop.

"Shut up," she says, aiming it at him but trying to make it look as if she is speaking to herself.

I stop Mr Schofield's hand with mine. He notices the stirring and laughs nervously. There is a silence. Neither of us knows what to say to fill it. We look around us at the other customers. We look at the door. We look at the counter. Occasionally we look at each other and catch each other's eye. He coughs. He seems to be about to say something. He changes his mind.

"I know what it is like to be the cause of someone's death," I say.

"You do?"

I tell him about my brother. He doesn't say not to be silly, that it isn't my fault.

"I don't sleep," he says. He glances around him, as if worried that others might hear.

"No?"

"No. I have all these what ifs going round in my head, you know? What if I hadn't been there? What if I had just been late, for once in my life? What if I hadn't been held up by my wife and her bloody cleaning rota? I even blamed her, can you believe that?"

I don't say anything. I'm not sure what to say.

"She's gone," he says. "She was going anyway, sooner or later. But this was it for her."

"Why did you lie?" I say. "To the police?"

He starts to cry.

"I really wish I hadn't," he says. "But I couldn't see what else to do."

I am touching his hand. Bloody Hell, what is happening to me? "I'm sorry," he says. "I'm so so sorry."

"I forgive you," I say. I mean it. "But you have to forgive yourself." This isn't me. Is it? I don't know any more. Everything is changing. The whole picture I had of myself is disintegrating and reassembling before my eyes. I'm not sure I want to be a zealous religious type. Mind you, I don't see Christine that way. I don't see Dad that way. Those two people seem very sorted with God. The Irises are the zealous ones, and I don't get the impression that they really believe what they say. So perhaps my beef with religious people actually stems from their lack of faith, rather than their faith.

"I don't deserve your forgiveness," he says.

"It isn't a matter of deserving or not deserving. It's about a mistake. You made a mistake. You need to look at the situation in your life that led to that mistake. You need to understand it, see it for what it really is. That's all."

"That's all?"

I am surprised at myself. In explaining to Mr Schofield, I seem to have found an explanation for myself. That is what I need to do too. I need to understand my actions, my motivations, my misunderstandings, my mistakes, myself.

Some more tears fall out of his eyes, but he smiles at me. "Thank you," he says. "Thank you."

Barney is waiting when I get back. He has let himself in and made himself a hot chocolate. "Want some?" he says.

"No, I'm all right," I say. I feel dazed, as if the world is padded with cotton wool and I can't quite reach it.

"You OK?" he says.

I look at him. Bless him, he is wearing an apron to make hot chocolate. "I always spill it, man," he says.

"I've had a strange day," I say.

"Where've you been?"

I wasn't going to tell either of them, but the words start to rush out of my mouth. I tell him about my visits to Christine and my trip home the other day. I tell him some of the things I have learnt both from her and my Dad. I tell him how I seem to be seeing things differently, although I still don't see how. I tell him that I seem to have started to believe in God, even though that's patently ridiculous.

He laughs.

"Oh, Mags," he says. "You always believed in God, you just didn't like Him very much."

"What?"

"I shouldn't be doing this, I shouldn't be doing that, I'll get punished. Is this punishment? God hates me, all that business."

He is right. Those words do sound familiar.

"Barns?" I say.

He takes a slurp of his hot chocolate. "Yep?"

He has chocolate round his mouth. "I went to see Schofield," I say.

He is careful to swallow, rather than to waste his drink by spurting it out.

"You what?"

I try to explain. It isn't easy. It was a realisation, and how do you communicate a realisation to somebody who just thinks it's common sense?

He smiles. He doesn't say, "I told you so." He says: "I'm so pleased for you, Mags."

"I'm not sure how to tell Emily."

"To tell her what?"

"Any of this. She's so against anything spiritual. Calls it flaky. I just don't think she'll be happy about any of this stuff."

"You know what? Situations change you. They make you see things more clearly. And they make you change. Friends know that. They understand it. And if they can't understand it, then you simply move on and find other friends." He is looking into the distance. I know he is thinking about his friends on the rugby team after his injury. I never asked him about that, but he did seem to have a very different circle of friends after he recovered. Some of his best mates before, he hardly sees now.

"I don't want to lose Emily," I say.

He nods, and pats my arm. He doesn't know whether I will or I won't. Neither of us does.

Thursday, 24th May

We have parked in a gravelled layby at Hollow Fell, and are now puffing our way up the steep climb towards the grouse moor. Stonesett sits 400 feet above us, which seems a long way up. Barney is carrying the urn. Emily couldn't come, because there is a big court case today that she couldn't get out of covering. Dad is helping Mum to pick her way around the big stones that have been put on the track to stop it eroding.

We are a quiet group. Each of us has our own thoughts, and that is understood by the rest. The steep bit makes us all breathe hard, and we stop every so often, in silent agreement that it is a beautiful view. There is the odd glug-glug-glug of a grouse, spooked as we pass. There is a slight murmur from the breeze. Other than that, and our breathing, there is very little sound up here. I think that's one of the things Patrick loved about it.

The initial steep climb is replaced by a gentler one as we ease our way to the top. A group of walkers appears, clattering along towards us, their laughter and chatter breaking into the peace around us, but they will very soon be past.

"It's gorgeous up there today," says one of them. "Absolutely gorgeous."

His smile is wide and genuine. I find myself smiling back. I find my spirits lifting. I try to hear my heart beat. Not too difficult today; it is pounding with the effort of climbing the hill. I am not sure what it is telling me. I feel empty. Not heavy, not light. Just empty. Distant. I look across at Barney. He gives me one of his quiet smiles, just raising one side of his mouth.

We reach the moon landscape of rocks at the top with nothing else said, and Dad looks up at them, no doubt wondering how he is going to get Mum to climb up there. After some thought, he turns and looks at me.

"Come on," he says. "Barney, can you pass Maggie the urn? I think you should do the last bit on your own, love."

He points at the rocks. I clamber onto the first one and turn to hoist myself up higher. One more big pull, and I will be on the top, looking down over the valley, as if standing on the top of the world. I place the urn ahead of me and pull myself up. There it is: Camberdale, in all its feminine beauty. Mum, Dad and Barney have walked a little distance away so that they can see me without the view being obscured by the rocks. I pull the lid out of the urn and walk towards the front, where the hill is cut away suddenly and there is a steep drop.

It seems hard to believe, looking back over my time with Patrick, how so 'much has changed. Years of total disbelief in anything he couldn't see or touch turned, with Lottie's death, into something else. A shame for Lottie, to think that what she so desired in her life could only happen after she passed away. And the same gift she gave Patrick, he duly passed on to me. I see Christine every week with more questions. I don't know where this new path is taking me. I don't know if I will be a healer, like Christine, like Lottie. I don't know what will happen. All I know is that, where life always seemed so limited before, now it seems limitless, as if anything I might dream up could potentially happen. I miss him every day. I question why he died. But at the same time I know the question doesn't mean anything. He did die. I may understand it one day, or I may not. Life continues on and I have come to realise that there is beauty to be found when I look for it, even without him.

Every day I look up and see light and wonder what I might become. For him. For me.

The quiet villages nestle over on the other side of the valley. A car, tiny in the distance, makes its way along the narrow roads. Life, going on.

I breathe in the beauty of the view. As I breathe out again, I turn the urn over and let the ashes fall out, a grey cloud dispersing and thinning as it is swept down the hill. "Forgive me," I whisper, but I know I don't need to ask it. The words fade and disappear into the breeze that carries the last remaining bit of the material Patrick away from me forever. I don't know where the rest of him is: the spiritual Patrick. Perhaps one day I'll meet him again, and we will finally tell each other the things we should have said. Or maybe we'll just sit, quietly, holding metaphysical hands, each accepting the other, in full knowledge of who we are and who we have been.